HD30.65 .C37 2012
Work the system :
33663005239211
HYS

D0566857

DATE DUE

BRODART, CO.

Cat. No. 23-221

PRAISE FOR THE THIRD EDITION OF
Work the System

" The best management book of the year. Follow Sam's path and your business will become orderly, disciplined, repeatable, and profitable."

—Thomas Cox, founder of Cox Business Consulting

"*Work the System* gives you the tools you need to take giant steps in adding value to your business and freedom to your life."

—Nancy Hagan, executive productivity coach, Effective Executive

"Instead of 'follow your bliss and the money will appear' Sam advocates, 'fix the mechanics . . . and the bliss will appear'."

—Rodney Sampson, Author, *Kingonomics*

"What Sam Carpenter teaches in *Work the System* will revolutionize your life!"

—Michael Jans, president, Insurance Profit Systems

"Sam Carpenter brings together the practices of the biggest and best companies to help you succeed in your small business."

—Rich Sloan, co-founder of StartupNation.com

"This book is a reality check for small business owners and department managers who are struggling."

—Susan Solovic, CEO, SBTV.com

"I usually do not rave about books I read. One way I judge if a book is good is if I actually take action as a result of reading it. I love this book and have taken action . . ."

—Jim Estill, CEO, Nu Horizons; author, *Time Leadership*

WORK
THE
SYSTEM

THE SIMPLE MECHANICS OF **MAKING MORE** AND **WORKING LESS**

Third Edition

Sam Carpenter

GREENLEAF
BOOK GROUP PRESS

Published by Greenleaf Book Group Press
Austin, Texas
www.gbgpress.com

Copyright ©2012 Sam Carpenter

All rights reserved.

No part of this book may be reproduced, stored in a retrieval system, or transmitted by any means, electronic, mechanical, photocopying, recording, or otherwise, without written permission from the copyright holder.

Distributed by Greenleaf Book Group LLC

For ordering information or special discounts for bulk purchases, please contact Greenleaf Book Group LLC at PO Box 91869, Austin, TX 78709, 512.891.6100.

Design by Greenleaf Book Group LLC
Cover design by Linda Carpenter and Greenleaf Book Group LLC

Cataloging-in-Publication data
Carpenter, Sam.
  Work the system : the simple mechanics of making more and working less / Sam Carpenter.
— 3rd ed.
   p. ; cm.
  Previous ed. published: Bend, Ore. : North Sister Publishing, 2008.
  Includes bibliographical references and index.
  ISBN: 978-1-60832-253-4
1. Organizational effectiveness. 2. Organizational change—Management. 3. Success in business.
I. Title.
HD58.9 .C377 2009
658.4/02   2008943859

Part of the Tree Neutral® program, which offsets the number of trees consumed in the production and printing of this book by taking proactive steps, such as planting trees in direct proportion to the number of trees used: www.treeneutral.com

TreeNeutral®

Printed in the United States of America on acid-free paper

12 13 14 15 16   10 9 8 7 6 5 4 3

First Edition: April 2008
Second Edition: April 2009

ACC LIBRARY SERVICES AUSTIN, TX

To Linda, of course

One should choose the simplest explanation,
the one requiring the fewest assumptions and principles.

—WILLIAM OF OCKHAM, FOURTEENTH-CENTURY ENGLISH PHILOSOPHER

CONTENTS

FOREWORD

"If I had eight hours to cut down a tree, I'd spend six sharpening my axe."

—Abraham Lincoln

I say this without hyperbole: *Work the System* is one of the most useful business books you'll ever read. I should know—I read business books for a living, and teach creative people from all over the world how to build businesses that are profitable, enjoyable, and sustainable.

Here are the top three questions I'm asked every single day:

- "Starting a business seems so complicated. Where do I begin?"
- "I'm working a lot, but not making much money. How can I improve my profitability?"
- "I'm constantly stressed and anxious. How can I run my business without going crazy?"

The answer to these questions is always the same: learn how to work the system.

Fundamentally, every business is a system: a collection of processes that, together, reliably produces an intended result. The more you focus on improving your business systems, the better results you'll produce. It's as simple as that.

When most people hear the word "system," however, their eyes glaze over. Most of us are trained to think that standard operating procedures, checklists, documentation, and the like are boring and bureaucratic.

Nothing could be further from the truth. Here's what happens when you begin improving your systems:

- You make more money, but do less work.
- You have more focus and energy to do your best work.
- You make far fewer errors and mistakes.
- You fix the mistakes you make quickly and permanently.
- You feel more calm, collected, and under control.

Solid business systems are largely a product of calm, rational, straightforward thinking. It's a skill that can be learned quickly, and a method that can be applied to improve every aspect of your life.

I use the ideas in *Work the System* every day when building my own business, and I've recommended this book to my readers and clients since the publication of the first edition.

I'm glad this book has found its way into your hands. *Work the System* will help you make better decisions, get more done, and have more fun along the way.

—Josh Kaufman, author of *The Personal MBA*

PREFACE TO THE THIRD EDITION

Working the System of *Work the System*

This book is different.

Its main thrust goes beyond providing new information, although it does that. The root purpose of *Work the System* is to guide you to a new way of perceiving your life so you can gain better command of it and therefore be better able to get what you want. I like to call this mini-awakening *getting it*, and I describe what it is and how to achieve it in part one.

I changed my life after a moment of insight, moving from a nightmarish, impoverished existence to a life of peace and prosperity. I now work two hours a week instead of eighty. Yes, I'm wealthy now, too: 100 percent self-made. I've had the same small business for twenty-eight years, and this is the story of how I transformed it from a chaotic ordeal into an ATM machine, pulling my staff upward with me while delivering the highest quality of service available in my particular industry. How I broke free, and how you can too, is described in detail. This is not theory; it's fact, and believe me, if I can do it, so can you! Career-wise, you may have to do something different than what you do now in order to reach your goals of freedom and prosperity, but probably not. People who follow my strategy become hyper-efficient, and most of them keep doing what they have been doing all along, as they finally leave the competition in the dust or suddenly streak up the corporate ladder. There are no gimmicks or mysterious theories here. No Six Sigma-type complexities. No hype. No BS. What I discuss, including the getting-it insight you will experience, will make perfect sense. Sound interesting?

The broad, nutshell premise?

There are an infinite number of puzzle pieces out there, and for each of us to get what we want in our lives it's just a matter of seeing those pieces, making a proper selection, and then assembling them in a way that produces the results we desire. And no, in focusing on the mechanical you won't lose your humanity.

Work the System is not rah-rah, pumping you up but offering nowhere to go. After you achieve the *systems mindset* perspective, I carefully explain the necessary mechanical steps for creating prosperity and peace in your life (in parts two and three). There's more beyond the book, too. I'll talk about that in a minute.

Despite the sly title, there is nothing sinister in these pages, and there's nothing that won't seem logical. It's a simple message presented in a thorough way: contrary to popular opinion, the workings of the world make perfect sense. There is an inherent order that is stunningly evident if one drops preconceived notions and quietly observes life-as-it-is. By internalizing this new insight—by going one layer deeper—it's an easy matter to arrange things in order to "get what one wants."

The added bonus: speculative, menu-driven presumptions about work, business, politics, health, and relationships drop away to be replaced by commonsense gut-certainties.

The most satisfying outcome is that life-theory and hard reality become congruent. This means one is no longer swayed by peers, public opinion, what feels good, or moment-to-moment expediency. Addressing raw reality head-on, one confidently makes up one's own mind about things and then consistently applies that certainty to the real world—and it works. It works because reality operates in the same way everywhere, all the time.

It's been four and a half years since I first released *Work the System*, and at the time I hoped it would help readers get better control of their businesses and their lives. At the risk of braggadocio, that has happened. More on this soon, too.

I'll say this here at the beginning: each of us has a mechanical aspect and an emotional aspect, and contrary to a boatload of pop-psychology books, tapes, videos, etc., I say it's a good thing to separate the two. If we don't, things get muddied and neither aspect turns out so well. And I take issue with the presumption that the road to freedom and prosperity begins with the elimination of personal emotional hang-ups. *Work the System* is about straightening out the mechanics of a life first: get the machine right, and emotional improvement will tag along naturally. Can one have emotional hang-ups together with wealth and freedom? Of course. We all know people like that. But hang-ups or not, obtaining wealth and freedom will go a long way toward making life better.

Yes, you can flip a switch and your life can become what you want it to be. This is because the switch is located in your head and therefore is readily accessible.

I've found that not everyone is interested in making more and working less. Some people want to make more while working the same amount of time or to just become more effectual at work and at home. And a large number of readers simply want to feel more in control of their lives, to have their worlds make more sense. *Work the System* serves all these purposes because it's about becoming more life-efficient.

Relative to the second edition, is there new material in the third edition? No, not a lot, and my defense is that base reality doesn't change over time. It can just be better explained, which is the primary reason I assembled this third edition. I've made massive improvement in how it reads. There are literally thousands of small enhancements. I want the reader to *get it* easier and faster. Also, I am finding some serious self-satisfaction in producing a better quality representation of what I believe.

A central fact remains: 90 percent of people struggle. On the surface it seems this is because they don't set direction, they don't get organized, and they spend too much time on trivialities. That's true. Yet, when the mechanisms of life one layer deeper are seen, the root causal reason for the struggle becomes strikingly obvious. Nevertheless, because most of us use up our days coping with bad results, we don't think about submerging to a deeper place to make adjustments where those bad results are propagated. We humans just have a penchant for thrashing around on the surface, complicating what isn't complicated.

Since the second edition was published three years ago, how was I able to make a "massive improvement"? For starters, after repeatedly delivering the concept to groups, individuals, and the media, I'm able to explain it better. Practice makes perfect. Another reason is that I've lived these concepts day and night for a few more years now; I simply understand the principles better and, in my head, have tied some loose ends together. Also, via reader feedback, I've witnessed the success of the method as I've seen it applied in a variety of situations, and this gives me a wider perspective of how it works outside my own experience. And, after three years of frequent posts on my website, I'm a better writer.

I'll borrow a common yet perfect descriptive term for an important thread that weaves its way through the book: "Bottom-up." From different angles, and beginning with the first edition, I've repeatedly touched on this concept, but I've never given it a name. In a business, bottom-up calls for system improvement ideas to be gathered at the customer and production levels and then passed on up through management for massaging and approval. It's not a declaration of democracy—I like to think a business is more of a benevolent dictatorship—but rather, it acknowledges the obvious: The best ideas come from the people on the front lines; the people dealing directly with customers or with the production of the product.

I'll go here at the risk of proselytizing: in group presentations as I begin to discuss my mechanical take on life, there is always some initial head shaking from the follow-your-bliss contingent (of which I used to be a member) who feel that they are called to rise above the mechanical world in order to focus on the spiritual. They believe the spiritual pursuit is noble and superior and shouldn't be hampered by the restrictive job of dealing with petty issues in the here and now. My response, which invariably gets them head nodding instead of head shaking, is that we are all spiritual beings existing in a mechanical world. Until we learn to assertively steer the raw mechanics of our lives, we cannot get to a place that gives us the freedom to pursue what is beyond this concrete reality because we will always be pulled back into it out of sheer necessity. *We must get our physical world, with all its boring and base considerations, straightened out before it will allow us to focus on anything beyond it.* Yet, having said that, this beautifully orchestrated mechanical existence that we experience from day to day can be perceived as a powerfully spiritual place if we can stop judging it and just see it for what it is. For ethereally-inclined Westerners especially, it's a reverse tack to use the mechanical to enter the spiritual. Give it a shot if the other sequence hasn't met your expectations.

And, back to the subject of producing a better-quality book: there is this system-improvement thing. *Work the System* is about systems, and a book is a system in itself. It's an enclosed entity, with a multitude of spinning wheels, all contributing to the singular purpose of that entity, that is, to accomplish a goal. And like our lives, a book is never perfect and so there is always room for betterment, for "system improvement." Herein lies a problem within the publishing industry that I have managed to circumvent. Read on.

I have an interesting contractual relationship with my publisher, Greenleaf Book Group. It's fundamentally different from 99.9 percent of author/publisher deals because I have been able to keep the rights to my manuscript. I can tweak it to my own heart's delight when I feel the need (of course, all the while paying close attention to the recommendations of Greenleaf's fine editors).

Normally, *getting published* means the author's rights to the work are forfeited forever to the publishing company. New authors, frantic to avoid permanent residence in the dustbin of the self-published, sell their souls to traditional publishing companies. The consequence is that, for starters, the original manuscript is handed over to an editor who, depending on competence, style, personality, attitude, mood of the moment, degree of belief/interest in the subject matter, and experience (often editors for first-book authors are just out of college), will often render the originally submitted manuscript unrecognizable. There is no recourse for the author. The editors have the final say on the content of the published book and any subsequent renditions.

"Here," says the new author to the publisher, "I want to be published so, yes, take my wife and do what you want with her."

And, beyond that profound abdication, good luck to the industrious scribe who wants to make changes and asks the publisher for another printing or, heaven forbid, requests a new edition. There's no going back to tweak the book without the publisher's line-by-line approval and 99 percent of the time that approval won't be forthcoming.

So, because I wanted precise control over this master statement of what I believe, I sought an alternative to the traditional publishing deal. I think you'll find the following chronology of the book's development interesting for that reason, and for another: the history of *Work the System* is a perfect illustration of the systems mindset that is the centerpiece of the book itself.

I self-published *Work the System* in the spring of 2008. This first printing was softcover. I had spent two years and thousands of hours getting the book right. It was the very, very best I could do at the time. It was perfect, I thought, as the manuscript headed off to the printer, sans publisher.

But when the boxes of new books arrived at our house six weeks later and I opened one, I gasped at a horrible miscalculation: the cover was an embarrassing gaffe. How arrogant was this, as a first-time author, to splash my photo across it? Then I opened a copy, and within seconds I blanched again because *it could have been said so much better*. There were clumsy sentence structures, flat-out grammatical errors, poor flows of thought, and way too much repetition. Nevertheless, disappointed, I put the book out there because the message was solid. It sold pretty well, and a month later I could see there would have to be another printing and this would give me the opportunity to make things right, to "improve the system."

Enthusiastically I went to work tweaking, working day and night to fix the deficiencies, including getting rid of the cover photo. I hammered. The message was unchanged but there was a lot to fix in the delivery and it was a satisfying exercise because I was certainly going to get it right with the second self-published printing. This upgraded version would also be softcover, and I decided on a plain white, glossy cover this time.

The shipment arrived. I opened a box with confidence that *this* would prove to be the penultimate, perfect representation of what I believe about work and life. Whoops. For starters, my minimalist cover was amateurish. And inside, I found that despite the countless additional grammatical and sentence-structure revisions and the continued soundness of the message, it was still structurally and grammatically butterfingered.

A few more months passed, Greenleaf Book Group accepted the book, we signed a deal, and preparation for a second edition/third printing ensued. This time, with two first-class professional editors via Greenleaf, the book's contents were shuffled around and literally *thousands* of additional enhancements were made. It would be hardcover this time, to be delivered in the spring of 2009.

When the books arrived, I was disappointed *again*! The new cover was awesome, but the experimental glossy cover material was too absorbent, instantly smudged by the fingerprints of anyone who picked up the book. And, yes, so much inside could have been better said!

For the fourth printing six months later, again hardcover, we fixed the cover and made many more internal enhancements. The books arrived and, sure enough, I was disappointed once more.

Arrghhh!

But what I haven't said until now—and this is my key point in all of this, so pay attention here—is that because of my serial disappointments and the resultant jillion improvements that I made because of those disappointments, the book's quality had improved enormously. Despite my nitpicky self-recriminations, I had to admit, the second printing of the second edition wasn't half bad, due to the incessant system-improvement gyrations of the previous three iterations.

And yet, this third edition has even more thousands of additional refinements, and my Greenleaf editors have again come in behind me to smooth things out even further.

As mentioned earlier, from the first edition through this third edition, the message itself is virtually unchanged. It's the delivery that's improved.

As I look back, it's clear to me that I should have known the book would never be what I wanted it to be the first time, or even the second, third, or fourth time. *I knew better!*

In any case, I've had the unique opportunity as a first-time author to repeatedly tweak my book through a total of eight printings, controlling the content completely while paying close attention to the advice of the top-notch Greenleaf editors and designers who have assisted me. The end result? Each additional version has been of better quality than the previous version.

I tell you all of this to make a point beyond self-aggrandizement: *Work the System*'s relentless evolution, in itself, is a perfect illustration of the system-improvement process that is at the core of its own message.

I'll also use this chronology to point out the beauty of personal freedom—of having the opportunity to chart one's own course.

It's my hope that with this book you will not just develop the capacity to see the processes of your world from moment to moment, but you will also reach deep down inside to discover that the key to reaching goals is to spend your time incessantly tweaking those processes, to make them better and better. Hunker down to relentlessly improve the systems of your world, and soon the fire killing will cease and you'll have the time and money to enjoy the life you have always wanted.

I hope you get that.

There are many examples and illustrations in this book, but it was never meant to be a collection of stories or anecdotes. I wanted to go a layer deeper and really help my readers to make changes in their lives by providing a set of clear, tangible instructions to follow. *Work the System* is written to be a master guideline to working the systems of your life. It's thorough. But if you wish to go further, there is a multimedia course that I've created. It goes far beyond the book in scope and is designed to jar procrastinating business owners out of their state of inaction. It's a one- to three-month program (the time necessary to complete it depends on the complexity of the business and the owner's availability to make changes). It's called the Work the System Academy (see appendix D and go to workthesystemacademy.com for the most up-to-date information). For some readers, the work the system method has literally become another department of their operation, such as accounting, IT, or sales. You could call it a blanket department because it overlays all other departments, making each one super-efficient and drawing all of them together into a single, super-productive business machine. The Academy provides business owners with a fast bolt-on installation of the method.

We've just launched a direct consulting arm, too. Go to Appendix F for details.

I've been wanting to write another book, one geared to the general public. I visualize it being one-third the size of this one. It would be an easy read, again emphasizing the systems mindset. But I haven't been able to start *that* book because up until now, *this* book remained incomplete, even after a careful birth and numerous subsequent re-births. Will this third edition/third printing be the final product? Probably not, but it's close, and in any case, I'm going to start that other book now.

My website is workthesystem.com, and I post when I feel inspired. Please join me there. Also take a look at my list of suggested reading at workthesystem.com/reading.

Something else regarding system improvement. My wife Linda and I were talking on the phone just as I was finishing this third edition manuscript (at the time, she was in Seattle; I was in Bend) and when, at the last minute, I asked her if I had missed anything, she said, "Well, yes." She said I had failed to emphasize—at the beginning of the book—the unavoidable it's-hard-before-it's-easy part; the it-comes-with-the-territory-trauma of an entrepreneurial start-up or company re-invention. After she explained, I asked her to write down her thoughts. I heard from her within 30 minutes. Here's what she emailed me:

> "I'm standing on the deck, looking out over Puget Sound—cup of coffee in one hand, phone in the other, as I talk to Sam, who is still in Bend. For two weeks I've been here in our Seattle apartment, working 16-hour days. I came up here to sequester myself in order to meet the deadline for my part of the Work the System Academy project. And Sam is using his time alone in Bend to work at the same demanding pace. We're collaborating on building an online machine which, once built, will of course be operated by others (per the Work the System methodology it advocates). We've been working for nine months on this venture and the launch is still a couple of months away.
>
> Sam and I are talking about the physical and mental demands of this work. The weight of it is heavy on both of us. And while we talk, I remember what I had forgotten . . . *this is the way it is at the start. This is how all new ventures are: it's crazy-busy in the beginning.* But what most of us forget is that we have a choice: we can stay suspended in this place of struggle, constantly fighting it . . . or we can relax and just go with the flow of it, knowing that *this is the only way it can be.* In a company's beginning—or in a company rebirth—the owner of the enterprise *must* be in the thick of it. *Things are hard before they're easy.* These are the steps we have to take to get to the other side. Zen philosophy applies: Stop agonizing about how this isn't the way it

should be, accept that this is the way *it is*, and put all of our energy into making it what we want it to be."

One more thing: know that *business is art*. The ability to patiently ascend the learning curve, to relentlessly plow through enormous obstacles, to keep improving things no matter what, to ultimately create something of beauty out of the miscalculations of the past—to weather the storms—is a beautiful thing. A successful business is a self-sustaining entity of worth that creates value for all involved. As you stumble, walk, and sprint to that end, don't underestimate your accomplishment and your contribution.

Sam Carpenter
Updated for third printing, December 2012

PREFACE TO THE FIRST EDITION

It's Just Mechanics

I work the system, but not just one. I work all the systems in my world—professional, financial, social, biological, and mechanical. You have your own systems. Do you see them? Do you control them? It doesn't matter whether you are an entrepreneur, CEO, employee, stay-at-home mom or dad, retiree, or student. Your life is composed of systems that are yours to command—or not command.

In the slang sense of the term, someone who works the system uses a bureaucratic loophole as an excuse to break rules in order to secure personal gain. But winning the life game means following the rules, for if we don't, any win is a ruse. Be assured that you will find nothing deceitful or unsavory in these pages. Nor does the work the system methodology have anything to do with esoteric theory, politics, or religion. It's about common sense and simple mechanics. I call it a workingman's philosophy.

Life is serious business, and whether you know it or not—or whether you like it or not—your personal systems are the threads in the fabric of your existence. Together, they add up to *you*. And if you are like most people, you negotiate your days without seeing these processes as the singular entities they are, some working well and some not so well.

In the complexity that is your world, what if you could distinctly see each of these systems? What if you could reach in and pluck one of these not-so-efficient processes out of that complexity, make it perfect, and then reinsert it? What if you could perform this routine with every system that composes your being? What if you could reengineer your existence piece by piece to make it exactly what you want it to be without having to count on luck, providence, blind faith, or someone else's largesse?

The foundational thrust of *Work the System* is not to educate you in the ten steps to peace and prosperity or to warn you of the five most common mistakes in seeking happiness. The method digs deeper than that, causing a modification in the way you see the elements of your world. And when this quiet yet profound mechanical shift in life-perception occurs— you will remember the exact moment you *get it*—the simple methodology will make irrefutable sense and you will never be the same.

I call this new way of seeing things the *systems mindset*.

The book also provides a framework—yes, a compendium of do's and don'ts—through which you can channel this new perspective to get what you want out of your life.

TWO VIEWPOINTS

In a broad sense, there are two psychological approaches to finding a way to lead a full, positive existence. The first holds that the events of the past and the mindset we formed as a result of those events determine today's happiness. In this view, we are victims of unpleasant circumstance and have a chance at peace only if we face and then disarm the psychic monsters planted in our minds long ago. That's the Freudian stance.

The second approach, the cognitive, maintains that the thoughts we feed ourselves today are what matter most, and the events of the past are just that—in the past—and gone forever unless we insist on swirling them back into the present moment.

The cognitive approach is more practical than the Freudian because it's simple and clean, enabling one to steer the thought process rather than wallow helplessly in mental negativity from years gone by. I believe that what we do today will determine tomorrow, and blaming the past or the world or someone else is a debilitating way to travel through this precious one-time event called life.

Blue-blood, old-school psychologists who see endless dour complexity in the human condition will sniff at the simplicity of the *Work the System* message. Things are more complicated than that, they'll say. I thank them in advance for the oblique compliment. This is an elementary, dispassionate, drop-the-load dispatch that describes lives as they really are: simple cause-and-effect mechanisms that can be logical, predictable, and satisfying.

No PhD necessary.

So take the title of this book at literal face value, understanding you will be working *your* systems. In these pages I challenge you to first see, then dissect, and then refine them one by one until each is perfect. (I call this process *system improvement*.) You will create new systems too, while discarding the ones holding you back, the ones that have been invisibly sabotaging your best efforts. Command the systems of your life and move toward inner serenity, prosperity, and the best for those around you.

LEADER AND HIGH EARNER

Five years ago I participated in Cycle Oregon, a weeklong bicycle tour. It was early September, and two thousand of us pedaled an average of seventy-five miles each day through remote eastern Oregon. At night we camped in ad hoc tent cities planted at various locations along the route—rural high school football fields, small town parks, and wheat fields. Seldom did we have cellular telephone coverage. That was just fine as we, en masse, divorced ourselves from the damn things for this seven-day break from the regular world.

At dusk on the last night of the tour, as my friend Steve and I were casually walking through the surrounding sea of tents, we encountered a group of young men sitting around drinking beer, being boisterous. We overheard them laughing, waging bets about how many voice mail messages one of them would have the next day when he was back within cell phone range and able to check his messages. Clearly, back in the real world these guys worked together in an office. One predicted the total messages would be 150, another, 250. The young man on the receiving end of the jest was robust and confident. He smiled at the fawning. It was obvious this man was important in his work. He was well respected, a leader, and most probably a high earner—a success. People depended on him.

For twenty-eight years I have been owner, general manager, and CEO of a small telecom business in Bend, Oregon. Centratel is profitable and has thirty-five employees and a solid, loyal client base. The part I play is important; in my world I'm also a leader and high earner. Many people depend on me, too.

When I checked my voice mail the next day as I began the long drive home, there was just one message. Andi, my COO, had left an update because she knew I would want to get caught up on things when I was again able to pick up my messages. She reported that all was well in the office, and she hoped I had had a fun week away from things. "Drive home safely," she said. That was it. She didn't need to address the obvious: during the week, without an ounce of input from me, and without a hitch, the business had functioned perfectly as it churned out thousands of dollars of profits.

It didn't matter that I was absent.

Who knows what that voice mail–inundated young man from the bicycle tour does for a living, but I tell you this: he is mismanaging things if his gig can't proceed for a single week without his direct influence; if the slew of processes in which he is involved all come to a halt when he is not available. Yes, all those voice mail messages (and God only knows how many e-mail messages) attest to his status and importance, but in the bigger picture he is a slave to his job—and the people who depend on him are slaves to his presence. They wait for his response and can't move ahead until he provides input. In his absence, because he fails to set up business processes that keep producing while he is gone, things come to a standstill in the same way water accumulates behind a dam.

He was probably twenty-five years younger than me. People and circumstances change with time. Not too long ago, my world was just like his.

HOOKED UP

Here's a more general observation: in the past thirty years the lure of instant gratification has seized a huge chunk of our population. For the hooked-up masses—those seriously addicted to smart phones, Twitter, Facebook, and the immediacy/pervasiveness of the entertainment industry—it's a stretch to dig down to consider the root of things. The gratification of the moment is a distraction from thoughtful contemplation of the reasons why events happen as they do. Today, unlike twenty years ago, a good *now* is available by just plugging in and tuning out. For too many of us, slowing down to examine things is not entertaining, and that's too bad because it's mandatory that we take the time to understand the machinery of our lives if we are to modify that machinery to produce the results we desire.

Yes, the work the system methodology is a throwback of sorts, back to an age when there was careful preparation with no expectation of immediate payback. But having said that, know that an investment in the strategy will show quick tangible benefits. Maybe not tomorrow, but certainly within a few weeks.

CLOSED-SYSTEM LABORATORY

Centratel is a high-tech telephone answering service. For fifteen years it floundered, my personal life a reflection of its chaos. Then I attained the new mindset, and immediately the pressure began to drop. Not too far down the line, as I continued to methodically apply the protocols described here, my workweek was reduced 98 percent while my bottom-line income increased more than twentyfold.

Moreover, my time away from work is smooth and easy now. In the morning I awake serenely, looking forward to yet another day of quiet, steady enhancement on all fronts. In the course of a week I spend far more time reading, writing, traveling, hanging out with friends, going to the movies, climbing mountains, and riding bicycles than working. My life is in control. It's what I want it to be.

What I've learned for sure is this: despite the almost visceral societal belief to the contrary, *there is a direct connection between happiness and the amount of control we attain.*

The nature of the telephone-answering service business, with its multitude of interacting processes both human and otherwise, made Centratel the perfect closed-system laboratory for developing the work the system methodology. It's logical and convenient to use my business as the explanatory platform for these chaos-to-order processes. And things can get too dry and theoretical without real-life examples, so describing the method within the framework of my business adds some fun to the party.

The strategies described here are not just for the small-business owner; they're also for those who work in a managerial capacity for a business owned by someone else. There are lessons for those born with a silver spoon and for those who are self-made wealthy, too. And based on feedback from readers, it's apparent there is much for those who engineer family life at home. It makes sense: We're dealing with reality, and reality works in the same way for everyone, everywhere, all the time; so when I offer a business illustration, read between the lines and find your own application.

When I refer to business and use the word "manager," understand that the label also applies to personal life. We are the managers of our lives, and as I said, the foundational protocols described here are universal.

The word "system" is a pointed and unique unit of language; it's so precise that it doesn't have a lot of synonyms. But it has a few almost-equivalents that I like to use occasionally because they add spice in certain narratives. They are the words "process," "mechanism," and "machine."

The principles are simple, but it is not enough to memorize or understand them. They must be internalized deep down. There is a difference between learning something new and undergoing an epiphany. On a gut level, *getting it* is key, and for this reason some repetition will occur as I approach the concepts from different angles.

Trust that the get-it epiphany will arrive soon, and probably when you least expect it.

A qualifier: I don't adhere to the work the system principles and guidelines every minute. I fall down on the job now and then. Nonetheless, because I have structured my existence around the methodology, the details of the day continue to take care of themselves despite any temporary distraction or physical/mental slump. My systems keep things moving forward no matter what.

The same will hold for you too, should you choose to take command of the systems of your life.

ACKNOWLEDGMENTS

Thank you to Sam Kirkaldie, my partner and friend, for your calm strength; Andi Freeman, for your faith in me and our systems—you really *get it* as you never fail to watch my back; Hollee Wilson, for being on top of every situation, and for never, ever letting me down; Pattie Casner, for enduring the hard times and for making our Quality Department sing; Lannie Dell, our longest-term employee, for sticking it out for over twenty years; Sandra Packard, our other twenty-year veteran, for your insistence on perfection and for weathering those storms with me; Linda Morgan, for your dependability and calm demeanor; Carla Hoekstra, for always being there to do what must be done; Denise Jones, for your nonstop, positive attitude; Dan Blomquist, master of the IT universe—and undisputed gadget-champion of the world, thank you for your quiet expertise and your subtle humor.

And to the Centratel TSR staff, how to thank you enough for your utterly incredible performance, day after day, year after year? I am profoundly grateful: you are the heart of Centratel's success.

A long time ago, Lindsay Stevens gave me my first inkling that a business should be directed, not indulged. Reese Shepard insisted there be a plan. Roger Shields, retired banker, smacked me in the head with his air bat when I needed it most. Robert Killen, formerly of Columbia River Bank, gave me a break when everyone else equivocated, and "RC" Roger Christensen, former president of Columbia River Bank, cut me some slack when the two of us were at the bottom of our respective career ladders.

Back in the '70s, the NYS Ranger School faculty taught me about common sense and hard work. And Lane Powell, my mentor at Central Electric Cooperative, now deceased, left an indelible mark on my being. There is much of Lane Powell in this book.

Special appreciation to the Greenleaf Book Group gang: editors Jay Hodges, Linda O'Doughda, Theresa Reding, and Jeanne Hansen, who edited this third edition. Also, Justin Branch and Kristen Sears for keeping the administrative balls rolling, and to Clint Greenleaf who makes it possible for authors like me to continue to own and therefore improve our work. You've earned your success.

Thank you audio engineers Tim Underwood and Jay Townsend of Underwood Productions for your patient and insightful input as I recorded the audio version of the book.

My gratitude to freelancers Sarah Max and Linda Chestney for preliminary editing; Bobbi Swanson for masterful indexing; *Shukria*, Khizar Abassi, for assisting me in helping the backcountry people of Azad Jammu and Kashmir and for welcoming me and Linda into your home; and to Ahsan and Mina Rashid for showing us the real Pakistan.

Gratitude to my father, Tom Carpenter, retired English teacher, who insisted I become proficient with the written word despite my strident resistance; my author-mother Nancy Fox, for your gang-buster inspiration that had everything to do with me becoming a writer; Anne Pietz, my wonderful mother-in-law, for your concise, nitpicky input. And Dad and Ma and Anne: thanks to each of you for proofreading this third edition. You are inspirational examples of vibrant, contributing, and engaged individuals who are well into their 90s.

You're a good man, brother Steve. You can put the abstract in a nutshell and do it with humor (and thanks much for your contribution to the space shuttle illustration); and thanks to Jack Cornelius for your "Great Machine" story.

And Linda Carpenter, I'm permanently beholden for your incredible patience and invariably on-target suggestions.

And my appreciation to my daughter Jennifer, for confirming that a penchant for living on the edge is indeed a genetic trait. I love you.

And, Mike Giles of England: cheers! It's an honor to be your business partner, and I am in awe of your marketing prowess as we launch the Work the System Academy. No small thing; you really do "get it."

To the men and women of our military: your song is not sung enough, but know without a doubt that there's a whole lot of folks who will never stop appreciating your sacrifice. You keep us free.

—Sam Carpenter, August 2011

INTRODUCTION

The Simplest Solution

Out of clutter, find simplicity. From discord, find harmony.

—ALBERT EINSTEIN

One should choose the simplest explanation of a phenomenon, the one that requires the fewest leaps of logic. Or one could say, "Keep it simple, stupid!"

My wife, Linda, and I live on the outskirts of a vibrant mountain resort town in the great American Northwest. Our house is not large, but it's open and bright, furnished in a pragmatic, people-actually-live-here way. For both of us, it is everything we have ever wanted in a home.

I sit at the dining room table in front of my laptop. Outside the window, the quiet of the late afternoon is tangible. It's June. The lawn is lush green and is the launching pad for a half dozen huge Ponderosa pines towering above the house. The weather is warm—another perfect, cloudless day in Central Oregon. Yesterday was like that, and tomorrow will be the same.

It's peaceful. Linda sits at the table next to me and we chat.

Meanwhile, in town, my telephone answering service business churns away whether we're thinking about it or not, providing more than a good living for us. It wasn't always this way. For a decade and a half, my business experience was a chaotic morass of endless work, fire killing, debt, health problems, and bad relationships.

Twelve years ago, at a point in time that I can pinpoint exactly, I experienced an unexpected shift in perception that began the transformation of my existence from chaos to calm. Now, truly managing my small business and the rest of my world, I am no longer enmeshed in minutiae. I'm an arm's-length observer of it. The numbers are good: compared to a decade ago, my workweek is two hours instead of a hundred, and my earnings in a month far exceed what I used to make in a year. My health is back, too; I'm climbing, cycling, and skiing again.

As for the subjective? It's no stretch to say my life has ten times more peace and freedom. As my day slides by, I feel like an athlete in the zone: powerful, relaxed, and efficient. I look at my existence now and feel a certain element of incredulity because my natural comportment has always included some flakiness. I've had a hard time focusing, sticking to things. I had no purpose, dropped out of college three times, got caught up in alcohol/drugs, moved from relationship to relationship at the spur of the moment, always dissatisfied with myself and my performance in life— clear up until the age of fifty. But now, when it comes to the big things, my personal bearing is centered and deliberate. It's true, I can still display a certain surface distractedness when it comes to things I don't deem especially consequential in life (amusingly so, at times!), but on matters that carry weight and when working toward goals that are important, I am determined and focused until I obtain the results I want. Linda, who came into my life just after the paradigm shift twelve years ago, says I am the most get-the-job-done person she's ever met.

Getting to this place wasn't hard to do once my mindset shifted to view each day from a more intimate angle. Since I seized upon this deeper reality I've been able to channel my efforts to get what I've always wanted. Did I have to work hard? Yes, for a short while there was some hard work, but in comparison to the nightmare of my previous existence the effort was not much, and I was happy to do it, especially as the results began to roll in.

How I did this—and how you can do the same—is the gist of this book.

I direct *Work the System* to those who have the following chronic internal dialogue: "*There are things I must do right now, and there is barely enough time to do them. I will bulldoze my way through these tasks, and as usual they will be completed just in time—but the results will be of marginal quality and my body and mind will continue to be stretched to the breaking point. I'm tired and stressed. There is too much chaos in my life and never enough money—my world is far from what I want it to be . . ."*

If you own or manage a small business, have a job, are a student, or engineer family life at home, there's a good chance this narrative caught your attention. The I'm-just-barely-hanging-on self-talk is endemic to every class and every age group.

I'm a low-key guy. Not a lot of flash, no frills, and no advanced college degree. I've run the standard gauntlet of ups and downs, successes and failures; and like a lot of folks, I've worked hard. It's clear to me that pragmatism increases with age, one lives by trial and error, and lessons can be learned from being banged around. And I'm not afraid to face cold reality, as I exhibit a knee-jerk suspicion of unsupportable theory. My existence has a limited time span, and I treasure this life-gift.

My life is engineered now, planned and maintained. Work or play, it gets my full attention.

No, of course I don't have everything neatly tied up in a bag (who does?), but I've found a way to take charge, to make my days orderly and calm. Nearly every day I awake alert and strong and happy.

COMPLEX JUMBLE?

What about you? How do you describe your typical day? Is it an amorphous, complex jumble of happenings or is it a relaxed and ordered sequence of events? Is it chaotic or is it under control? Do you have enough money? Do you spend enough time with friends and family? Through the day—and through your life—are you in an endless race around a circular track or are you climbing slowly and steadily toward a mountaintop? Are you getting what you want? If not, could it be a personal management problem?

Don't confuse these questions with right, wrong, good, or bad, and don't inject some abstract theoretical, political, or religious bearing into your answers. Keep this mechanical and—equally important—keep it simple. And take heart. If you tend toward defining your existence as a complex jumble of happenings, rest assured that you already have 100 percent of the resources necessary to eliminate this too-common story line.

The work the system methodology is almost silly in its simplicity, but, and I risk hubris here, nothing less than profound in its capacity to transform. That's why I chose the words of William of Ockham for the epigraph of my book. To paraphrase, the simplest solution *is* invariably the most correct solution. Here, as I begin to discuss recognizable events and scenarios, habits, goals, successes, failures, and plain old common sense, you will relate to the methodology because it is believable. It's about simple mechanical improvements that will combine to transform your existence.

Yet what I describe in these pages is not apparent to the casual observer.

This book is not about feel-good, pie-in-the-sky promises. You won't find new-think premises, nor is there pseudo-intellectual blathering. You will not be asked to write down tedious lists, memorize odd platitudes, repeat affirmations, make daily journal entries, publicize your newfound direction to your friends and family, or worst of all, wait to see if yet another mysterious theory will make things better. This isn't a matter of blind faith.

But if you think sheer energy, clever thinking, and unbounded enthusiasm are enough to secure the freedom and income you want, think a bit further. Certain structures—certain mechanical processes—must be in place before these important attributes can take you where you want to go. Independence and wealth occur *after* the system mechanics are put in good order.

So is there something you must do, some work that you must perform? Yes, some written documentation. And, if you lead people, you will teach them your new vision. But you're putting in your time and working hard anyway, right? For a while you'll simply channel a portion of this time and energy toward step-by-step, one-time building efforts that will lead to permanent freedom, prosperity, and peace.

And think again about racing around an endless circle versus steadily climbing upward. Effort is required either way, but know it is the climbing you want. Instead of expending precious resources on getting-nowhere, churning tedium (which is the hardest and most frustrating work of all), you will expend that same time and energy in a step-by-step steady ascent that will provide a geometric return on investment.

We'll be dealing with a perfunctory fact that most people overlook due to a pervasive can't-see-the-forest-for-the-trees myopia. The system-based protocols discussed here are quietly used in large, successful organizations everywhere, but they are not often present in small businesses. And although the principles of the method are scattered among scores of time-management, business, spiritual, and pop-psychology writings, here they are grouped together to form an everyman's methodology that is rooted in one fundamental truth: *a life's mechanical functioning is a result of the systems that compose it.*

And the simple crux? It's this: if it is true that a life's mechanical functioning is a result of the systems that compose it, then reaching your goals does not lie in coping with the bad results of unmanaged systems. Doing that is a wasteful distraction. Rather, getting what one wants requires delving one layer deeper in order to *work* the systems that *create* the results. Hence, the title of this book: *Work the System.*

The first step—the *getting it* part—is to experience an awakening that will make you constantly aware of the separate systems of your life. Once you *see* your systems, working them is just common sense. Work your systems and good results will spontaneously appear.

CONSCIOUSLY PAYING ATTENTION

All of us have recurring individual systems we employ to good advantage. We have a multitude of these processes down pat, and we perform them efficiently and quickly today because we have practiced them over and over in the past. We've perfected walking, driving a car, fixing breakfast, and playing a game. Why are we expert in these small system proceedings? Because they are simple, yes, but mostly because at some point we consciously paid close attention to the elements of the processes; we analyzed and adjusted and practiced the bit parts so that after a while we could execute the complete protocols with little effort, almost without thinking. But for many people, there is no deliberate effort to dissect and then perfect the sequential workings of more complex, wide-angle system processes like careers, health, and relationships. Too many of us just churn along, wasting time and energy revisiting the same problems over and over again because we aren't focusing on the elements of the equation.

So, to tackle the more involved challenges—the challenges that have stymied you because of their complexities—we're going to redirect the perceptive, investigative, and analytical skills you already possess.

OVERVIEW OF YOUR NEW SYSTEMS MINDSET POSTURE

The systems mindset is different from the mental paradigm most people pack around day to day. Instead of seeing yourself as an internal component of circumstances, enmeshed within the day's swirling events, your vantage point is outside and slightly elevated from those events. The day's happenings are visible as separate and individual elements, arranged in logical sequences. You are an observer looking down on your world, examining the comings and goings of the day as if they are tangible, physical objects. You see the separateness of the systems of your life; the components are simple and understandable. Wherever you look, the machinations of the world make sense: step by step, one thing leads to another as the systems around you continuously execute.

Your job is to work your systems. *This is what you do*. One by one you take your systems apart, examine them, and then make them better. Over time, complexity and confusion decrease to be replaced by order, calm, and rock-solid self-confidence. There is little fire killing and no confusion, and as you peer down at your handiwork you feel an intense self-respect and you are proud of what you've accomplished. All by yourself, you've created the life you've always wanted.

I COME TO YOU AS A PROJECT ENGINEER

With blue-collar roots, I have a mixed-bag background: land surveyor, heavy-equipment operator, union-man factory worker, door-to-door salesman, technical consultant, hamburger flipper, house painter, department store sales clerk, construction superintendent, design engineer, ditch digger, sales professional, builder, janitor, journalist, public speaker, book publisher, retail store owner, lab technician, logger, mill worker, machinist, stocks and commodities investor, writer, photojournalist, telecommunications entrepreneur, real estate salesman, kitchen worker, handyman, corporate CEO, and business owner. I founded and operate a nonprofit organization that assists earthquake victims in northeast Pakistan, Azad Jammu and Kashmir, and in India (see kashmirfamily.org). Through my business, Centratel (centratel.com), my special expertise is in the practical methodology of telecommunications: taking information, processing it, and then passing it on. My personal comportment? I'm a handshake, not a man-hug kind of guy.

Now my overall life role is as a project engineer: that is, someone who accepts a problem, designs a mechanical solution, and then makes that solution work in the real world. I'm a project engineer in every aspect of my being, including the personal roles of father, son, brother, husband, and friend.

Metaphorically, here's my day: after a solid night's sleep, I bounce out of bed, shower, eat a big breakfast, and jump into things full bore, plunging into the new day. Today I am working with my crew to build something tangible out of the design I created on the drafting table just yesterday. I'm on the job in clean jeans, work boots, and a decent shirt. My persona is relaxed, with a slight smile on my face just under the surface of my focused comportment.

Again, metaphorically, I pull the levers and push the buttons of the unfolding day. My crew and I are lighthearted, relaxed, powerful, and efficient—and we're fast. *Work feels good* and time flies as we cut a wide swath, making positive things happen as we translate yesterday's paper design into the reality of the physical world today. We're creating something worthwhile. We're permanently improving things.

This is what I want for you.

A NONHOLISTIC APPROACH

Is there a holistic or global side of you that balks at separating things to examine them individually? You may say everything is connected and we're all one, and we must stop seeing ourselves as distinct from the world around us. You may think our lives are immeasurably complex, beyond human comprehension. That's fine for the big picture. I tend to think that way myself when I'm relaxed and daydreaming. But for now, here on this material earth where we must physically navigate each moment, put that aside and go with the case for separation and simple mechanics.

Understand that fixing an entire scattered conglomeration of a life in one fell swoop is impossible. It can't be done holistically, despite the rightness that term suggests. Fixing anything of complexity requires proceeding one step at a time, one component at a time—a decidedly nonholistic approach.

I don't care for the term *holistic solution*. Instead, I like the term *holistic result*, which suggests that each component system within the organism is functioning at peak efficiency, resulting in an entity that is superb in fulfilling its purpose.

So it's OK to take your world apart to examine it, to get things straightened out piece by piece. You can view it holistically later, when you're not working on the details. There will be plenty of time for that.

CHANGES IN YOUR LIFE

Because this isn't a mystery novel, and because preparation is at the heart of the work the system method, here's a two-part summary of how it will affect you, and what it asks.

First, here are four points about how acquiring the systems mindset will impact you personally:

1. **You will undergo an elementary yet fundamental shift in perspective.** The systems mindset will probably arrive suddenly, as a stark awakening in a moment of time rather than over a long, drawn-out learning experience. After the mindset takes hold, moment to moment you will dispassionately observe the separate human and mechanical systems that comprise your world. These systems will stand apart from each other, starkly visible and sharply defined. You've turned a corner.

2. **There will be no turning back.** You can't go back! So point two is a warning of sorts. Because of the obvious logic of it, the systems mindset is something you won't be able to shake.

3. **You will not be swallowing unsupportable theories of reality.** This is just a matter of more clearly seeing the world's mechanical workings. There's plenty enough reality without having to delve into questionable feel-good theory. Deep down you will know the truth of the work the system method because it makes sense. And be assured that you won't sound flighty when you explain your new point of view to those around you. You're not going to lose your friends and family because you are not going to ask them for anything. You have nothing to sell. Instead, should they ask what's up, you'll explain what this is about, and they will be intrigued with what you have to say.

4. **There is some heavy lifting.** Yes, you will undergo an exciting change of perspective, but that is not enough. At the beginning of the process there is some sit-down work as you create documentation in order to better define your targets and to keep moving efficiently toward them. It's a superb investment because the end product will be a relaxed persona, plenty of money, and lots of free time. In all probability, it will be the best investment of time you will ever make. (Boring but true: what is the single major operational difference between a large successful business and a small struggling one? Documentation and procedures.)

Here's the second part of this nutshell summary, the three steps of the process:

1. **Separation, dissection, and repair of systems:** The satisfying process of exposing, analyzing, and then perfecting work, personal, and relationship systems. This ongoing effort includes creating new systems from scratch as well as eliminating those that are holding you back.

2. **Documentation:** Creating written goals, principles, and processes that are guidelines for action and decision making for you and for the people who work with you. This is not a feel-good exercise. It's the mandatory foundation for creating tremendous efficiency. This is the one-time heavy lifting. But it won't take

long (and if you lead a team or department, you'll teach your people to do it).

3. **Ongoing maintenance of systems:** Greasing the wheels. This is easy. The positive tangible results of the work the system method are motivating because it's obvious the systems you've created are carrying the ball. You'll happily oversee your systems in order to keep them operating at peak efficiency.

TWO ITEMS OF NOTE

First, at the end of most chapters I've placed real-life examples to illustrate various aspects of the new approach. Some relate to the previous chapter, some don't. The examples will remind you that *a mandatory element of the method is to view your world from a new perspective.* The systems mindset vantage point is removed from the day's machinations. Only from an exterior position can system mechanics be properly examined and adjusted. From this outside observation post you reach down to adjust those mechanics so they produce the results you want.

Second, it's important we speak the same language. Here I define words and terms as they apply to the work the system method. I advise you to get familiar with them now, at the beginning.

99.9 percent of everything works fine: Look around! There is a penchant for efficiency in the world. The systems of the world want to work perfectly, and 99.9 percent of them do.

Business: One does not have to show up in order to earn money.

Closed system: Self-contained processing entity, easily discerned from its surroundings.

Error of omission: A less-than-perfect situation that occurs because someone didn't do something.

General Operating Principles: The second of the three primary work the system documents; a two- to four-page collection of *guidelines for decision making* that is congruent with the Strategic Objective. Essential for the work environment and in a simplified and shorter format, useful in one's personal life (see chapter 10).

Job or profession: One has to show up in order to earn money.

Linear: This is how most systems execute, in a 1-2-3-step progression. A linear process is not chaotic. Within its context it is logical, reliable, and simple to understand.

Mechanical system: A physical car, house, tree, etc. that, because of its physicality, doesn't fluctuate in its form or execution of purpose. But also, within the work the system context, a formerly organic work process that has been made mechanically tangible via written documentation.

Off-the-street people: These are the people who will do the work as viewed by business owners or managers. Depending on the context, off-the-street workers can be novices or professionals.

Organic work system: Recurring human communication or work process in which the components (and therefore the outcome) vary according to personality, mood, time of day, etc.

Outside and slightly elevated: The essential (and almost metaphysical) perspective is external and above. The view downward also encompasses the observer—you.

Perfect: In the work the system world, 98 percent accuracy is perfect because trying to achieve that additional 2 percent demands too much additional output.

Primary system or system of systems: Composed of subsystems, a whole encapsulated entity with an ultimate purpose. An organism unto itself.

Project engineer: The role of a business owner or manager who adopts an outside, system-improvement posture rather than an inside, doing-the-work role. For personal life, it's in-the-moment positioning in which one's systems are contemplated, analyzed, adjusted, and maintained.

Recurring system: An enclosed process that occurs over and over again.

Strategic objective: The first of three primary work the system documents. It's a single page that defines goals, describes methodology, lists strengths, and prescribes action (see chapter 10).

System, subsystem (or process, mechanism, machine): An enclosed entity, with numerous spinning wheels, all contributing to the singular purpose of that entity, that is, to accomplish a goal. Within the work the system context, we are especially interested in *recurring systems*. The terms *system* and *subsystem* are interchangeable depending on context.

System improvement: The heart of the method. In the workplace it's the relentless search-and-repair process of tooling a process closer and closer to perfection all while documenting and maintaining that process so its hyperefficient execution will recur every time.

System management: A focus on maximizing the efficiencies of processes in order to prevent recurring problems, increase production and quality, and save time. It is the opposite of fire killing.

Systems mindset or work the system mindset: The embedded vision of the world as an orderly collection of processes, not as a chaotic mass of sights, sounds, and events.

Tweaking: The antithesis of neglect. The assertive, dogmatic, boots-on-the-ground work of making incremental, subsystem enhancements that will ultimately produce a hyper-efficient primary system.

Work the system methodology: The mechanical process of establishing goals and then perfecting the systems that will ensure attainment of those goals.

Working Procedures: The third of the three primary work the system controlling documents. These are written instructions that describe how individual systems of the workplace are to operate. They are the end products of the system-improvement process. Written Working Procedures are not often necessary for personal life (see chapter 11).

Workingman's (or workingwoman's!) philosophy: A set of beliefs stemming from the hard, cold, sometimes dirty realities of the job site. The pragmatic view that a carefully composed blueprint directs the assembly of individual pieces into an excellent end product.

PART ONE

THE SYSTEMS MINDSET

CHAPTER 1
Control Is a Good Thing

My father says that almost the whole world is asleep. Everybody you know. Everybody you see. Everybody you talk to. He says that only a few people are awake and they live in a state of constant total amazement.

—Patricia (Meg Ryan) from the movie *Joe Versus the Volcano*
(Warner Bros. Pictures, Amblin Entertainment, 1990)

For many, hearing a version of the adage "To get what you want, you must have more control" evokes the knee-jerk response that seeking control is a bad thing. They counter that one should relax and go with the flow, stay loose, and not worry so much about details . . . and that seeking more and more control can only mean one is devolving into a nervous control freak. There is an almost cosmological sense—a carryover from the '60s, no doubt—that "we're all one," and the problems in our lives and the world around us are created by people who don't share our brand of let-it-be spirituality. If my boss, my spouse, my parents, my children, my neighbor, and my government would just lighten up and be sensible—like *me*—then everyone would be happy!

Confident in the truth of it but confounded by reality, we are eager to proclaim that the states of our lives—and conditions in the world—are not good. We exhort that people are too uptight, too concerned with tiny details.

Allow me to retort.

Notwithstanding the possible metaphysical truth of the "we're all one" mantra, it's my contention that being in control of the details of our lives is mandatory if we are to find peace and success—if we are to find happiness.

Conversely, while we're focusing on those factors that are in our control, we must lighten up about those that are *not* in our control. If we attempt to influence events that are out of our reach, we are in for disappointment.

Is it difficult to determine what we can and cannot control? No, it's not.

My generation emphasized a great and useful truth: what's happening now *is* the most important thing. But I also know that the satisfaction I feel in any particular moment has much to do with the details I've carefully managed in days past. Yes, I try hard to be here now, but I spend some of that here-time focusing on actions that will ensure future moments will be what I want them to be.

WALLOWING

With my younger brother as an ally, I was brought up in my grandparents' house in the small town of Port Leyden in upstate New York. It was a chaotic, unsettled family.

At seventeen, I was on the streets of the Haight district in San Francisco. It was 1967, the Summer of Love, when I discovered an intriguing escape from the not-so-perfect family situation back home. For two years I wallowed in sex, drugs, and rock 'n' roll. (Well, maybe not that much sex.)

In the summer of '69 I ended up at the Woodstock Music and Art Fair, the famous gathering of five hundred thousand in rural upstate New York. *Far out*, I thought. Afterward, I continued to fruitlessly seek a better state of mind, and another year wafted by. I was the poster child for the freewheeling '60s.

In my self-imposed stupor there was little I didn't complain about. I tried college but dropped out my second year, distraught in my loneliness and with my vision of a planet gone mad. In 1970, during a Washington, DC, political demonstration, I was teargassed. Literally, as the mist of gas swirled down on me in the middle of the cordoned-off street, I met the woman who was to be my wife and the mother of my two children. Then, within weeks, with my new love in tow, I revisited the now dangerous streets of San Francisco. We lived on those streets for two months and then returned to rural upstate New York.

Through it all I balked at everything that didn't align itself with my idea of rightness, chafing at the unfairness of it all. It was the system, I thought. It's stacked against me. I ranted that too many narrow-minded, selfish people were manipulating things, conspiring to ruin my life.

Of course, I was a beacon of equanimity.

In truth, I was a pain to everyone who had to deal with me, while my life was a series of dead-end jobs and personal frustrations. Profoundly unhappy, dropping out of college twice more, I was a narcissistic complainer haunted by self-imposed psychic hooligans.

In the middle of all this, I married my teargas love. Not surprisingly, my bride was equally frustrated with the unfairness of things. We were two peas in a pod, loud and bold, convinced of our rightness and everyone else's wrongness.

Then, after six years of wallowing in this foggy existence, the chains suddenly fell off one August morning in 1973. Hungover and depressed yet again, I sat at the kitchen table in our dumpy apartment in Inlet, New York. I was earning minimum wage as a seasonal worker at a State of New York recreational campsite, collecting garbage and cleaning public restrooms. I was late for work that morning, but nevertheless sat there immobile, looking inward. I declared to myself, essentially, and in not so many words, *"I'm not living like this anymore. Until now my point of view has been wrong. No longer will I try to change the world by whining about it. There is very little outside myself I can direct, so I will stop agonizing over events outside my reach. I will arrange to go back to school this fall to learn something that can be used to create a future for us. From now on there will be no more complaining, no more blaming. Rather than rejecting the world as it's presented to me, I will get inside it—as it is—and see what I can do with the parts of it that are within my grasp."*

Little did I know that my desperate acquiescence to "the system" in my mid-twenties would be the first step toward writing a book thirty years later that would point out the beauty of systems and the freedoms they can provide. But unlike my preoccupations back then, what I write about here has nothing to do with politics, wishful thinking, or right or wrong. It's about simple mechanics.

I enrolled at the New York State Ranger School in the Adirondack Mountains of upstate New York to study forestry and land surveying. I put my head down, worked hard through the winter, and graduated the next summer with a technical degree. Continuing to pay attention to the details, my wife and I, and our five-month-old son, headed to Oregon with $400 in our pockets and everything we owned packed into a homemade trailer attached to the back of the Plymouth. I had made a stand. I was improving my life—and the lives of the two people who were depending on me—by expending my energy only on details that I could control. The fog in my head had lifted due to an absurdly simple adjustment in my thinking process.

But despite those first steps toward dealing with the real world as it is, I had not yet recognized the next necessary step that would lead to control of my environment and thus the ability to forge freedom and wealth. In this ignorance, I would bang my head against the wall for another twenty-five years.

PERPETUAL DISAPPOINTMENT

The best illustration of the baggage I carried is a photo taken at Wood-stock. It's one you may have seen. It's of a lovely, slender, long-haired girl who is maybe eighteen years old. She's beautiful, and she's dancing in a farm meadow in a long, sheer dress. There's a flower wreath in her hair, and she's laughing as she whirls with her arms stretched above her head in a casual way. Her thin, handsome, ponytailed boyfriend is dancing, too. They share a peaceful ecstasy, and anyone who sees that photo would, at least for a moment, want to be one of those two young people.

The image is a declaration of pure bliss with the clear message that unrestrained happiness *is* attainable, and the path to it requires no more than an unrestrained persona, hip music, and an unlimited supply of drugs. With a broad metaphorical brushstroke, the message that photo paints is that freedom will arrive as soon as we drop our uptight preoccupations and dance in the meadow.

Let it all hang out. Stay loose. Go with the flow.

Back to the real world. The photo is an enticement for a state of mind that exists only for brief moments. Its message on how to live is a sham. One can't just lighten up and expect ongoing happiness. Life isn't that way. But many of us who evolved from that era think it *should* be that way, and so we live from day to day in perpetual disappointment within a world that refuses to conform to our expectations.

We bask in wealth never seen before but wonder why we are unsatisfied. Forty years after the '60s, that silly self-absorbed perspective has carried over to our children and grandchildren.

(Don't get me wrong. I don't like focusing on negatives, and it's a bit painful for me to discuss the unhappy contortions of my generation. But it's a necessary discussion for presenting the work the system premise, so I have to start here—in the negative—in order to set the stage for the rest of the story, which I promise you will find uplifting.)

So we finger point and complain and wonder at our dissatisfaction. It's too bad we do that because it's not just a waste of time, it's a distraction from what we really need to do to find life satisfaction. Excuses, generalizations about the alleged dire state of the world, and under-the-radar as well as overt attempts to change the people around us are ineffectual to the point of paralysis. These preoccupations are diversions from the actions we could take that would produce what we want in our individual lives: peace, prosperity, and control of our own destinies. And pursuing peace, prosperity, and control are noble goals because the sure way to realize them is to contribute to the people around us.

What about the generally accepted notion that someone who seeks firm control is an unpleasant personality, someone who needs to loosen up? I submit that this ubiquitous generalization is wrong. Back in New York, at the age of twenty-five, I learned that happiness would not be found in the control we have over others or in complaining about world conditions or in finding the perfect drug. It would be found in the firm grasp of the moment-to-moment trajectory of our own lives.

But as the three of us drove west to Oregon back in 1974, what I didn't see—as illustrated by the dancing girl photo—was that gaining command of one's life can't arrive from approaching it from the outside. Personal control will only occur after a mind shift inside.

Your Circle of Influence

A concept made popular by Stephen Covey, the circle of influence analogy illustrates one's level of control. In years past I was hardly able to direct my own comings and goings due to whatever psychological funk was swallowing me up in the moment. My circle of influence felt like it was inches in diameter. Now, my circle feels as if it's miles across, as my days effortlessly sail by and I am able to accomplish nearly all that I set out to do. This impact gives me enormous satisfaction, as the wheels of progress keep turning due to my previous input, not because of my immediate presence.

Take a moment to imagine your own circle. How large is it? Is it just six inches in diameter? If it is, when you look down, is the top of it hidden underneath your feet? If the tiny circle is just twelve inches in height, you can barely balance on it. Do you spend all your available energy and attention just trying not to fall off? If this is your situation, your tenuous balancing effort doesn't leave much time for anything but complaining.

Instead, what if you could channel the time and energy expended in this constant balancing effort into making your circle larger?

Wherever you are, whatever the size of your circle of influence, focus on making changes inside of it, not outside. Don't spend precious time agonizing over big-picture issues you can't affect while neglecting the elements of your own life that you *can* change. Expend your limited and precious allotment of time and energy on the matters you can affect, the matters within your circle. Do that, and your circle—and influence—will expand.

LIFE IS A STREAMING VIDEO, NOT A SNAPSHOT

Outside of brief moments within that encapsulated era, the unbridled approach of the '60s was just another great idea that didn't work. It was a theory of living that didn't consider how we actually were, but instead, declared how we should be. If the Woodstock meadow-dancing photo had been a documentary movie, the hours and days surrounding that dance would tell a different story.

The truth of Woodstock? The nonstop music was good but few bands played their best due to the confusion and pervasive drug ingestion. Yes it was peaceful, but after that first glorious day it was cold and wet, and we sat in the mud shivering, drenched, hungry, and thirsty. Huddled in the rain, a half million of us worked hard to relax, insistent in our success at finding freedom and joy outside the system. Peace, brother! In the downpour, over and over again we told ourselves that all we needed was love. We really had jumped outside the everyday world, but in our T-shirts, jeans, and little else, we were utterly unprepared as the relentless torrent hammered down. It was no contest as soft theory met bare-knuckled reality.

With the inevitability of a wave washing onto shore, the enthusiasm faded as the filth that comes with neglected crowds began to accumulate. After forty-eight hours of this, a general paranoia swept through the cowering drug-addled horde, and my friend John and I got out of there. We left before Jimi Hendrix had taken the stage. It was that bad.

As we headed home in my beat-up wreck of a car, listening to the radio, we were reminded of Vietnam, racial unrest, and political deviousness. And beyond those negatives, we both worked graveyard union jobs in a small-town paper mill, and as we drove through the night exhausted and depressed, it was clear that the joy we experienced at Woodstock fell within just a narrow sliver in time.

John was eighteen years old; I was nineteen. We were college-dropout party guys and proud of our chaotic lifestyles. We never thought of the relationship between our undirected lives and our unhappiness. As I think back and make judgments, it occurs to me that the ones who were creating something worthwhile were the straight kids. They were not immune to down times, but in their willingness to conform to the reality of planet earth and to face existence head on, they were more in control and yes, happier.

The lure of dancing in the meadow is an invitation to illusionary bliss. Truth is, orderliness and attention to detail are the roots of peace. Proof? Consider the indisputable reverse logic: in any setting, the opposite of peace—disorder—always leads to desperation. It's this way for any out-of-hand situation: a natural disaster, riot, war, car accident, or family argument. The outcome is never a pretty sight.

Too many of us are paralyzed in the static picture of how we think the world should be instead of working with the fluid mechanics of how it actually *is*. Life is not a snapshot. It's a real-time, streaming video—and the video plays on whether we understand it or not.

DISTRACTED

So, forty years later, what is the relevance? For those who still buy into the '60s mystique, an unfounded assumption smolders. It whispers there is chaos all around, that systems and organization are bad and that Big Brother is right there behind the curtain, always steering things in the wrong direction.

This thread of paranoia leaves too many of us obsessing about conditions that are not in our control, and the obsessing distracts us from taking the actions that would truly make us free! It's not the system that holds people back. It's a flaw in individual perception.

Back in 1974 as I moved my small family west, what I still didn't understand was that freedom and peace lay in seeing the mechanisms of life and then attending to them. Back then, I didn't know there could be a breathtaking internal shift in perception that would not only allow me to see the machinery that was producing the results of my life, but also would reveal the enormous power I had over my own destiny.

It didn't occur to me that by being blind to personal systems, the mistake of a lifetime could be waiting just around the corner, ready to flatten me when I least expected it, and, less dramatic but more endemic, that small inefficiencies could quietly accumulate and take me to the same dark place. The logic that this churning flow of life would be at my command only by paying close attention to the nuts and bolts that composed it, was beyond me.

Back then, I didn't understand that peace and prosperity arrive *after* the mechanics are in order.

Mood Adjustment

In the Western world, 10 percent of adults are alcoholics, 70 percent drink copious amounts of caffeine, 25 percent are addicted to tobacco, and more than 10 percent rely on antidepressants. Throw in the other legal and illegal drugs, and it is safe to say that each day, 98 percent of us ingest at least one mood-altering substance in our endless search for a better state of mind. Of course, many of us are multisubstance users, for instance, consuming caffeine in the morning and alcohol at night. One addictive substance counters the negative effects of the other in the classic, endless loop of Western chemical mood adjustment.

A DEARTH OF SYSTEMS

From a systems perspective, what happened at Woodstock? One system that worked well was the one that delivered the music. The technicians were adept and the equipment functioned adequately. The musicians showed up, which meant the transportation process worked—the entertainers were delivered by helicopter. The location (Yasgur's farm) worked.

What systems did *not* work? Outside of what I already mentioned, you name it. The ticketing process failed, with all the surrounding fences coming down the first day of the event—a disaster for the promoters. The sanitation and medical systems were overwhelmed. And if overt police protection had been required it would have been mayhem because there was little more than a tiny contingent of informal private security guards.

Of course, few in the audience were physically prepared, even in a rudimentary way. To compound the external challenges, drug use was hampering rational thinking. Everyone was in the middle of everything and chaos was a breath away, held back by no more than the luck of the draw.

One day of peace and music? Yes, OK, that's true. Two days? Well, the drugs helped maintain a certain calmness, but circumstances were deteriorating quickly. Three days? Whew! It was an exodus out of there! If there had been four days? For those diehards who might have remained, it would have been a sordid, nasty affair.

For a while, it was the love and goodwill of the people that made the festival work. But that sliver of bliss time was narrow and can't serve as an example of how a life can be lived day to day. "I love you, man" is not nearly enough for the long term.

A Potent, Visceral Reminder from the Folks at NASA

A space shuttle is arguably the most complex machine ever built by man, and a launch was perhaps the most magnificent display of human system control. I never missed an opportunity to watch the event on TV in real time.

The shuttle program ended in the summer of 2011, but one can still consider the precision of the countdown, which relied on thousands of simultaneous and automatic monitoring processes, all overseen by engineers and technicians. Launches were executed, and tens of thousands of active processes, both on the craft and on the ground, operated independently and in concert, each a precision entity unto itself.

There was a total of 135 space shuttle launches, two of which were spectacularly horrible failures. Yet, considering the incredible complexity of the endeavor, and acknowledging the human penchant for error, one could legitimately wonder why there were not more catastrophes than this.

Like countless minor failures of the past, the two tragedies provided space shuttle engineers with information they used to prevent future problems. As time moved on, the chances of failure decreased steadily as the shuttle was tweaked ever closer to perfection.

Each shuttle launch was a keynote celebration of human potential and a potent, visceral illustration of the beauty of the countless systems that comprise our existences.

CHAPTER 2
Events Did Not Unfold as Anticipated

King Arthur (Graham Chapman), after chopping off both of the
Black Knight's arms: *Look, you stupid bastard. You've got no arms left!*
Black Knight (John Cleese): *Yes I have! . . . It's just a flesh wound!*

—FROM THE MOVIE *Monty Python and the Holy Grail* (EMI FILMS,1975)

ONE REASON I USE CENTRATEL TO ILLUSTRATE the work the system
framework is that it is an easily understood primary system that is composed of subsystems. It's a closed system of systems that provides simple
cause-and-effect depictions of the principles. As I go through the details
of my business, read between the lines and understand that the picture I
paint is also applicable to personal life.

CENTRATEL OVERVIEW

For fifteen years Centratel struggled for survival, always at the brink of
disaster. Why did this primary system begin to prosper in year sixteen?
Yes, focused attention, terrific staff, targeted marketing, and a consistently
high-quality product went a long way, but they were not the *cause* of the
turnaround. Instead, these were by-products of the cause. The reason for
the turnaround was the discovery and application of the principle that
leadership must focus on improving processes, not on performing the
work or on repeatedly snuffing out brushfires. Quality products or services, a stable staff, and profitability are the result of the quality systems
that underlie them, not the reverse.

Centratel is a high-tech, national telephone answering service (TAS). As a third-party outsourcing business, a telephone answering service employs telephone service representatives (TSRs) who process incoming telephone calls (from *callers*) for various businesses (*clients*). Essentially a private 9-1-1 dispatch center, an answering service's purpose is to take messages from the client's callers and then deliver those messages to the client. Clients include medical and veterinary clinics, hospice and home health care services, funeral homes, public utilities, property management companies, HVAC operations, high-tech firms, and the like. These are businesses that must provide 24/7/365 human interaction to their customers or patients. Since these businesses can't cover their phones 24/7, they must employ an answering service to screen and process their after-hours calls. And, a significant number of businesses use an answering service during daytime hours when incoming phone traffic is more than can be handled in-house, or if the company is tiny and has no physical office.

At Centratel, up to twelve TSRs at a time (depending on call traffic) sit at workstations and field one call after another, with the incoming calls arriving randomly from any one of approximately one thousand accounts. Sometimes when traffic is heavy, calls come in like machine-gun fire. One will be from a nervous husband whose wife is on the way to the hospital to have a baby; the next one from the panicked owner of a horse stricken with colic; the next from an apartment tenant who has accidentally locked herself out of her unit. You get the idea.

Our TSRs take messages, record them in a database, and then deliver them in a variety of ways including pager, cell phone, voice mailbox, e-mail, or fax. It's a complex enterprise, with multitudes of human and mechanical processes executing simultaneously. Caller, client, and TSR communication is constant and nearly always time sensitive. Each of our accounts provides unique and exact instructions on how to handle callers and process messages. So within any TAS business there is enormous opportunity for error, and without strict systems protocol and superior staff, it's an understatement to say an answering service is a breeding ground for chaos.

The TAS industry stretches back to the first days of telephones. As they were then, today's answering services are nonstop operations. This all-the-time activity engenders another interesting challenge: odd work-ing hours for TSRs as they come and go from the office at all times of the day and night. It's a tough way to earn a living, a major challenge for those who field calls after hours and on weekends. Our more senior TSRs have worked themselves into daytime shifts, but new people must earn their stripes, enduring the tougher schedules until they can move into better slots that open due to staff attrition and company growth. In any case, the pay and benefits are very good at Centratel, close to double industry averages.

It's a fascinating industry, but it's in decline. In 1975 the total number of TAS businesses in the United States was more than twenty thousand, most of which were small mom-and-pop operations. Now, survivors are larger—but less than two thousand total—and as a percentage of the over-all population, the number of TAS clients has also decreased considerably. Smart phones, voice mail, the Internet, and telephone company switching options have cut deeply into the potential client base. Nevertheless, plenty of businesses still require a real-live human being to process their incoming calls, and the core market will not be disappearing any time soon.

Twenty-eight years ago I contemplated entering the TAS industry for three reasons (and these reasons are still good general considerations for anyone going into business).

First, it intrigued me that it was all about people and communication.

Second, revenues would be passive. If managed properly, I would not have to be physically present in order to receive income. I was new to busi-ness, but it seemed to me that making money without having to show up to do the work would beat being a doctor, attorney, teacher, psychologist, working man, or any number of occupations where a specific individual is the centerpiece of the endeavor.

Third, revenues would be recurring—clients would continuously use our services and pay us over and over again. If clients paid monthly, gener-ating new income would not be a full-time daily challenge. I reasoned that if the product was superior and our clients were happy, the money would constantly flow.

So on December 1, 1984, at the age of thirty-five, I bought Girl Friday Telephone Answering Service, an ailing TAS. The total purchase price was

$21,000; the down payment was $5,000. There were seven employees, 140 clients, and 400 square feet of office space.

Now the owner of a business, I changed the name of the company to reflect the changing times, and—per my arrogant cockiness in those days—announced to anyone who would listen that we would someday be the highest-quality telephone answering service in the United States. Despite my bravado, I had no idea how we would achieve such a goal. (As I think back on those days and how I performed, the words "brash" and "clueless" enter my mind.)

Events did not unfold as anticipated. The new business was a disorganized nightmare, and in the chaos of it all, my personal world devolved into a shambles. Within a year, there was a divorce, and then I proceeded to do my best to bring up my two children as a single custodial parent. All this was compounded by a deep economic recession that had especially affected the Northwest, which was still reeling from the recent virtual destruction of the supporting regional industry: timber harvesting. (For my beautiful hometown of Bend, Oregon, however—and lucky for me— tourism would soon fill in the gap.)

Yet, although always on the brink of disaster, Centratel grew in volume—but profits never increased. It was an epic struggle, and as the first years passed, the best-in-the-U.S. goal disappeared behind the cloud of disarray.

For a decade and a half I endured moment-to-moment turmoil, working long, long hours—consistently in excess of eighty hours a week—always just scraping by financially. I got sick from the pressure but powered on anyway. The only thing that would stop me would be if I dropped over unconscious from stress and sheer fatigue, and after fifteen years of relentless pressure, this became more than a possibility.

Then I had an unforeseen insight. An earthmoving event, the new vision deeply affected me as it profoundly changed the way I perceived the world. Per this mini-enlightenment, I immediately began to interact with my surroundings in a new way, and instantly the turbulence began to subside. Centratel became a better place because I was viewing it more precisely.

Just after my mini-enlightenment, I brought a partner into the business—a good man, an acquaintance I had always respected who said he knew about my company and thought it had a future—and I was no longer in it alone. Now I had a second set of professional eyes, and with his stock purchase, a financial boost. Interesting that as I began to delve deep into the mechanics of my business and my life, odd synchronistic signs emerged. For one, my new partner's name: it's Sam.

The next few chapters describe the odyssey in detail. As you read, think of parallels in your own life.

Installing a Preventative System

Sometimes we install a system that doesn't do much. We achieve the desired effect by the mere existence of it. At Centratel, we knew that a few of our TSRs spent time cruising the Net while on duty. For security and focus reasons, that's not a good thing. It was impossible to track these sleight-of-hand excursions, and the closest we could get to managing the problem was to walk around a corner and find a TSR covertly closing a non-Centratel window upon our approach.

So we installed special software that tracks and logs all Internet activity. The software solved the problem instantly and completely.

Have we ever tracked down bad behavior with it? Yes, when we first installed the software without announcing what we had done, the expected suspects emerged. Did we say anything to them? No, it wasn't necessary because we knew that once we announced the installation and noted it in our Employee Handbook, the people who were violating the rules would change their behavior. Did they? Yes. In routinely checking the monthly logs, have we had subsequent abuses? No.

In our society, other examples of preventative systems include drug testing, the police, the military, and laws. These mechanisms provide consequences for bad behavior but are mostly intended to halt problems before they occur.

Think of preventative systems and mechanisms in your personal life: the seat belt in your car that doesn't just protect you from injury but reminds you that a defensive driving posture is paramount; the routine backups on your computer; the small courtesies you show to loved ones and strangers alike. As you go through your day, think of systems you can implement that will prevent problems down the line while they keep things smooth in the present.

CHAPTER 3

The Attack of the Moles

Gwen DeMarco (Sigourney Weaver): *They are so cute!*
Guy Fleegman (Sam Rockwell): *Sure, they're cute now, but in a second*
they're gonna get mean, and they're gonna get ugly somehow, and there's
gonna be a million more of them.

—FROM THE MOVIE *Galaxy Quest* (DREAMWORKS SKG, 1999)

ALL ANSWERING SERVICES PERFORM THE SAME FUNCTION for their clients, and my newly purchased TAS was no exception. At all hours of the day and night our TSRs took incoming calls from our clients' callers. When clients called in, TSRs read their transcribed-by-hand messages back to them. It was the mid-1980s, when word processing and computer database programs were little more than future concepts for small businesses. We were a mom-and-pop service, and for a flat rate of $35 to $45 per month, we processed as many calls as the client could send us. During the day, two TSRs handled calls; after hours, one.

From the beginning and for fifteen subsequent years, I called the shots on all aspects of the operation. From the first day of ownership, it was a madhouse because most of our clients had taken advantage of the flat-rate arrangement and used our TSRs as their full-time telephone receptionists. TSRs were overwhelmed with call traffic and so the quality of call handling was abysmal. At first, all I could do was watch and wonder because I had no understanding of the internal mechanics of an answering service. That first day, I didn't even know how phone calls were routed to us.

When I bought the business, the monthly total gross revenue of $5,500 was not enough to cover wages, rent, telephone company costs, and everything else, including supporting myself and my two children. The business had been mine for only two months, and disaster was already at hand. ("Disaster at hand" was to become a serial catchphrase over the ensuing years.) Standing by and not taking some kind of action would be a quick ticket to failure, so with my staff and my eight- and ten-year-olds depending on me, I had to do something immediately. Here, my brashness would be useful.

It was ironic that although the business was in terrible shape when I bought it, some positive aspects lay hidden. After just a few weeks the major problems were obvious even to me, someone with zero knowledge of the industry. It was clear I must immediately correct the most glaring inefficiency: a customer pricing schedule that was in the basement. It was fortunate that our service rates were extremely low—we could raise them enormously and still remain competitive.

I informed our clients by letter that service rates were going up and we would start charging for the actual call traffic we handled for their individual accounts. I told them that a large price hike was the only choice if we were to stay in business. So, for each client, we dropped the monthly flat-rate billing plan and began counting the number of messages we processed, billing them for the exact number of messages we handled.

On average, this *tripled* our customers' monthly costs, and immediately one-third terminated service, while others dramatically cut back the traffic they forwarded to us. The decrease in incoming calls allowed our TSRs to spend more time on each call, and because they were less rushed, the quality of service improved—the first of many incremental quality improvements that were to accumulate over the years ahead.

As a sidelight, and to illustrate just how low our service rates had been, even with the 300 percent increase, our prices remained lower than our much larger local TAS competitor.

Despite losing more than a third of our total client base, monthly revenues doubled overnight to $11,000. The huge increase in income was terrific, but equipment had to be upgraded and wages raised. So even with the additional cash boost, the company was still not profitable. We raised rates again in six months and then again six months after that. One year later we did it again. Nonetheless, we continued to struggle.

This just-barely-hanging-on predicament endured. Over the next decade and a half, we couldn't get ahead even though we were able to multiply income by a factor of twelve. Our revenue growth was due to rate increases, a booming economy, and the new clients we gained because of our growing reputation for quality—quality that had risen from terrible to marginal (but marginal quality was better than our local competitor who remained at the terrible level because of their own self-perpetuated chaos). Nonetheless, the rise in income was always matched by increases in operating costs. The largest hikes were in wages, health insurance, retirement, and other benefits for the TSR staff.

Within three years we moved to a larger office space. We stayed in that location for twelve years and then moved to an even larger space. We continued to grow, but there was little profit, and the turmoil and cash flow problems mounted.

In all those years, my small salary didn't change while my eighty- to one-hundred-hour workweeks continued unabated. I had no life outside the business, and any off-work time went to my two children.

As the years passed, I learned the ropes thoroughly, priding myself on being expert at every facet of the business. I was able to perform any function and address any challenge. Within moments I could move from scheduling staff to handling customer complaints to solving telephone company problems. I could interview a job applicant for a TSR position one minute, and in the next put together a plan for adding a computer. I could prepare payroll while I signed up a new account and then head to the bank to plead my case for yet another small loan. I did it all, including being an effective single parent to my kids (the task juggling at home rivaled the task juggling at the office).

What a feeling of power as I simultaneously solved multiple problems. I was a master of survival juggling, a fire killer extraordinaire! How heroic! But in my arrogance, and as I was swept up in the endless fire killing, I was spinning my wheels and headed for destruction.

The Numbers Are Gloomy

Statistics show that of one hundred new business startups, only twenty will remain after five years. Then, in the next five years, only four of those remaining twenty will still be functioning. In another five years, three of those four will disappear, leaving one out of the original hundred. That's a 99 percent small-business fatality rate over a fifteen-year period. This is in accordance with my admittedly anecdotal conclusion that nine out of ten new small businesses are mismanaged.

Gauge your own situation and look ahead. Are you an employee of a small business? If so, the numbers are not on your side. Or do you *own* a small business? If so, there is hope because you have the power to direct it.

Too often, what ends a business or a job, or what casts an onerous spell on a life, is death by a thousand cuts. This is relentless erosion caused by recurring inefficiencies and their toxic offspring, fire killing and distraction. These time wasters undermine efforts to create and sell a good product that has a viable market. And in personal life? You've seen it in those who can't seem to break out of the bad-luck syndrome. It's not mysterious tough luck that takes people down; it's serial inefficiency. The great news is that inefficiency is easy to correct if one can see the cause of it.

THIS SURVIVAL THING IS KILLING ME

With the exception of whatever happened to be going on in my mind on any given day, there was no direction for the company. Centratel grew because of the booming local economy and my knack for foiling the reaper at the last minute. Long-term planning didn't happen, and routine maintenance was a vague concept for the future.

My days spiraled downward into ever-deepening chaos. I leaped from one predicament to the next. Crises multiplied. The days were crammed with cash flow crunches, chronic staff absenteeism, and innumerable customer complaints. The office temperature was too cool—or too warm. We would run out of critical office supplies and not have the time to leave the premises in order to replace them. Turnover among TSRs was incessant, and scheduling was haphazard, put together at the last moment. In year ten, we went through more than sixty new people—and my total number of staff was twelve! TSR trainees would start work, stay for a week, and then quit. My employees were unhappy, and the same held true for our clients as they endured a still marginal quality of service.

Making payroll was always a challenge: every two weeks it was a last-minute, hold-your-breath epic as we gambled that payroll checks would clear. Twice they didn't, and I went to employees' homes with cash to cover their bounced checks, pleading with them to give me another chance; to come back to work.

Through it all, I was the heroic jack-of-all-trades, the master fire killer who would work as long and as hard as necessary.

The years drifted by. My teenagers would wait for me at home as I flailed around at the office late into the night. When I finally came home, I would check to see if they were sleeping OK, and then stumble into bed myself. I would lie there exhausted with that deep, deep fatigue way down inside the chest.

Bills were not paid on time, both at Centratel and at home. Collectors called day and night. Checks bounced and NSF fees accumulated, sometimes over $100 at a time. The people at the bank felt sorry for me as they marveled at both my endurance and my ineptitude.

We lost our house and then my truck. My two teenagers shared the office space with me because we couldn't afford a place to live. They went to school during the day and at night slept on bunk beds in the back room of Centratel's small office. When I could, I slept alongside them on a cot.

Then, after the kids had gone off to college, in one long stretch of seven months, I answered calls as the sole TSR on the midnight to 8:00 a.m. shift *every night*. Here's the kicker: during those seven months, Monday through Friday of every week, I also worked in the daytime from 8:00 a.m. to 5:00 p.m., taking care of all administrative tasks. This meant each weekday my shift began at midnight and ended no sooner than 5:00 p.m. the next day. Weekends were a relief because I had only to work the midnight shift. My workweek exceeded a hundred hours and so there was no time for a social life or personal relationships.

Financially, those midnight shifts as a TSR helped, and I was able to get an apartment and a small used car. The kids were OK. They were out of town, off to school.

During those seven months of graveyard shifts, I was sleeping just a few hours each night and never in a single stretch because, as the lone TSR, I had to wake up each time a call came in to the service. Throughout the shift the medical and veterinary emergency calls came in at a steady pace. There was the occasional straight hour of sleep as I lay on the floor with a pillow and blanket. After the long stretch of graveyard shifts ended and I fell back to my normal eighty-hour workweek, it was impossible to sleep through the night because my body had become hardwired to per-form a day's work with three hours of rest.

There was no relief due to my critical involvement with every aspect of the operation, and I wondered how soon my physical and/or mental collapse would occur. Of course, that would be the end of things because the business would immediately fail if I wasn't there moment to moment.

For the body and mind, there is little worse than long-term sleep deprivation, and eventually I succumbed to the stress. It was a depression and exhaustion that inhibited every thought and action. My performance became clumsy in the face of escalating problems. The situation was get-ting worse by the day, and after fifteen years of accumulated trauma, the end was near.

If things were so bad, why didn't I throw in the towel and get a regu-lar job? I was terrified of rejoining the workforce as someone's employee. The thought of having a traditional job sent shivers down my spine. After all those years of being on my own, working for someone else would be a nightmare for me *and* for my employer. I rationalized that if I was in hell, at least it was *my* hell.

PLAYING A GAME I COULDN'T WIN

I had no idea what to do other than what I had always done, to dig in and take care of whatever came up. It was horrible, and the fire killing got worse. I kept at it. My existence was like the Whac-A-Mole game in which little grinning-faced moles keep popping their heads up in any one of a dozen holes. I would whack one mole and two more would emerge. My hammer would respond in a flurry, and the mole heads would be rammed back down into their tunnels, one after the other. It was a beautiful performance, a remarkable demonstration of dexterity and power.

But despite the heroics, the mole whacking was distracting me from seeing what was necessary to fix my business and my life. The incessant disaster control was blinding me from the reality that I was playing a game I could never win.

The problem wasn't how I was playing the game. The problem was the game I was playing.

The Whac-A-Mole Game, per Wikipedia

According to Wikipedia,

> "Once the game starts, the moles pop up from their holes at random. The object of the game is to force the individual moles back into their holes by hitting them directly on the head with the mallet, thereby adding to the player's score. If the player does not strike a mole within a certain time or with enough force, it will eventually sink back into its hole with no score. Although game-play starts out slow enough for most people to hit all of the moles that arise, it gradually increases in speed, with each mole spending less time above the hole and with more moles outside of their holes at the same time. After a designated time limit, the game ends, regardless of the skill of the player. The final score is based upon the number of moles the player struck."

 Jim Morrison and Mick Jagger

Jim Morrison and Mick Jagger are arguably the best lead singers rock has ever produced: Morrison's comportment and lyrics, Jagger's energy and flair. Jim Morrison's short wild ride was fueled by his enigmatic stage presence and brazen thought images, built around a mystique of chaos. He wallowed in the haunting darkness, enamored with the great unknown beyond death. He lived in chaos, too, awash in alcohol and drugs, abusing his physical and mental processes. He died at the age of twenty-seven after just four years of performing and recording. His too-short existence was the antithesis of systemization and order.

Mick Jagger, however, has been hammering away for literally fifty years, more than ten times longer than Morrison. Essentially, Jagger is the Rolling Stones' GM and CEO, carefully attending to the operational detail of the band's enormously sophisticated touring/recording machine. Eschewing drugs and alcohol in his twenties, and now approaching seventy years of age, he is as fit as a thirty-year-old. Whether he's creating music, performing, recording, or managing the complexity that is his world, he is a master of systems management.

CHAPTER 4

Gun-to-the-Head Enlightenment

It is often darkest just before dawn.

—Sojourner Truth

For fifteen years I pounded my small business into some kind of subservient yet mocking submission, carrying on like a perpetual motion machine. But of course, it was tenuous. Everything depended on me, and if I let up for one moment, everything would come crashing down.

Then, on the heels of my seven-month double-shift epic, I hit a brick wall. In my arsenal of last-minute bailout strategies there was no solution to the looming deathblow—my inability to cover even part of an upcoming payroll. My staff would walk out when there were no paychecks, instantly ending my business as our clients raced elsewhere to find another answering service to handle their urgent calls. In a single moment, Centratel would close its doors and everything I had built in the past decade and a half would be lost, not to mention that my staff of sixteen would be jobless and my three hundred loyal clients would be in crisis.

I was a mentally and physically wrecked fifty-year-old single guy facing financial and career oblivion, and it was more than an interesting coincidence that Centratel's imminent demise was dovetailing with my almost certain physical and/or mental breakdown. I was desperate—and for the first time, angry—and the doomsday clock was ticking.

DAWN

The payroll was due in just days, when I lay awake in bed late one night, exhausted as usual. But that night, for the first time, I stopped thinking about work details, business philosophies, elaborate theories, or some last-minute divine intervention. It was the end, and there was nothing left to examine or ruminate about; nothing left to salvage—except one small thing. In a last gesture of raw defiance I could at least end this long sad epic with some small bit of self-respect. As a final last-gasp effort I would go down in a blinding flash. This would not end with a whimper.

Since everything was lost anyway, why not find one last moment of command?

This time there was no salvation and I lay there in the 3:00 a.m. darkness and began to review the blinding-flash possibilities. I remember a morbid yet satisfied amusement at engineering a final death throe. What would it be?

But something was odd. I was suddenly at peace. How could that be? Without coaxing and for no apparent reason, two simple, pragmatic questions emerged out of the blackness: *What have I been doing wrong all these years? And since the end is coming, what is there to lose if I abandon past assumptions and look at my world from a completely different angle?*

My what-is-there-to-lose posture was the catalyst. The certain end of Centratel gave me the freedom to consider anything. No matter how outrageous, any new idea was an option because there was no further possible downside. I had a few more days to stretch into unknown territory and do some experimentation, maybe even relax and have some fun with it, because . . . what did it matter?

Then, answers came out of nowhere.

I underwent an enlightenment of sorts. It sounds corny, but in my mind I rose up and out of the jumble that was my life. I was no longer an integral part of it. Floating upward, outside and slightly elevated from the chaos, I gazed down at the details of my business, spread out neatly as if on display on a tabletop. From this bird's-eye perspective it struck me that Centratel was a simple self-contained mechanical device! It was—and is— nothing more than the sum of an assemblage of sequential mechanisms:

answering the phones, sales presentations, payroll preparation, scheduling, handling complaints, etc., with each protocol executed in an orderly, linear fashion whereby one step follows another step until the sequence for that particular process is complete. I knew instinctively that the rest of my life operated in the same way: as a collection of separate and independent processes, each functioning in a predictable, reliable 1-2-3 sequence according to its own construction. (Yes, I thought, of course these systems intermingle and affect each other—a holistic assemblage to be sure—but that holism can't mask the wonderful separateness of each; of the beauty of their individual existences.)

Late that night a new vision gripped me, never to let go.

My thoughts raced at light speed as I marveled at the simple beauty of it. I understood that my previous vision of the world had been wrong. The planet earth is not a huge, amorphous, seething mass of people, objects, and events swirling in disarray. It's a place of order and logic, a place of predictability. The world is a collection of logical systems!

For the first time, I saw Centratel as a closed package, a primary system—an independent, stand-alone mechanism, a machine—a separate entity, like a human body, an airplane, a tree, or a city. And I knew that the primary system I called Centratel shared a commonality with all other primary systems in that it was simply the sum of the numerous separate subsystems that composed it.

The logic of it was crystal clear, exquisite. I felt a quiet joy I had never felt before. To this day, I remember every moment of it.

A line from an old rock song by The Fixx went round and round in my head as I lay there: " . . . one thing leads to another . . . one thing leads to another . . ." I looked down and saw that my leadership in the business had been reactionary and therefore horribly inefficient. *I had taken the wrong stance because the mechanics had been invisible to me! All I did was kill fires, unaware that those fires were the products of dysfunctional subsystems.* The subsystems had lives of their own and were acting out their 1-2-3 sequences without direction, constantly producing random bad results—results that had to be fixed or covered up.

The primary system that was my business was out of control because it was composed of uncontrolled subsystems!

My world was chaos, not because I was some kind of loser or unfortunate victim of circumstance, but because so many of my subsystems were not being controlled. Unsupervised, these chaotic processes composed the dysfunctional primary systems of my existence: business, health, and relationships.

WHO IS IN CHARGE OF ALL THIS?

Exhausted yet exhilarated, I lay in bed floating above it all, looking down on my world, savoring the delicious new vision. It was borderline mystical, a sort of near-death experience but without the tunnel and bright light. For the first time in my life, it was clear that my perception of reality had been murky and undefined. How does the saying go? "One thing I know: once I was blind but now I see."

From depths beyond my physical and mental despair, more questions surfaced, questions I had never considered before: "*Who is in charge of all this?*" and "*How does this world continue to function day after day, year after year, millennium after millennium?*" The answers came fast and hard.

I was startled to grasp that there is no human King of Everything who directs the goings-on of the world. On its own and no matter what, this earth keeps turning, and life carries on in an overall structured and organized pattern, and . . . *no one is in charge!* The indomitable laws of nature ensure systems work perfectly according to their construction. On this earth, gravity works all the time, everywhere. Over here, one plus one equals two, and over there, one plus one also equals two! The laws of nature cause the mechanics of the world to be dependable and predictable, and the gift with which we humans have been blessed is the ability to get in the middle of it all, to manipulate it, to direct our lives to be what we want them to be, to use the laws of nature to our advantage. *And no single human, or group of humans, is in charge!*

I floated in my thoughts and wondered at the silent and invisible background of organizational strength that keeps this earth chugging ahead like a train despite our human race's best attempts to derail the process. Cyclically, methodically, and for whatever reason, this complex world moves along on its own, adjusting, balancing, and counterbalancing. And at the root of it all, and in the middle of it all, uncountable separate linear systems are at work.

THE WORLD IS 99.9 PERCENT EFFICIENT

This systems rationale is not another feel-good, think-positive invocation, and it's not about faith. It's about stone-cold mechanical reality. Think about the processes of our lives and then do the numbers. We wake, shower, dress, eat, go to work, and proceed through the day to return to our loved ones in the evening. Then we watch TV, read, and go to bed early—or stay up late. We go to sleep and then we awake again the next morning. And everything works fine 99.9 percent of the time.

That's the cursory overview. Break it down and sequentially note the other events of the day's chronology. It will be thousands of items long as it includes contributing components such as the coffee maker that works every morning; the car that—despite all of its internal intricacies—operates with the turn of a key and then the turn of the steering wheel; the office we occupy; the complexities of the work we do; the paychecks we receive for doing that work. Consider the processes of sharing information back and forth with those around us: one on one, voice mail, cellular phone, e-mail, the written word. Each is a system, and 99.9 percent of the time each works flawlessly!

Envision the system we call a TV. By simply pushing a button, this incredibly complex mechanism jumps to life every time! Beyond the physical TV itself, consider the myriad organizations that put together the programming that appears on it. Then, switch gears and think about the lawn mower, the water that flows from the kitchen tap, the ubiquitous electricity that comes to our homes to animate a host of devices, each a complex system of its own.

Contemplate the clothes we wear, the shopping we do, the work we perform. Consider the gas pumped into our cars at gas stations. In some faraway place, sophisticated mechanisms extract oil from the ground. Then people transport it via high-tech ships, trucks, and pipelines to refineries where it is converted into gasoline via complex refining processes. Next, truckers deliver the gasoline to an uncountable number of convenient locations so we can pump it into our cars whenever we feel like it. We never think twice about the intricacies of the drilling/refining/delivery systems. And these are just a few of the millions of systems that touch our daily lives.

And what about the human body? Consider the amazing complexity of chemicals and mechanics that make it work. For each of us, as we progress through the day, billions of cells simultaneously cling to each other making us who we are. And all the while, as we function moment to moment, trillions of concurrent electrical signals execute without direct supervision.

Incredible!

Consider the miracle of what you are doing this moment, viewing and translating the characters on this page—or perhaps you are listening to my words in the audio version. You are transferring my thoughts to your mind where you instantaneously interact with what I am saying, making immediate judgments, agreeing or disagreeing, line by line. This is happening *now*, in this instant.

Yes, these complex systems sometimes fail. Nonetheless, it's a numbers game and it is unquestionable that the systems of our lives, taken together, work perfectly more than 99.9 percent of the time.

So far, I have focused on human systems, which are just a fraction of the total at work in any given moment. Uncountable natural systems add to the numbers and dwarf what man has created, and they all work perfectly according to their scripts.

Once one accepts the world's beautiful systems dance for what it is, the mystery of it goes even deeper. Consider that primary systems depend on subsystems, and those subsystems depend on sub-subsystems branching outward and downward, further and further, to subprimal levels.

And see that these processes repeat themselves over and over, as they incrementally create new forms and dissolve old ones.

The world is *alive* and it churns ahead with power and purpose!

Stop for a moment and attempt to draw it all in. The depth and intricacy of life's fabric is astonishing beyond comprehension. Grasp the beautiful complexity of life's workings and know that all by itself this world gurgles and percolates along with no overall human supervision. The countless systems that comprise life surge on and on while most of us remain oblivious to the mystery of it, to the sheer beauty of it.

It's interesting that the two most opposite groups of people imaginable share a similar wonder of the world's mysterious workings: scientists and the religious.

The relentless flow of life carries on with purpose. The sun comes up and later goes down. Grass grows in the spring and lies dormant in the winter. The tides rise and fall. We go to bed at night and wake up in the morning. The microwave works! The car works! Love comes, love goes, and then it comes again. We live, then we die, and another is born.

Systems, systems, systems—everywhere!

We Are Machines

Five years ago, as I was charging down a city street on my mountain bike, a sixteen-year-old driver veered across my path. I slammed into the side of her SUV and was launched over its roof, landing on the pavement on the other side. To this day, I don't remember either of the impacts.

I was knocked unconscious, coming awake only as I was loaded into the ambulance. On the way to the hospital, the paramedic asked my name. I answered correctly. She asked who she could call to inform that I was going to the hospital. I told her "Linda." Then she asked me where I had been on my bike and . . . I just couldn't remember. It was several hours before I could put the pieces together, to recall the details of my ride before the accident. With a slight concussion and some bruises, I was released from the hospital shortly thereafter.

From this experience, a lesson was hammered home: our minds and bodies are elaborate *machines*: machines that perform—or don't perform. Each of us is an indescribably complex collection of subsystems, operating via countless sequential and cooperative protocols. Our intricate minds and bodies work well most of the time, but because of the occasional mechanical glitch within a subsystem, sometimes they don't.

We should never take for granted our connection to the reality around us; never underestimate the tenuous grip we have on our worlds. We must handle our bodies and minds with care; we should be careful about upkeep and maintenance yet challenge them so they stay strong. We must attend to them and never take them for granted.

A PROPENSITY FOR EFFICIENCY AND ORDER

Late that night I asked myself, could it be that the common presumption that the world is functioning badly—that it's a mess—is *wrong*? Yes, I instantly realized, that presumption is wrong because in any given life, on any given day, countless systems work perfectly. We don't notice them and so we take them for granted, never appreciating their impeccability. We hyperfocus on individual, mechanical, and geopolitical systems that are not to our liking and conclude that deficiency is the default way of the world. Swallowed up in this, we see perfection as an anomaly and imperfection as the norm. That conclusion is backward.

Overall, the systems of this world work absurdly well: 99.9 percent of everything works just fine, and even the parts we consider imperfect are that way only because we think those parts should be different from what they are. (In truth, this world is 100 percent perfect if we discount what we want. However, for our purposes let's not discount what we want. Being pragmatic, let's characterize it as 99.9 percent perfect.)

I lay in bed in wired stupor, thinking about how life insistently plunges ahead, all within a framework of countless efficient processes. And I thought, since there is no human King of Everything there has to be an underlying cosmologic propensity toward efficiency and order. Some incredibly powerful force out there prefers events to go smoothly and, in fact, has inserted itself everywhere. It's holding the world together. It's making it work . . . *God?*

This new understanding was the reverse of my previous vision of existence in which I saw my world as a place of barely controlled mayhem, tenuously held together by its human masters. The colossal misperception of my life was that I had visualized perfection as an occasional harmonious chord in a universe more comfortable in its cacophony.

Oh yes, I thought. Indeed, there *is* a God.

My mind continued to race that night in 1999, and it struck me that if the universe has a predilection for order, it should be a simple thing to climb on board. And *since system inefficiencies comprise such a small percentage of my life's events—there wouldn't be that much to fix—I should be able to methodically isolate those problematic systems and then, one at a time, adjust them to produce the outcomes I want.* It should be easy to get things straightened out because cosmological bias is on my side—and this bias isn't just rooting for efficiency, it's demanding it!

OVERWHELMING STRENGTH AND INEVITABILITY

Is there a real-time analogy for the relentless power that propels the processes of the world? Yes. Find railroad tracks and stand nearby while a train slams by at full speed. Feel the overwhelming strength and inevitability of it. As the enormous mass of the train surges, feel the invincibility. This is an in-the-guts sense of the universe's mechanical potency and purposefulness. It's *that* deliberate.

The world's turning is powerful and methodical, and that is the point. Why it behaves that way is the human mystery—the ultimate question—but it is not the issue at hand. For our purposes, what matters here is this: despite the common assumption that chaos reigns, the truth is that the mechanics of the world work very, very well. And if we can proceed from the premise that there is a proclivity for this powerful efficiency, rather than blindly buying into society's ubiquitous assumption that all is chaos, we will stop fighting events. Instead, confident and deliberate, we can dig a bit deeper to construct the lives we want, step by step.

GUMMING UP THE WORKS AND THE ENIGMATIC POWER

Of course, it must be said that although there is a regulatory force disposed to keep things flowing smoothly, human free will enables us to cause havoc on personal and global scales. When a process or mechanism doesn't produce the outcome we want it to produce because of something we did or didn't do, we must recognize this is the downside of the human race's gift of being able to influence and manipulate.

Dysfunctional systems may constitute just a small percentage of all systems, but for the record let's state the obvious: we humans are inclined to disrupt our affairs, and for this reason there have been horrible problems in the world. The worst of it? In the last century, in fits of narcissistic insanity, tens of millions of people were slaughtered by Hitler, Mao, Stalin, Mussolini, and Pol Pot. These were human systems gone haywire.

And still the agony continues, at its most virulent in third-world, non-democratic countries.

Then there is the self-generated personal pain that resides within our own thought processes. Add to this the self-inflicted damage caused by the neglect and abuse of the body mechanisms that we inhabit, not to mention no-fault setbacks, such as accidents and genetic irregularities: the Forrest Gump "shit happens" scenario (a brief yet profoundly meaningful phrase).

Large or small, cultural genocide or a missed appointment, the life events that go wrong are due to component irregularities within systems. When a process does not produce what we want it to produce, something within the process is not as it could be. Something is gumming up the works.

Despite all this, and notwithstanding the general media's allegations otherwise, the majority of lives move from beginning to end with a minimum of true, overt pain. When there is trauma, it is most often short-lived. Because of the universe's inclination toward stability and efficiency, real discomfort is a small slice of the pie, and when it happens it is usually the result of self-inflicted mental anguish and fear—negative constructs within our thinking. Yes, again, of course there are the notable exceptions. I am not a Pollyanna.

Systems want to be efficient. If a system could talk, it would say, "My single goal—and I am passionate about it—is to accomplish the task that I was built to accomplish!" This means that our efforts to make circumstances right are aided by an enigmatic power that works hard to propel those efforts to success. Within one's life, getting things to work swimmingly is not a difficult task if one pays attention to the mechanics.

Late that night, lying awake in bed, I realized the force *is* with you.

Safety, Comfort, and PC in the First and Third Worlds

Why are there major differences between life in the Western world and, say, Afghanistan or rural China? Why is life in the West easier than in the East? A part of the answer is that in the West, there are far more safety and protective systems than in the East, and therefore our lives are less in jeopardy. A simple example: In the West, we wear seat belts in our cars 99 percent of the time. It's the law—and the law is a system. In the times

I have been to the rural Far East, I have seldom seen a driver or passenger buckle up. In most third-world countries, there are no enforceable seat belt laws. (Are seat belts actually *in* the cars? Yes, they usually lay buried in the seat cushions—but sometimes the driver has altogether removed them.)

Another example: Here in the developed world there are quick and severe penalties for anyone's unprovoked, assertive aggression toward another. In the third world there are few protections, and meager justice mechanisms can be corrupt and impotent, encouraging undeterred person-to-person crimes.

And the flip side? It is telling that the annoyance of the politically correct is nowhere but in the West. This is a result of a culture trying too hard to regulate. It's system thought taken to the extreme by people whose basic needs are satisfied and who therefore have the time and energy—and proclivity—to attempt to channel the thoughts and actions of others. Busybodies! For the rural African there is no PC thinking, as life is negotiated via just a few systems, systems that have to do with survival. In most of the world, people don't have the luxury of expending energy on PC gyrations.

For a Westerner, it is a good thing to live for a while in a third-world household. It's a crash course in establishing fundamental priorities and humility.

FLOAT THROUGH THE DAY IN FASCINATION

For me, one plus one equals two. For you, one plus one also equals two. The natural mechanics of planet earth are reliable and can be trusted. And human-devised systems will also operate reliably if they are put together properly and then routinely maintained. If they are not put together correctly and then coddled, they will fail to produce the results we want.

Few people think their problems are a result of personal process failure. Most see their troubles as isolated events, blaming fate, horoscopes, bad luck, karma, God, the devil, neighbors, competitors, family members, the weather, the President, Congress, liberals, conservatives, global warming, too much TV, lack of money, too much money, the educational establishment, or just a world gone bad. And most see problems as overwhelming in number: an onslaught from out there, only to be fended off by superhuman efforts. For many, the excuse/blame list is endless. I had been a card-carrying resident of that camp, but when the new vision engulfed me there was zero chance I would ever live in that place again.

I now float through the day in fascination. Instead of wallowing in a hodgepodge of unpredictability and fire killing, I see events and objects as part of one structured system or another. This real-time, outside-and-slightly-elevated perspective has channeled peace and prosperity into my life and into the lives of those who depend on me.

I call it semi-enlightenment.

Negatives will sometimes worm their way into my day, most often due to my own failures. It's not often, though—not any more.

This life I lead is a result of actions, actions rooted in my gut certainty that *in the systems that compose the world's workings, there is not a cosmic inclination to chaos. Rather, there is a default propensity toward order and efficiency.*

Without question, I understand that inefficiency and its attending pain occur because of rare and isolated component problems within otherwise perfect systems.

IT WON'T TAKE LONG

By perfecting your life's individual systems—by identifying them and then rebuilding them one by one—order and peace accumulate incrementally. However, the enhancements in these rebuilt systems must be made permanent or the systems will slip back into dysfunction due to random outside influence. In the workplace, permanence happens first by creating written descriptions of how systems are to operate, and second, by making sure responsible parties follow the steps described in the documentation. We'll get to those details soon.

Once systems are examined and flawed components are exposed and repaired, systems will produce desired results. (Creating new contributing systems and eliminating unnecessary ones will add to success.) And since this is all mechanical, when the changes are performed and then locked in, tangible improvement is both instant and permanent.

For your own situation, not only can you count on an overwhelming bias toward efficiency, but also you probably won't have a whole lot of systems to adjust, create, or delete. It won't take long to get your circumstances straightened out.

Now we are at the heart of the work the system method. Your existence is composed of countless linear systems, many of which are under your direct command. These are the invisible threads that hold the fabric of your life together. If there is an outcome that doesn't suit you, you can change that outcome by making a component adjustment within a system, adding a system, or eliminating a system. In your life's rejuvenation, it will typically be all of the above.

Whether an outcome is to your liking or not, the underlying process is performing exactly as it was constructed. You are not at the mercy of mysterious conspiring forces or the swirling backwash of chaos. If it is in your power—and so much that affects you *is* in your power—you can fix things!

What about those systems you can't repair because they are out of your influence? Relax. If you can't fix something, don't worry about it. Do what you can or walk away, but certainly don't spend time or energy agonizing over it. If you live in a democracy, vote and then don't complain. If you have a problem with a coworker, talk to him or her and then don't obsess about the outcome. Metaphorically speaking, if you don't like the TV program, change the channel or turn off the set. Save your energy for efforts that will provide tangible positive results within your circle of influence.

THE OBJECTIVE

Back to my story and the looming crisis at Centratel. That night, yet another realization struck: my business needed at least one solid objective. From my new vantage point I could see we had been operating without any pointed purpose. The closest I could come to a reason for the existence of the business was that I hoped we would make money and be successful. That is the single mantra of the typical small-business owner or corporate middle manager. It is not concrete and directed, but ambiguous and wishy-washy.

Not only had I never considered its individual components, Centratel had no direction! Despite my jack-of-all-trades/fire-killer-extraordinaire attributes, I didn't have a grasp of the *why* of the organization. This realization engendered the birth of the Strategic Objective document. I'll talk about that in part two.

THE CRUX OF CONTROL: THE SYSTEMS MINDSET

Without prodding, nor willing it to happen, I stepped outside my life, rose above it and looked down, never again to settle back into the morass that had been my existence. There was nothing airy-fairy about this new vantage point. It was mechanical and logical. I saw that the solution to my business problems did not lie in becoming more proficient at whacking moles—the solution was to find a way to eliminate the moles altogether. I had to put aside the hammer and dig down into those tunnels to find out exactly where those moles hid. When I found them, I would ruthlessly strangle them one by one. Their grinning furry faces would not deter my genocidal mission. And while I was down there taking care of mole extermination, I would find a way to prevent any mole relatives from returning later.

Ruthless? Yes.

Late that night I understood, deep in my gut, that perfectly executing systems were at play everywhere and all the time, and that imperfection was the anomaly. *I realized that my business—and for that matter, my whole being—was the sum total of the efficient and inefficient processes that composed it.* Confident, I would look down on these systems and isolate them one at a time, viewing each as a separate autonomous entity. Per a solid directional plan, one by one and over whatever period of time it would take, I would disassemble and then rebuild each system so that each contributed to my stated goals. In addition to the reconstruction, I would add new ones and discard useless ones.

This, I finally realized: the leader's role is to keep the wheels of the machine turning with maximum efficiency.

It was logical. Creating efficient subsystems should cause the primary system to be efficient too. And to take this a step further, it seemed to me that if the individual subsystems could be made more than efficient, if they were to be made potent and powerful, then my primary systems—my business and my life—would become potent and powerful too. Who could argue with that logic?

I just needed to identify individual subsystems and then, one by one, optimize them. The primary system would take care of itself, the end product of the subsystems that composed it.

I hadn't been looking for a revelation, but in my desperation I got one. It was a vision that bared the simple mechanics of the world, mechanics that had been cloaked by the dissonance of the day. It was a permanent shift in perception, and in the big picture and in the smallest snapshots of my life, I would never again specialize in killing fires, spinning my wheels in futile attempts to stop chaos.

The crux of control? *I would no longer deal with the bad outcomes of inefficient systems. Instead, I would expend my energies on perfecting those systems—and good outcomes would come along naturally.*

For a decade and a half, although the simple reality had been floating right there in front of me, the mental turbulence of my fire-killing approach had relegated this simple, earthshaking reality to invisibility: a life's condition is not the result of luck or of being good or bad. And it's not about intelligence, karma, education, social class, political stance, religious affiliation, or how hard one works. Life is about simple mechanics—the dispassionate mechanics of the systems that compose it.

What I now knew for sure was that there is a very simple difference between happy people and unhappy people. *Unhappy people are not in control of their lives because they spend their days coping with the random bad results of unmanaged systems. Happy people are in control of their lives, spending their days enjoying the intentional good results of managed systems.*

My new perspective was not just an interesting new concept; it was an electric, life-changing revelation. Late that night, the moment the switch flipped in my head, there was no going back. I was a changed man.

CENTRATEL WOULD BECOME A MACHINE

It was uncanny. My thoughts raged on. Supported by indisputable logic, an entire strategy unfolded as I lay there.

I thought, if Centratel is an organism—like a human body, or a car, or a TV—smooth and efficient operation will depend on a multitude of simultaneously functioning processes that operate automatically.

In other words, the business mechanisms I would fix and/or create would have to function without direct moment-to-moment supervision by me, the majority owner, GM and CEO of the company. To be sure, people would be watching the details, but I would not be one of those people. The watchers would be employees who would supervise the mechanics of the business without my constant over-the-shoulder intrusion. Centratel would become a self-perpetuating organism.

Centratel would become a *machine*.

Further, this machine would be the highest-quality telephone answering service in the United States. We would accomplish this in five steps:

1. We would exactly define the overall goals and strategies. It would be done on paper by creating the Strategic Objective and the General Operating Principles.

2. We would break down Centratel's workings into subsystems we could understand: processing calls, staff management, client services, equipment, quality assurance, the methodology for handling client and customer requests, bookkeeping, purchasing, customer services, etc. Then, each of those subsystems would be broken down into even smaller contributing sub-subsystems, including receivables software, customer complaint protocol, employee recruitment, equipment maintenance schedules, and so on.

3. Once isolated, exposed, and understood, we would refine and perfect those systems—one by one—so each would contribute 100 percent toward the stated goals of the Strategic Objective. As needed, we would create new ones from scratch. We would discard useless ones. We would document each process into a Working Procedure, thus making the perfected system permanent. The execution of the perfected systems would be automated so they would recur without prompting.

4. We would implement fail-safe, recurring maintenance schedules for all processes.

5. "Replacements" would be identified and trained. Every employee, including me, would have someone in the wings who could instantly take over, should that become necessary.

FROM ORGANIC TO MECHANICAL

Why does a car perform the same way every time? Why does a city stay in the same place without spontaneously moving to a new location? Why do we, in our lifetimes, continue to be ourselves? The reason is hard mechanical reality: physicality. With the obvious exceptions of fluids and gases, physical objects don't morph into other physical objects or dissipate into the ether. They are mechanical—dependable and predictable.

On the other hand, human communication processes—organic processes—are the antithesis of physical substance. For example, the execution of a nondocumented recurring communication protocol not only varies among the individuals performing the process but also, for any one person, with the time of day, the weather, or mood. Untamed, these organic processes are feathers in the wind.

In the workplace, the challenge and the solution is to make these organic human processes as solid and reliable as the mechanical objects that surround us. On planet earth, we accomplish this with documentation!

STRENGTH AND RESILIENCE

In the process of rebuilding Centratel system by system, strength and resilience would evolve as by-products. Outside events would continue to challenge us with unexpected shake ups, but if we constructed the new systems properly, the business would become rugged and adaptable. Potential earthquakes would be reduced to tremors. Until this point, earthquakes had been earthquakes, and there had been too many of them.

And if what I saw for the business was true—that it was a primary system composed of component subsystems, each of which could be brought to high efficiency and strength—then it was logical this would be true for the other primary system that was in immediate crisis: my physical and mental self. The process for fixing my body/mind problems would be the same process I was going to use to fix Centratel. The systems mindset is effective in every life situation because it deals with fundamental cause and effect—the basic truth of how the world mechanically operates everywhere and all the time.

Learning How to Sleep

For any recurring problem, there is a path to getting things fixed: take the inefficient process apart and fix the pieces one by one. Earlier I mentioned my problems with getting enough sleep. Sleep intertwines with numerous other biological, social, and relationship processes, but in that broad context one can't begin to find a solution to improving it. What did I do via systems methodology to cure this problem? I envisioned sleep as a primary system composed of subsystems.

My new posture led me to a doctor who specializes in sleep disorders. The doctor's recommendations had a strong theme, reduction of stress, and this led me to the subsystems of yoga, more sensible exercise, and meditation. Also, I would substantially reduce my intake of caffeine, alcohol, and sugar. There were other subsystems to modify, including changing the layout of my bedroom, removing the clock from the nightstand, and going to sleep at the same time every night. I would adopt a more consistent routine for preparing for bed. Another thing: testing indicated my requirements for sleep were less than average—six hours was enough—and so I should avoid tossing and turning in bed expecting to get eight or nine hours. Waiting to drift off was stressful in itself, so instead of lying there mentally churning away, I should get up and read, work, or even exercise.

With the help of my regular doctor, I found my blood chemicals were out of balance. Those chemical imbalances affected my sleep pattern, and with my doctor's guidance, I began to fix those subsystem imbalances with supplements.

I had to reduce my hours at the office and that meant getting the company to run itself without me being there every minute. Of course, that transformation was already underway, using the same systems thinking.

I got back to a healthy sleeping routine over the course of just a few months, literally doubling each night's sleep duration.

Now if I find that my sleep is less than what it should be, I can trace the problem back to a violation of one of the dozen or so sleep-system guidelines I listed initially.

I attacked the overall problem by isolating the primary sleep system and then breaking it down into subsystems that could then be analyzed and manipulated. By taking an outside-and-slightly-elevated vantage point, I was able to tweak my sleep process to more and more efficiency, one component at a time. The process was pure mechanics.

CHAPTER 5

Execution and Transformation: Creating the Machine

If there's a bustle in your hedgerow, don't be alarmed now,
It's just a spring clean for the May queen.

—From the song "Stairway to Heaven," written by Jimmy Page and Robert
Plant and performed by Led Zeppelin (Atlantic Records, 1971)

Until I woke up, my vision of Centratel was of an amorphous mass of interrelated and confused sights, sounds, and events. Unraveling was impossible because of my presumption of chaotic complexity. Observing the workings of my business in a holistic way, I could not detect the internal inefficiencies that continually churned the business into bedlam.

On a subliminal level, the feel-good precept that everything is related to everything else so we should consider each of our actions in a global way encourages paralysis while it masks mechanical disarray. Any possibility of internal enhancement is subverted by the assumption that tampering with things over here will upset things over there. Inaction prevails. The notion that a butterfly flapping its wings over the jungles of Brazil will have an impact on the weather patterns over the state of New Hampshire is an interesting concept, but it evokes a nonsensical paranoia. Although the precept illustrates the interrelation of life elements, taking it literally casts a spell of impotence over an individual's inclination to make changes. In the real world of day-to-day existence, the Brazilian butterfly doesn't make a damn bit of difference.

The reason I had felt helpless to fix my business was because I had seen it as a hopelessly complex, impenetrable entity. I never considered dissecting Centratel into simple subsystems that could be optimized one at a time. Instead of fixing the individual mechanical inefficiencies within the faulty mechanism, I had been spending my time cleaning up the recurring problems the faulty mechanism produced.

So the years crawled by as I whacked the moles. It had seemed there was no other option but to wallow in the middle of it and hope for some kind of magical, holistic solution: a huge loan from the bank, the perfect employee, client, or consultant.

I could have spent my whole life like that!

But finally, I knew what to do because I saw Centratel for what it truly is, a collection of separate subsystems. It would be my simple task to optimize those subsystems one by one. How could that not be a good thing?

A NEW WORLD

My mini-enlightenment arrived just days prior to the payroll I was going to miss. I had to find the money to pay staff and keep them working so the repair process could begin. With newfound emotional energy, I convinced my credit card company to raise my credit limit a bit so some cash could be drawn. A friend gave me a loan. Offering a discount, I talked a high-volume client into paying for a year of answering service in advance. Several staff members agreed to delay cashing their paychecks.

We made it through the payroll crisis, and I immediately turned my attention to creating three sets of documents that would get Centratel on track. First, I would create the Strategic Objective, which would define us and set goals. Second, I would put together the General Operating Principles document, which would serve as our guideline for making decisions. Third, we would begin to write out our Working Procedures, which would exactly define every recurring process of the business. These Working Procedures were the end result and the tangible evidence of our system-improvement quest. (I have been asked where I got the idea for these specific documents. Truth is, they sprang up instantly and out of nowhere, late that night. I have not modified their names or their intent since that moment.)

I completed the first draft of the Strategic Objective and began the Principles document. Then I explained the new vision to my staff, outlining what we would do next and how they were going to assume new leadership postures. Tentatively at first, to get the hang of it, we began creating our Working Procedures: isolating, fixing, and documenting processes one at a time. For examination and repair, we first selected the most flawed process and then moved on to the next most flawed.

From the moment of my late-night epiphany, we were on a new path and there was no turning back. Marching ahead without pause, we quickly began to see tangible results as confusion immediately began to subside and cash flow came under control. In the first six months my workweek dropped from eighty hours to sixty. Then, in the next six months, it fell below forty.

Much of our early success had to do with the perfection of our internal communication system. Every moment, each of us knew what was going on in other parts of the business, and each of us could make decisions without stumbling in semantics or bureaucracy. (You'll read more on communication in part three.)

We made all critical systems, human and mechanical, redundant. The first year passed, and we confidently hammered on. Customer and staff complaints continued to decline, and chaos dissolved into serenity as we relentlessly improved our processes and mechanisms one by one.

Precisely targeting our efforts via the Strategic Objective and Operating Principles documents, we tackled the obvious recurring protocols, gobbling up inefficiencies by generating Working Procedures. Plunging ahead relentlessly, we rebuilt and documented several hundred existing systems. We perfected all of our departments, one by one. At the same time, we created new systems from scratch and discarded useless ones. Whew!

Through it all, there was some employee turnover. A couple of managers wouldn't accept the new systems theory and attending documentation. They were replaced by fresh faces who understood the systems mindset approach. (Today, we attract and keep smart, loyal, goal-oriented people because of *how* we operate. Also, because of our strict methodical approach, we are expert at sizing up people in job interviews. Another reason for our great staff is because our compensation/benefit package is much higher than that of other businesses in our region, as well as the TAS/call center industry at large. The high wages we pay are possible because we are internally hyper-efficient. We have just a few people accomplishing a lot of work. (More on staffing in chapter 16 and in the appendixes.)

As error rates plunged, the overall quality of service dramatically improved, light years better than industry standards. The growth of the business went into high gear, and within two years of instituting our new paradigm, we bought out three of our local TAS competitors (and we bought five nonlocal ones as well). We absorbed both of our local voice mail service rivals, too. In that two-year period, our TAS client base grew from three hundred to seven hundred.

It was system improvement at its finest, and although we finished the heavy lifting long ago, we still spend most of our time working our systems.

It took a long five years to fix Centratel. That's understandable because we were figuring out the details of the process from scratch. We invested (and sometimes inadvertently wasted) time and money as we experimented with new concepts, tried to find the right management people, and stumbled with the documentation.

But also, during this period, our relationship with a third minor stockholder had an enormous negative impact. Unrelated to our new tack, this partnership began in the middle of the rejuvenation and included outsourcing some of our call processing chores overseas, which resulted in a severe loss of clients. In turn, this led to full-blown legalities. In the end we were able to buy the partners out of the company based upon a settlement agreement, but it's my guess that the bad partnership and resulting litigation cost us between two and three years of progress and an overall loss of over 20 percent of our client base. For a while, our new growth was swallowed up by this serious dysfunction.

If we were to do this again without having to develop the work the system process from scratch, and without having to deal with a partnership dissolution, I'm guessing it would take twelve to eighteen months to fix things.

There was a lot to do because in addition to the rebuilding efforts and the litigation, we had a business to run. But obviously there was enough energy to do what was necessary. It was a long five years but I recall them with satisfaction and nostalgia.

As mentioned, despite the setbacks and the additional workload, my physical involvement with the company's daily operations continued to decline. Today, I spend just a couple of hours a week working on Centratel business. One of those hours is for our weekly staff meeting, and the other is for paying bills and attending to various R&D efforts with my staff.

The Price to Be Paid

Abusing personal systems too often means introducing foreign substances into the miraculous, near-perfect mechanism that is the body. Perceiving themselves to be unhappy, people complicate their already flawed thinking processes by contaminating themselves. The ice-cold reality? One plus one always equals two, and with the same utter reliability, a drunken night out on the town equals days of subpar physical and mental performance as the human body works overtime to repair itself from the chemical assault. We make our worlds worse in the long term by violating bodily systems in the short term, as we ignore the simple truth that disruption of an efficient process always has its price. One could say that substance abuse is a criminal attack against one's self.

HEART AND MIND

In parallel with the business resuscitation, there was no time to delay in regaining my health. As with the business, I had to change course right away, and it was obvious what I must do. I would handle my physical problems with the same systems methodology I was using to fix the business. Here's what I did:

1. I changed my viewpoint. What, exactly, was making me ill? My doctor thought I was depressed, but after belaboring that theory for way too long, it became clear to me this was not the source of the problem, but merely a symptom. My so-called depression

stemmed from undergoing too much stress, lack of sleep, and my long, long workweeks. (I thought, "*Of course I'm depressed! Under these circumstances, anyone would be depressed!*) I got outside and above, looked down, and saw my body was a collection of subsystems. My physical being was not a jumble of random happenings to which I could only react; it was a logical collection of processes, and some of those processes could be adjusted or altogether eliminated. And I could add others. So I modified or removed a number of external stress-inducing systems in order to prevent stress events from occurring. The biggest relief was in cutting back my office hours through the rebuilding of Centratel.

2. I created a personal written plan. I wrote a simple one-page management document in which I described my goals and guidelines—a personal Strategic Objective. I also created a personal Operating Principles document that included a series of stress-reducing action items.

3. Once circumstances got better, I continued to perform the stress-reducing action items on a regular basis. Always working toward the ideal, but not always reaching it, this preventative maintenance was what I would have to do to stay healthy. That's it! The mantra is to isolate–fix–maintain. *It is not enough to know what to do. One must take action.*

Stress-Reducing Action Items

It started with a simple list. I wrote down five or six actions that would reduce anxiety. I carried the note in my pocket for a couple of weeks, jotting down additional ideas as they came to mind. My final list included fifteen action items, each a separate subsystem of its own. These items were not special in any way; most people would agree that any one of them would help eliminate stress.

Here's the original raw list: work fewer hours, lose ten pounds, go to the sleep disorder clinic to find out how to sleep (and do what the doctor suggests!), stop ingesting caffeinated drinks, learn and practice meditation and yoga. Exercise vigorously, but not excessively, at least four times a week. Eat good food. Drink lots of water. Ingest less sugar and salt. Get a blood test every three months and per those tests, take supplements until my blood chemicals come into balance. See friends at least once a week. Spend more one-on-one time with my family. Read a minimum of one hour each day: one book and half a dozen periodicals per week.

While I compiled the list, my thought was that it would be sensible to choose just some of the items on the list, whichever ones seemed best. However, when the list was complete I decided to implement *all* fifteen items, leaving nothing out. Why should any of them be dismissed if each one contributed to my well-being? It was a challenging list, difficult to fully implement, but I gave it my best shot. I viewed each of my action items as a separate subsystem and incorporated them into the primary system that is my life. Because I had become such a physical mess, it took two years to get healthy again. Fifty years of stress damage was not unraveled overnight.

Today, do I live every minute by these standards? No, but I get close.

 ## Paying the Bills

Here is an example of replacing an old system with a new one:

For years, a nagging problem at Centratel was the time and effort it took to pay the bills. The time I spent performing this function contributed nothing to the bottom line, and each month required ten to fourteen hours of my time to process the sixty to eighty payables to our various vendors. I wrote the checks, entered the transactions into the check register, stuffed the checks into envelopes, and mailed them. Then there was the filing and the bookkeeping entries. As we grew, it became too time consuming for me, and in my new systems quest to automate and delegate, I hired a part-time bookkeeper to do the task. But that created an unintended consequence: the expenditures were not being examined and questioned by our bookkeeper in the same way I, as owner of the company, would examine and question them. There were double payments as well as payments for services that we no longer utilized. There were late fees, too, as some bills simply weren't paid on time.

The solution: our bank's online bill-payer feature. It's a perfect illustration of systems thinking and methodology. Now, writing a hard-copy check seldom happens. Ninety percent of recurring monthly bills are the same amount each month, and the bank software is programmed to pay these bills automatically. QuickBooks automatically logs these monthly payments too, so there is literally nothing to do in order to pay these bills. For a payable in which the billed amount changes monthly, it's an easy matter for me to review the statement and then insert the exact amount both online and in QuickBooks.

Now, again paying the bills myself, I am able to keep a close eye on every cent of expenditure.

This is a prime example of investing time to set up a new mechanism and then benefiting forever from the effort. Over several weeks, it took maybe fifteen hours of additional work to program vendors into the bank billpayer software—the same amount of time that had been required *each month* to pay bills with the old method. Now I spend maybe two hours a month processing these payables, and unlike before, there is never an error; never a late fee. The overall time-savings has been staggering: twelve hours per month multiplied by ten years. That's thirty-six forty-hour workweeks.

At home we use the same system. The homeowner association dues, water, electricity, and everything else are paid on time with little or no input from me, and it takes just minutes per month.

Are we outside and slightly elevated? Yes! Bill-payer is the quintessential illustration of systems methodology, an enormous time saver/efficiency enhancer both at work and at home.

CHAPTER 6

Systems Revealed, Systems Managed

A person needs new experiences. They jar something deep inside, allowing him to grow.
Without change, something sleeps inside us, and seldom awakens.
The sleeper must awake!

—Duke Leto Atreides (Jürgen Prochnow) from the movie *Dune*
(Universal Pictures, 1984)

Note to the reader: *You* **must** *get it* if this new approach to life is going *to stick, so I present these next two summary chapters in a meditative, almost hypnotic tone. There is some repetition as I explore and summarize the core of the mindset.*

CONVERGING CHAINS

Your day can be under your command. Chronic shortages of time and money, emergency decision making, and dealing with less-than-amusing people can be history. Starting with a subtle yet penetrating shift of perspective, elimination of chaos is possible.

The pathway to control is to discover, examine, optimize, and then oversee your mechanical and biological processes.

The dictionary's definition of *system* is "a group of interacting, interrelated, or interdependent elements forming a complex whole." That's perfect.

Systems don't operate randomly. Like computer code, they relentlessly execute in linear 1-2-3 sequence. In your world, they are embedded wall to wall. You wake, study, read, exercise, and eat. You breathe, walk, digest. You go to work, talk to friends, drive to the store to pick up groceries for dinner. You put gas in the car. You earn money and put it in the bank. Later, you pay the bills.

Some of your systems are aligned to help you reach your goals, and others silently sabotage your best efforts. Sometimes they work alone, but things are best when they work together.

You can make refinements in the dysfunctional systems, manhandling them into efficiency, pointing them in the directions you want them to point, producing the results you want them to produce. You can create useful ones from scratch and discard the bad ones.

Examine the primary system that is your life. See that it is composed of subsystems, and each one of those subsystems is composed of sub-subsystems. Explore your way down further, through the multiplying, expanding, and intertwining rootlike chains. Then turn it around and work your way back up to the top of the converging chains. As they come together and thicken into a single trunk, see that they add up to the ultimate primary system that is you. You are a system of systems!

The essence of your work, health, and relationships lies within systems, and although they are veiled behind the buzz of everyday consciousness, there is nothing magical or convoluted about them—or about their management.

You see life better. You're one layer deeper than the people around you. In this more concise reality you extract, examine, and perfect your systems one by one, and the wonderful reward for this incremental enterprise is that peace and prosperity silently enter through the side door.

NEARING YOUR EPIPHANY

This minute, slow down. Find a place where you won't be distracted. Let's work toward the magic moment when the systems mindset takes hold.

Visualize each of the following processes and note the commonality: *sequential execution over time.*

In this moment you must consciously concentrate in order to visualize a world of systems, but trust that soon you will naturally carry this perception through the day, always living in this place of one-layer-deeper, constantly observing the mechanical processes that generate the happenings of the day.

Suspended in this deeper layer, this *right here, right now place*, you will discover the spiritual wonderment you have been seeking.

Consider your mechanical reality. Start by imagining the closed set of sequential actions necessary to drive a car from point A to point B. (Open the door, get in, put the seat belt on, insert the key in the ignition, turn the key to start the engine, etc.)

Describe to yourself the specific linear steps—both mechanical and human—involved in finding a potential customer, making a presentation, and closing a sale. Think about the process of interviewing and hiring a new employee and then what you must do to keep this person for the long term while maximizing his or her contribution. Think about nurturing a relationship with a spouse, coping with the terminal illness of a parent, giving birth. Then there are the mundane processes of preparing a financial report, writing a paper for a college course, raking the yard, dumping the trash, or doing the wash.

Ponder the miraculous human-body mechanism that propels you through this material world with its umpteen individual biological and mechanical subsystems, nearly all of which function without any overt guidance, but many of which you can abuse or enhance.

Use your imagination, and in your immediate proximity—right now—look around yourself to see uncountable sequences in motion, most going unnoticed until *this* moment. You see that some of these processes don't matter too much, but others have an enormous effect on your happiness and the happiness of those around you.

Yes, systems intertwine and affect one another, yet first they are separate entities.

Although almost all of your life processes are automatic, there are many you perform consciously. Either way, by focusing on the systems that are within your circle of influence, you'll see that tweaking them to higher efficiency is almost always possible.

You'll know when you *get it* because within your moment-to-moment reality you will clearly see the individual systems around you—on the street, at the airport, at home, and in the mirror. No longer will you feel suspended in a swirling conglomeration of sights, sounds, and events. The new vision will be natural and unforced and you will wonder why you didn't see with this clarity before.

The moment you *get it*, you'll know it.

It could be right now, as you read these lines.

The Work the System Methodology Is a System

It's the primary management tool used to analyze and maintain all your other personal systems. It's the master mechanism for engineering an efficient life; one of serenity, prosperity, and contribution. *Focus on the method*. Study and experiment with it. Make it as efficient as possible.

SYSTEM MANAGEMENT

Each of your personal systems has direction and thrust. Each is headed somewhere, attempting to accomplish something. They are channeled by genetically determined patterns, learned formulas, cultural codes, bias based on race and gender, humanitarian predilections, simple self-interest, and of course the standard physical predispositions for appetite, sleep, sex, and survival. And all of them are propelled by a mysterious force that many of us choose to call God.

So, each of us is a system of systems. But here's the problem: some of them—each of which, always remember, can be visualized as a distinct entity—are headed in oblique directions, dissipating our efforts to reach conscious goals. At best, a system combines with other systems to help us reach desired targets. At worst, an errant component within a system creates problems that manifest themselves subversively, contributing to the gnawing sense that one is not in proper control of one's life. That horrible feeling is not rare. Most people are not in control of their existences, especially if the definition of control includes the qualifier, "I am getting what I want in my life."

Life can seem complicated, but the complexity doesn't leave you helpless to get a grip on circumstances because, one at a time, you can take action on specific system components that you pluck out of the chaos. This is system management in its most elemental form, and the beautiful aspect of it is that neither the sheer intricacy of it, nor your propensity to lean in certain directions, will stop you from improving the mechanisms that turn the wheels of your life.

You can list a multitude of minor individual systems that are necessary for just getting through the day, not to mention major primary systems—such as running a business or holding a job, coping with college, raising children, making retirement vibrant and meaningful—or just staying levelheaded while balancing a household, negotiating with family members, and providing an income. (I was a single parent of two children for fifteen years and—don't argue with me—this role is the supreme test of a human's ability to simultaneously kill fires, build something for the future, and stay sane.)

In our culture it is common to call the simultaneous handling of the day's umpteen events *multitasking*. This is a flawed expression because it suggests that the conscious, hands-on command of multiple concurrent undertakings is some kind of laudable accomplishment.

Instead, the term *system management* is what we're after. The term defines a thought-out orchestration in which one has a firm grip on details and is not living at the edge of crisis, floating along on hope, fingers crossed, prayers recited, and obsessions indulged.

If solid goals are established and the majority of time is spent manipulating systems toward those goals, great results will materialize naturally. Conversely, think about holistic solutions that cover life's complexity like a blanket: another market for the product, a better manager for the company, a larger house, a new boss, a new spouse. These are attempts to straighten affairs out all at once, and although occasionally they are necessary, they are opposite of the dig-down system governance efforts I am proposing here.

So stop looking for an immediate hand-of-God solution, and drop the idea that life is convoluted and mysterious. Burrow through the complexity and get to work repairing the underlying inefficient mechanisms one by one. Trying to find peace and life control through drugs, food, work, money, silly psychobabble, fanatical adherence to religious or political dogma, running away, or excessive preoccupation with the extraneous—obsession—is an abomination of the simplicity of it all. These are whole-sale applications that falsely promise to soothe life's complexities in one fell swoop. Easy buttons! Instead, you'll go inside and fix building-block components one at a time. This is about making small, mechanical better-ments in subsystems that over time add up to a primary system made of steel. *This* is how you will get where you want to go.

Set aside the complexity and begin to work your systems. The first steps you'll take include setting direction and deciding on strategy. (You will begin this process by creating the Strategic Objective and the General Operating Principles. These documents are fully explained in chapter 10.)

AGAIN: THE SUBVERSIVE HOLISTIC THOUGHT PROCESS

In the last thirty years, the terms *holistic* and *global* have inserted themselves into the fabric of our culture, and we often suppose an entire mechanism is faulty, so we think we must completely replace it. This overreaction is too many times rooted in a quick-fix mentality coupled with feel-good emotionalism, and it can obscure a more sensible path in which one sim-ply examines a primary system's mechanical construction in order to fix a faulty component or perform an update. From the start, the primary sys-tem is probably better than OK, working well in most situations. Rather than starting from scratch, could we simply make an internal adjustment?

HOW SUCCESSFUL PEOPLE NEGOTIATE THEIR DAYS

If you are like most people, you have not *consciously* considered the involve-ment of systems in your daily life. Therefore, you have not *consciously* thought in terms of adjusting them in order to eliminate problems from occurring in the first place. For most people, whacking emerging moles is how life is played out. There is no thought of burrowing deep into the mole hole for some serious mole extermination.

The little moles are cute-faced decoys that distract us from the critical moves we should be making. I say, let's burrow deep inside their tunnels and eradicate them all. And then, before we leave, let's do some serious manipulation—let's do what we have to do—so no more moles show up later. Then, confident that moles will never distract us again, we'll climb back above ground and start fixing the other processes of our lives that need fixing.

Here is a mechanical truth: *one can compensate for the negative outcome of a recurring problem, but without repairing the errant process that caused the problem, the problem will undoubtedly occur again.*

Few people understand the systems approach of successful leaders who intuitively grasp that a seemingly isolated problem is not isolated at all. These leaders see problems as the result of a flaw in an errant system—an errant system that can be fixed. For these leaders (more often from the private sector than the public sector), a problem is not a disappointment just to be corrected and then written off. It's a wake-up call. This means that once the manager corrects the immediate negative effects, there is a second step. It is this second step that is key. The problem's cause is traced to the errant subsystem, which is then modified so the problem doesn't happen again. *This is how successful people negotiate their days!*

So, through the astute leader's observation, a problem in the primary system calls for a subsystem modification. The leader makes the permanent enhancement, causing the primary system to be incrementally more robust and reliable than before the problem occurred. Addressing the problem, and then taking this second step to fix the cause of the problem, distinguishes people who are in control from people who are not—the successful from the unsuccessful.

The improvement of a system is a system improvement, and the documentation of that improvement is a Working Procedure. The documentation of each revision is critical. Making an enhancement without it guarantees that the improved system will revert to an inefficient unpredictability borne of shortcuts, outdated but comfortable methodologies, the pressures of the day, and/or confusion infused by assorted personalities and talents. Documentation converts an organic process into a mechanical entity. It gives permanence. It has to happen.

Again, by focusing on repairing problems in this way, the primary system becomes ever more efficient and rough edges disappear. It's a beautiful thing because as time passes the mechanism gets better and better.

Imagine a system that improves with time rather than wears out!

At the start, these one-by-one efforts can seem daunting. You work at them for a while and then ask, "When will the problems cease, and when can I stop fixing and documenting?" But you carry on. After plugging along for a short while, you notice the pace and quantity of incoming problems have decreased. You see the fire killings aren't coming so fast, and this is the moment in time when a powerful belief takes hold. Now, with fervor, you accelerate the process so even fewer errors occur, and your organization and personal life become ever more smooth and efficient. The bottom line improves while vitality increases. Now you're managing your life, working your systems. You'll never go back!

Your Job

Your task is to fix one system after another, not careen through the day randomly taking care of whatever problems erupt. Your job is not to be a fire killer. Your job is to prevent fires.

RIPPLES AND HEAVY SEAS

For Centratel, the system-improvement process continues twelve years after the implementation of the method. Now problems are so few that when one surfaces, my staff pounces on it with a vengeance. It is hard to describe the satisfaction of leading a company that operates this way. Like Centratel, my personal existence still has its occasional unexpected ups and downs (that's life!), but now it's enormously more resilient, and I am well prepared to absorb unexpected blows. For the apple vendor, an overturned apple cart is a disaster, but an apple falling off the side of the cart now and then is a small, easily dealt-with occurrence. There is no getting away from random problems that are caused by an unexpected circumstance or unpredictable human error. No one is perfect!

In organizations and in individual lives, outright mistakes account for only a small percentage of total errors. Most problems stem from nonexistent process management and show themselves as errors of omission. Your new positioning will *dramatically* reduce this form of inefficiency. (Errors of omission are addressed in chapter 13.)

What about the unexpected heavy seas of a debilitating injury or the loss of a loved one? Here it is again: strength and resilience are by-products of the work the system method. A life that is stronger and more resilient will be better able to navigate the inevitable dark waters.

ROUTINE MAINTENANCE AND TWEAKING

Once your new processes are in place and functional, you will focus on routine reviews of the entire collection. This ongoing analysis is a beautiful thing. The percentage of overall work time spent fixing systems decreases with time, while the percentage of time spent maintaining them increases with time. (We'll talk more of routine maintenance in chapter 9.)

Business *Is* Art

I write these words spontaneously, from a downtown coffee shop in early March 2011, as I proceed with the face-lift of this third edition. I've been thinking of this for a while, and the concept was suggested to me by a reader who explained it briefly: who says art must include a canvass, sculpture, or musical instrument? Art *is* creativity, and is there a better example of a creative enterprise than the machinations of building a successful business? Indeed, business is art in its purest form! The painter and the musician shouldn't scoff at the business entrepreneur or corporate chief who must take hard, cold life—sights, sounds, events, things, people—and stir them into an efficient enough mixture to produce a successful business or corporate department. *Business is art*, it's a heroic endeavor, and within it lies two superb by-products: tangible value to others—employees and customers—and a bottom line for the creator.

NOTICING POOR SYSTEM MANAGEMENT

When you get a feel for system management in your daily life, you will notice when it isn't happening around you. As you interact with the world you'll find yourself critiquing what works and what doesn't, hyperaware of the processes others control. This new posture as an informal service-quality observer will go with you everywhere.

You will understand the real reasons why people who promise to call don't call; why there is lousy service in certain restaurants, retail stores, and hotels; why there is haphazard communication with a service provider. You will develop a knack for instantly recognizing shoddy workmanship, missed deadlines, promises not kept, bad attitudes, and sloppy execution. You'll recognize these dysfunctional human performances as the logical end result of poor process engineering and/or maintenance, both organizational and personal. Human dysfunction is pervasive. As soon as your new systems vision takes hold, you will begin to notice these inefficiencies. But when you encounter efficiency in an organization or another individual, you will notice that too, and you will appreciate it for the beautiful thing it is.

When you're at the receiving end of poor service, remember that the ultimate problem is not with the person who is facing you, who may indeed be rude or uncaring, but with the individual at the top of the organization who is not managing properly. Even so, be sympathetic with the absent leader. Most people don't understand the system-improvement methodology, or even that there is such a thing. With best intentions and working hard, they stumble along, batting off the fastballs as they come hurtling in from all directions. I was like that.

What about selfish people who circumvent the rules and don't consider others? Be careful here, too. Don't confuse someone's personality flaw with their mechanical problem, which is a simple lack of attention to the details of individual relationship systems. How one goes about cultivating good relationships is also a system, and the methodology must be set up with care and executed with consistency. For thoughtless people, the base problem is not usually a personality flaw, but the lack of a functional *relationship maintenance system*. This error of omission creates a vicious circle. These people do not return calls, remember birthdays, say hello to strangers, spontaneously smile, send thank-you notes, extend invitations, or really listen while in a conversation. They don't show interest in the vicissitudes or successes of the people right in front of them. The consequence is that they receive little positive attention in return. These lonely people feel rejected and alienated yet dig themselves deeper and deeper into loneliness, getting ever more sour on life. Is it their fault? Well, mechanically speaking, yes it is.

It sounds antiseptic, but it's the reality: some people don't apply the recurring relationship fundamentals necessary to make and keep friends. Maybe they don't care enough, or more likely they just don't understand the mechanical reality that having friends requires routine forethought and effort.

Despite the near perfection of our natural world, look around right now and notice that the human qualities of dependability and consistency are in short supply. And because they are in short supply, people accept that condition as normal. Actually, people should accept it as normal. It *is* normal. And happily for you, this means standing out from the crowd won't take much effort. The people around you will start to notice your quick execution of detail, your consistent reliability, the congruency between what you say and what you do. And especially they will feel your calm, confident comportment and that you are in control of things. People can depend on you and know what to expect, and this makes you attractive to them. New customers, great employees, and reliable friends will be drawn to you because you doggedly adhere to the simple system-management tenets for cultivating great relationships.

YOUR LIFE: PROBLEMATIC OR ORDERLY?

So, bottom line, how do you perceive your life? Do you see it as problematic—unfair, unpredictable, and inhospitable? Or do you view it as orderly and directed? Yet again, this isn't a matter of having a positive or a negative attitude or adopting some philosophical stance based on feel-good theory. This is about simplicity, mechanics, and logic.

How do you see your life?

A Certain Billionaire

We were on vacation in Siena, Italy. We'd been there just a few days, and at night the jet lag of crossing ten time zones had me entertaining strange dreams. A lucid midnight sojourn inspired this 2:00 a.m. writing session.

A well-known multibillionaire asked me to take the equivalent of the chief operations officer position for his conglomeration of several hundred international corporations.

Upon receiving the offer in this tycoon's ad hoc boardroom located on the tarmac of an airport somewhere, my central dream thought as I faced him was that I would succeed. I would succeed despite my small-town heritage, my lack of an advanced academic degree, and the shortage of other seemingly necessary background requisites. My challenges would be prosaic, limited to dealing with frequent travel, the certain inevitable corporate personality clashes, and whether or not being a part of the enterprise would cause me to feel trapped in a cage (my current world is much smaller, but at least I roam it at my whim).

In my dream, why was I confident? It was because my position would entail dealing with the same simple mechanical realities of cause and effect that I deal with now, just on a larger scale. I would work my systems in this enormous corporate structure where, symbolically speaking, one plus one would continue to equal two, just like everywhere else. Other than the scale of the endeavor, my tasks would be no different from the day-to-day tasks I was already handling.

CHAPTER 7

Getting It

I'm trying to free your mind but I can only show you the door.
You're the one who has to walk through it.

—Morpheus (Laurence Fishburne) from the movie *The Matrix*
(Warner Bros. Pictures, 1999)

First you work your systems, then your systems do the work. Imagine the following metaphorical scenario.

Recently it became clear that one of the managers in the company where you work had neglected his department. It showed in the lack of output and the general chaos.

Yesterday, he was fired.

You feel bad the department manager lost his job, but you understand why it happened. This sometimes occurs, and when it does you usually see it firsthand. You are a troubleshooter for your organization, and your role is to get the apples back on the cart when they fall off.

You make your way to the department, which occupies a single room in your building.

You walk through a door into a large, dimly-lit room. It's one you've been in before. The room is empty except for several dozen wooden boxes varying in size. The containers, each with a hinged wooden lid, are scattered around the room. You begin by replacing the burnt-out light bulbs and then pushing the boxes around so they are in order, taking time to organize them so you can perform your work in a logical way.

You've brought your toolbox, and of course you have written technical instructions if there are questions. The repair and maintenance procedures are understandable and well thought-out. You know this because you are the one who supervised their creation.

Because of the previous neglect of the contents of these boxes, you knew before you came here that completing this job would require a long day. You hunker down and get to work.

You open the lid of the first box and find a mechanical apparatus within. It's made up of gears, wires, and levers, and because you are a technician trained in understanding the construction of such devices, what you see makes sense. It is clear to you what this mechanism does and how it is put together. Peering deeper into the box to examine the intricacies within, it is apparent that adjustments are necessary. You make them. In the course of your work you notice an obsolete component. You replace it with an updated version (you always carry spares). This revision will make the device more efficient and reliable.

Then you oil the moving parts and finish by cleaning up the mechanism, wiping it off.

Finally, you thoroughly test it to make sure it's working perfectly. It is.

On the inside of the lid of the box, you write the date and your initials, along with a brief summary of what you did so that when the new department manager shows up for the first day of work, he or she will know what you've done, and when.

You close the lid and move on to the next box. You repeat the process. One by one you move through all the boxes, making each of the unique mechanisms within them perfect, closing the lids afterward.

It indeed takes the entire day to complete your work, but the time went quickly as you spent your hours in a creative, constructive flow space.

You've finished, and you stand in the doorway and take a last look around the room. The boxes are in neat rows, their lids closed, and you are confident the devices within the boxes are working perfectly. You know the department's output will be very good now because each of its mechanisms is working flawlessly. How could it be otherwise? You also know the new department manager will be system-improvement oriented, watching over the details of the department, not allowing it to fall back into disarray. There will be routine maintenance. As you turn off the lights and walk out the door, you are intensely satisfied with your work and with yourself.

There it is—the systems mindset approach in which one sees life as a collection of individual systems (or call them processes or mechanisms or machines) that are to be, one by one, isolated and then made perfect. And once perfected, they are routinely coddled for maintenance and upgrading.

Here's the no-brainer that eludes most people: in the course of a day and in the course of a life, each movement we make is a single step in a linear sequence of steps intended to accomplish one or another goal. *Each thing we do is a component of a system, a system that has a purpose.*

You are a project engineer and you direct the events of the day; you're not a leaf in the wind, blowing around at the mercy of whatever wind happens to be blowing.

My intention here in part one has been to present illustrations and evidence from a variety of angles so you will see the mechanisms of your own life on a visceral level. I'm being repetitive, hammering the concept home. Are you there yet? If not, continue to be patient as I replay the elements of the new perspective while slowly introducing the how-tos.

If you don't experience the aha! moment soon, it's OK. The fake-it-'til-you-make-it routine is a potent way to get there.

THE FIRST STEP: MAKE YOUR SYSTEMS VISIBLE

You know this by now. First, make the various systems consciously visible. Second, one at a time, bring them to the foreground for examination. Third, adjust them. Fourth, document them. Fifth, maintain them.

By plucking individual systems out of the amorphous mass of your real-time existence—that intense conglomeration of sights, sounds, and events that is your life—you can examine and then precisely manipulate their workings. But first you must see them.

Reaching the point where you see the systems around you is the first and most significant step. It's a mini-enlightenment. When the epiphany occurs, you will have internalized the fact that *systems make up your life,* and you will know that assertively directing them is leadership at the most fundamental level. You will view your existence with new clarity. Details will be sharper and more vivid, the colors more vibrant. No more will you perceive your world as a confused assortment of people, objects, and situations.

What seemed complex will suddenly appear elementary.

Certain in your new vision, you will change your strategy from fire killing to system improvement because it is the most sensible thing to do.

YOU MUST STAND OUTSIDE OF IT

If you want to see where you fit in the machine that is your life, you must observe it from an external vantage point. *You must stand outside of it if you are to see how you are a part of it.*

There is nothing shadowy in this. This is only about seeing your existence more precisely.

There is no need for me to list a one-through-ten-step process for making the method produce results. You must simply see the processes in your life with the same clarity with which you perceive the physical objects around you. Once that happens, the rest will be fill-in-the-blanks sensibility.

Again, here's how you will see your world: the day's happenings are visible as individual elements, arranged in logical sequences. It's borderline metaphysical as you hover above your world. You are the watcher, the observer of your life.

Considering your new mindset, you think, "Why couldn't I see this before?" You look back on your previous life and observe that, embroiled in minutiae, you were blind to the processes that lay beneath the happenings of the day. You remember the day when the shroud lifted, when sequential life systems became visible and your perception of the world's workings shifted. You also remember the first inklings of the potency of systems methodology and how soon it proved itself in action. Tangible rewards came quickly. You remember that removing the shroud didn't take a whole lot of faith or hard work, just some quiet observation.

IT'S WHAT YOU DO

Now you know, and thus you will act. Consider the following points.

First, *it's what one does that counts*. Good intentions, a positive attitude, and enormous enthusiasm are not enough. Really, thoughts don't even matter. What matters is the action one takes, right here in the tangible world.

Second, *getting things right most of the time is good enough*. The things that don't come out well are just part of the overhead: the cost of doing business, of taking risks, of external confusion, of coping with events that are sometimes one step ahead of your best efforts, of being alive. As by-products of your advancement forward, accept that less-than-perfect events are going to happen. Three steps forward and one step back is the way it goes.

Third, remember that *most people don't fail by making overt mistakes*. They fail because they don't take action. If you fall into this category, prepare to change your ways.

YOUR DAY WILL NEVER BE THE SAME

It is incredibly satisfying to have control; for the world to make sense, and to have direction over your own destiny. And you'll become tenacious about maintaining this new direction because as time marches on, life just gets better and better.

I belabor this point because it is key: *once the work the system methodology is internalized and applied, you will be a different person*. No more feeling anxious in the morning, your head filling with encroaching worries even before you get out of bed. During the day, no more long hours spent killing fires. No more evenings spent buried in paperwork or sitting exhausted, zombielike in front of the TV, with no hope of relief tomorrow.

Instead, at the end of the day you look back to see that you spent your time immersed in one-time creative projects and productive conversations with staff, customers, friends, and family. You feel gratification that the day's efforts were further incremental steps toward even more freedom and prosperity. You don't pine for the big break because it's clear the big break is already occurring piece by piece, step by step.

In charge of your life from dawn to dusk, you know you are building your destiny in a solid and honorable way.

In your day, you have not just made incremental progress toward your most important goals, you have also spent time with the people who matter most to you, and you have done what you wanted to do.

There's plenty enough money now, and your circle of influence is growing.

You are happy with yourself. You know why your life is what you want it to be. It's because of you: *you did that to you!*

The systems mindset is logical. But it's magical too, as what you used to take for granted erupts into magnificence.

Violating a Social System

In Italy, we were staying in a small guesthouse in the tiny coastal town of Monterosso. One morning while Linda still slept, I sat alone at a breakfast table in the corner of the dining room. Other tourists surrounded me, quietly enjoying their cappuccinos and pastries. I worked on my laptop, putting the final touches on the first edition of this book, my breakfast dishes pushed aside.

The manager of the guesthouse approached. In halting yet perfect English she asked, "Are you finished with your breakfast?"

I answered, "*sí.*"

Then she said, "Please. To work, take your computer to the lobby downstairs. This is a place of breakfast."

That elegant phrase—"*This is a place of breakfast*"—was perfect. In her wonderfully nuanced English, my host got directly to the point and I instantly understood. There was no quibbling with the logic. I was working in a place of breakfast, and working there was wrong. Italians consider eating a semisacred process that should never be sullied by work. My incursion was callous. I was not respecting a process that had been operating for scores of generations.

I moved downstairs to the lobby, a place where many things—including a busy American with his laptop—were welcome.

It's understandable how Europeans can sometimes consider Americans crass, as we too often fail to leave our overbearing nuances at home. It was a humbling reminder that I must always respect the systems of others.

PART TWO

MAKE IT SO

(CRITICAL DOCUMENTATION)

CHAPTER 8

Swallowing the Horse Pill

There are some people who live in a dream world, and there are some who face reality;
and then there are those who turn one into the other.

—Douglas Everett

Having your protocols written down is as important as what you think or say.

This part of the book describes the fundamentals of work the system documentation. They are presented here as we use them at Centratel, but you are welcome to copy and customize them. (And to make the process simple and thorough, investigate Business Documentation Software in appendix J and at workthesystem.com/documentation).

With your documentation you will transform ephemeral, feather-in-the-wind organic processes into iron-clad mechanisms that do your exact bidding every single time.

Linda came up with the following analogy for the three work the system documents (and it will especially resonate for residents of the United States). The Strategic Objective is your Declaration of Independence, your mandate for a better future. The General Operating Principles document is your constitution, a set of guidelines for future decision making. The Working Procedures are your laws, the rules of your game. Can you imagine a representative government not having its foundation recorded in written form? Why would it be any different for your business or your job—or your life? (Does a dictator require documented guidance/structural documentation? Not so much. It tends to get in the way of the tyrant's self-serving, day-to-day manipulations.)

First you will create the Strategic Objective, then the Operating Principles. These documents establish your bearing; they will keep you sailing straight. Putting them together won't take long.

Then you will begin your Working Procedures, and it is here that you will spend most of your time. Again, the enhancement of a system is a system improvement, and the documentation of that improvement is a Working Procedure.

THE UNASSUMING NATURE OF WHAT MUST BE DONE

One day not long after the light bulb switched on in my head, I realized that creating the necessary documentation would not be flashy. The process would sometimes be tedious as it was clear that cataloging all of our systems would take time. The Working Procedures would not fall into place as easily as the first two controlling documents, the Strategic Objective and the General Operating Principles.

Firsthand I saw that within my own TAS industry, few owners perceive their businesses from an outside-and-slightly-elevated perspective. They thrash within the inner workings, smacking those moles as their little heads unexpectedly yet inevitably pop up. I realized immediately that my industry was not unique. Few small businesses document their direction, and still fewer chronicle their processes.

Why is that? I thought. If this methodology is so simple and potent, why aren't more small-business owners doing it? Could it be because the documentation work is too much of a challenge? Too hard? Too labor intensive?

It's all of that! And the unassuming nature of what must be done is smoking-gun evidence of its viability! This revelation instilled in me a powerful desire to tackle the cataloging tasks that lay ahead.

In any case, if I was to establish solid direction, hone processes to perfection, and then expect those processes to continue to be perfect in the future, it was logical the direction and processes would have to be written down. And then—there was no getting around it—the next prosaic task would be to ensure that my staff precisely followed the documentation.

My next moves were obvious, but creating the documentation would take time away from the ongoing efforts of keeping the business afloat day to day. Business demands would not step aside while we improved processes and wrote up attending paperwork, and I wondered if we could find the time to write everything down. But then I realized this was a moot question. Accomplishing the work was mandatory because if we didn't do it, the company would fail—and my guess was that if we *did* do it, the company would flourish. So I swallowed the huge horse pill that there was some serious work to do—unexciting yet quietly potent documentation work—and plunged ahead full steam.

Motivating Yourself

To get off the mark, remember there will never be an Easy Button you can push to make everything instantly better. Documenting systems takes time and focus. But you are already working hard and long, so what's the big deal? Simply tell yourself that you must continue to work hard for just a bit longer. And think about heroics. Yes, documentation can be seen as boring, but having the fortitude to accomplish it is courageous.

PREPARATION LEADS TO COMMAND

Yes, the one-time heavy lifting of creating your documentation will be intensive at first, but once in place, your ongoing workload will dramatically decrease. In my case, I transformed one-hundred-hour workweeks into two-hour workweeks. (That's one way to look at it. The other way is that if you wish to keep working your long hours—or for whatever reason you *have* to keep working them—why not dramatically increase the quality and quantity of your output? For the salesperson, this means more money. For the corporate manager, it means a faster climb up the ladder.)

You will generate extra time, so you will be better able to prepare. And proper preparation leads to better command of future events, which leads to higher efficiency. Higher efficiency produces more available time—and some of that available time you will reinvest in additional preparation.

This is the opposite of a cycle of diminishing returns. It's a cycle of *increasing* returns, a cyclical mechanism that builds upon itself to ever-higher positive results.

So, the largest obstacle to better preparation is the reluctance to invest the necessary time to better prepare! At the beginning, even if you have experienced the insight that systems make up everything in life, you must be patient and self-disciplined. You must keep your head down and grind out those Working Procedures until prosperity and free time begin to arrive, thus confirming deep down in your belly that this is a smart thing to do. When the results begin to materialize—and it won't take long—I promise that you will become a fanatic for documentation.

Note that some documentation will be useful in your personal life, but it will be informal and less intensive.

As a preview, here is a summary of what you'll create (there will be much more detail in chapters 10 and 11):

1. Strategic Objective. The one-page Strategic Objective will provide overall direction. You will create it yourself. Spread out over several sessions, it won't take more than six to eight hours to complete. (Caution: This is not a job for a committee. It's a job for the leader, you.) Once it's completed, you will get feedback from your staff (and superiors, if any). Over time, you will adjust it as necessary. As the years pass, it won't change much. Create a separate one for your personal life. (In appendix A you will find Centratel's Strategic Objective.)

2. General Operating Principles. Upon completion of the Strategic Objective, you will begin to put together a list of General Operating Principles. Just two or three pages long, this condensed *guidelines for decision making* document requires ten to twenty hours to complete, but these hours will be spread over a period of a month or two as Principles come to light. (Yes, the creation of this document is also a job for *you*, although you will want to get input from others.) You will extract these principles from your everyday experience while formulating them from the perspective of your new systems mindset. *These principles are what you believe.* Don't rush them. Be thoughtful and patient with yourself. Put them together carefully, and your Principles will change little over the years. You'll want a thorough set for your business and a more informal

set for your personal life. (Centratel's Thirty Principles document is in appendix B.)

3. Working Procedures. Instead of killing fires, you will spend your time creating a fireproof environment. Your Working Procedures will be the on-the-job, blue-collar tools of this effort. This documentation will be a collection of protocols that outline exactly how the systems of your business or your job will operate. (Working Procedures are not often necessary for your personal life, although the concept should travel with you everywhere.) Brief, concise, and authored by you and other key people (your staff, peers, supervisors), 95 percent of your procedures will follow the same simple 1-2-3-step linear format. The other 5 percent will follow an open narrative format. (In fact, the Operating Principles document is itself a narrative-format Working Procedure.) Every system process will have its own written Working Procedure. As you did with the General Operating Principles, you will begin creating your Procedures documentation just after you complete your Strategic Objective. You will start with the most troublesome critical processes and then work down through dozens, if not hundreds, of additional ones, depending on the complexity of your business, job, or profession. But even over this initial period, it won't be a full-time job. And, if you have staff, remember that it's a bottom-up strategy: train your best people to do the legwork. Foundational to your everyday business experience and adjusted with evolving circumstances, Working Procedures are fluid (see samples in appendix C).

Lifestyle Requirements

If you choose to live a certain lifestyle, that lifestyle has certain requirements. There are tasks that must be accomplished. These are task requirements, not when-I-get-around-to-it or if-I-feel-like-it undertakings. To achieve your desired lifestyle, you must accomplish these tasks whether you enjoy doing them or not. No matter how onerous the task, or how little you want to do what is required, the payoff will arrive as long as you take the steps! Carry this thought around with you: *I do not have to like the steps I must take. I just have to take them.* Nine out of ten people don't understand this. They think, rather, "If I don't enjoy what I'm doing, then what I'm doing is incorrect." Bad presumption.

The documents you will create are mechanical aids. However, there is something else that is important about them. They are tangible. Their physicality makes what you are doing and where you are going *real*. With written guidelines, you can put your hands on your work and your future. Every day you will see your goals and methodology, and this will be a reminder to stay on the path. Always remember that surging thoughts, desires, and hopes are intangibles and they can divert you, but documentation is real and it will keep you straight.

Your controlling documents do not have to be perfect in the first drafts. They can be grammatically incorrect, the sentence structure can be less than optimal, and they can be brief. What is important is that you begin to create and use them. Just begin! You will clean them up later.

EMOTIONAL FLUCTUATIONS

Like bedrock, your three master documents will stand against the storms that blow across your world. And what storms create the most havoc, reversing forward progress? Your own emotions.

Documentation lays out everything that is important for getting you to a place of control in your life: your beliefs about how the world works, what is most important to you, your goals and how you will achieve them, and how you will operate. Because of it, your forward progress will ebb only slightly as you encounter the inevitable emotional surges that are part of the human condition. With the new methodology in place, you will minimize the impact of your personal downtimes. It may be slower progress during those times, but it *will* be progress.

THE KEY: GET OUTSIDE YOURSELF

No matter what, there will be times when you think you are sinking. Nonetheless, when those times occur, your documentation will reach down and yank you to the surface before you drown.

The Strategic Objective, General Operating Principles, and Working Procedures are your self-created guiding lights. In the tough times, they remind you that your business is a system of systems and that tweaking certain external and internal subsystems is what you must do. When you are not feeling strong and your emotions are negative, your guidelines are right there, ready to get you back on track, or at least keep you from straying too far. As Mick Jagger said, "It's alright to let yourself go as long as you can get yourself back."

When you realize you are watching your temporary depression from the outside, you will know you have reached a higher level of control. This is cognitive self-command, the ability to examine and adjust your own thinking from an external vantage point. You see your thoughts as independent of you, mechanisms unto themselves: singular, tangible entities, just like any of the other system-mechanisms under your direction.

Your new perspective will remind you that the reasons for the downtimes are usually quite simple: too little sleep, low blood sugar, excessive work or TV, negative people, gloomy environment, the payback for ingesting a mood-altering substance, and so on. Get outside these influences; look down on them to see them for what they are. Then, next time, delete or minimize them so they will no longer drain energy or create depression.

In my own life, being tired drives me downhill faster than anything else. Like clockwork, every afternoon between 1:00 p.m. and 2:00 p.m. I go into a physical and mental downturn, and I either nap it off or crawl through the mid-afternoon, understanding that my physical body—and my thinking process—is at low ebb. I never make important decisions or handle sensitive issues in that time frame. By 4:00 p.m. I'm fine again.

Discover your own cycles and work with them.

STORMS OF THE CRIMINAL MIND

The criminal mind has a certain grasp of the base mechanics of the world, maybe more so than the average law-abiding citizen. In the classic colloquial sense, the criminal works the system, as he or she strips away the niceties, examines the raw mechanics, and without concern for others, manipulates those mechanisms to selfish benefit. Yes, the criminal approaches life with a malefic bent, but one can't deny that it's a systems approach.

In any case, criminality is a losing game because it's a flaw in the over-arching primary societal machine, a machine that automatically works hard to eliminate flaws one way or the other. Consider the plight of the chronic lawbreaker who gyrates outside of common expectations, ignor-ing accepted notions of how one is expected to act. For greedy reasons, the criminal takes shortcuts, exploits exposed system components, and makes small-time gains. As the societal system is manipulated without regard for fairness and compassion—the bulwarks of a just society—personal pain arrives in an overt way: jail time, for instance, or a more covert lack of inner peace. The criminal is afloat in a stormy sea. The TV series *The Sopranos* perfectly illustrated the paranoia of fighting the system. The characters were diabolical and tormented, and ultimately doomed. If you are a criminal, the force is *not* with you.

If one is working outside the system, what is the solution? It is to make the decision to step back inside; to accept the general human process as it is; to play the game like an adult—to follow the rules. Things are just smoother that way. The universe welcomes manipulation if it results in a better, more efficient process, but it will fight manipulation that is disruptive.

In the free world there is huge opportunity to fit in, and to get ahead. One has unlimited options to succeed without going outside the boundaries.

A BACKBONE OF STEEL

Look forward to this: in the midst of a less-than-perfect day, from your outside-and-slightly-elevated vantage point, you will watch yourself drag your emotions out of a black hole rather than allowing them to swallow you up. Later, you will witness this self-rescue again. These incremental successes will strengthen your control, and after a while this even-keeled response will come effortlessly. Soon you will find you won't be so inclined to resort to the old antidotes of avoidance; no longer will you bludgeon your way through the downtimes with overwork or excessive alcohol, coffee, sugar, or drugs—the temporary fixes that used to rescue your mood in the moment but guaranteed more intense downtimes later on.

The learning cycle will continue upward until you have a solid grip on your world and you realize your Strategic Objective, General Operating Principles, and Working Procedures have pushed you to become one of those rare individuals whose backbone is made of steel. It seems odd that dispassionate documentation could have this kind of effect, but as you can see, there is much more to this than the written word.

OUTSIDE AND SLIGHTLY ELEVATED

At Centratel, when we took action from our new external stance, turmoil evaporated and was replaced by order. Once we began the new methodology it was easy to continue to implement it because great results accumulated quickly. The more we invested in system improvement and attending documentation—working the system—the more positive results we experienced.

Centratel is highly profitable now, and I spend little time managing it because the business is self-propelling. As project engineer I watch over it from a distance, nudging here and there to keep it traveling in a straight line and at full speed. Centratel is not under control because of my presence as a detail chaser. It's under control because of my insistence that we spend the majority of our time perfecting the mechanisms that compose it. Of course, another critical element of our success is my staff's enthusiasm for the method they helped put into place. They are project engineers, too.

Centratel is a pleasant place to work. Calm efficiency pervades. Concurrent with the business strategy, the systems perspective flows through my personal life where I have the same levels of efficiency and freedom. I regained my health years ago and today consider myself more than robust.

One might think my adoption of the new perspective came about because I was courageous, but that wasn't the case. It was fear and exhaustion. It took impending doom to see life was not going to conform to my wishes just because I thought it should.

Why weren't the answers obvious to me *before* there was a gun to my head? Part of the reason was that although the year-to-year struggle was killing me, it was more comfortable—more convenient—to acquiesce to predictable day-to-day pain than to question my overall vision and methodology. Don't let that happen to you.

There was also arrogance. It was easier to posture myself as a hero, facing and then overcoming incredible external odds, doggedly marching on, rather than to question my presumption that the world would someday get a clue and adjust to my requirements. But when catastrophe was finally upon me, everything distilled down to the indisputable raw fact that I was not managing the processes of my life.

Am I happy the insight came as the end-result of trauma? If that was what was required, yes. Do *you* have to have a gun-to-the-head experience to get to the same place? No!

Late that night twelve years ago, when I first got outside and looked down, it struck me that although there was some work to do, it would be simple to repair my business and my life. All I had to do was identify systems, isolate them, and then fix them one at a time! Does this make sense now? Do you see there is no need to undergo a cataclysm in order to change your perspective and then get your circumstances straightened out?

In retrospect, the almost humorous aspect of my outside-and-slightly-elevated enlightenment was the realization this was not some kind of divine blessing bestowed upon me alone. The systems perspective is already permanently etched into the minds of those who direct large, successful organizations everywhere. Yet many of the people who innately embrace the methodology, as simple a concept as it is, can't describe it, much less identify it, as the critical factor of their own success.

System Questions

By dispassionately dealing with stone-cold reality, the odds of getting what you want are infinitely higher than waiting for a ghost to communicate good tidings, a horoscope or tarot card to predict a prosperous future, or a multimillion-dollar lottery winning to land in your lap. Be mechanical. Can you imagine how you will feel as you watch yourself get a grip on life and create what you want due to your own actions, not because of improbable fate, magic, dumb luck, or someone else's benevolence?

There are system questions—system filters—you can pose to yourself in order to really see the hard and cold reality of any given situation. Ask, "Without regard for my personal preference, what *exactly* is going on here?" Carry that question around with you everywhere, and when the necessary action is obvious, but you are still hesitant, ask, "Is not wanting to take action in this moment enough of a reason to not take action?"

FLOW

You watch in fascination as the world's endless processes ripple on. It's flow, and you like being part of it. You view your existence from this very nearly metaphysical perspective that is a step away and a little bit above yourself and your world. In your life, your job is to modify your systems, gently goading each to more and more efficiency. (Regarding systems that are outside of your control, you make no attempt at adjustment because it is a waste of time and energy.)

This world operates at 99.9 percent efficiency because there are unalterable physical laws that are powered by an unfathomable strength—a strength that hungers for order and efficiency. In the systems that make up our lives, results occur in a cold-blooded way; outcomes don't mysteriously conform to our individual desires just because we want them to. But this is a good thing because this mechanical reality is predictable; it is something we can depend on and therefore confidently use to our own benefit.

When you understand the relentless dependability of reality's mechanics and then carefully work those mechanics, you will get what you want in your life.

THREE LARGE STEPS AHEAD

In the middle of my business and health rejuvenation, I was pounded hard by two unexpected, earthshaking blows. One was the nasty legal battle mentioned earlier. The other was a bone-crushing personal family loss. Those two nightmares arrived at the same time. The first lasted two years; the second, three. It was painful during those dark times, but I was able to roll through the days with sanity and effectiveness, watching the goings-on from my outside-and-slightly-elevated vantage point.

Swallowing that horse pill so long ago was well worth it.

The new posture is natural and unforced. Here is how it will be from this point forward: you wake up in the morning with an immediate focus on what is most important for the day ahead. The day's tasks will be one-time, creative efforts, each aimed at carrying you closer to the objectives outlined in your two Strategic Objective documents—one for your business, one for your personal life. Although you will minimize stepping backward, there is no avoiding it because that is what getting through the day includes. You accept those imperfect movements as part of the overhead that comes with the much more significant movement forward—three large steps ahead for every one small step back. And the inevitable earthquakes? You'll be ready.

And at the end of the day, you feel satisfied because there has been tangible advancement toward your prime objectives. Working or relaxing, you don't float or obsess anymore. You direct, build, watch, and enjoy. It flows.

 The Giant Machine

The world's largest manufacturer of computer printers keeps a factory running 24/7/365. The nonhuman mechanical and electronic workers don't take breaks, and they work their entire lives in this fixed location. A daily line of transport trucks delivers raw materials and picks up fully packaged products. A few cars in the tiny parking lot indicate there is merely a small contingent of human workers present.

Given the proper security clearances, issued from the lone guard minding the front gate, a brave person can walk through the center of this giant machine. Doing so, one quickly learns that even human visitors are under the machine's governance. Standing at one end of this system of systems, one can barely make out the other end. It's a huge *machine*, as wide as it is long. Approaching a well-defined walkway, the human intruder is warned by red flashing lights to stop while a part of the mechanical line physically retracts in order to allow passage. Once the visitor passes, the track closes and the machine continues at an accelerated pace to make up for the time lost by the encroachment.

This is not the place for the faint of heart or the claustrophobic. There are no escape routes. Should the machine fail to detect your presence, there are no humans readily available to intervene on your behalf. Yes, you are free to leave but only at the mercy of this primary system and only at a pace that doesn't compromise system requirements.

The colossal machine is made up of subassemblies, and those subassemblies cooperate with one another until complete products are rolling off the end of the line. The fully tested printers are packaged and shipped to a local store near you, and in all likelihood the first human hands to touch the printers are those of retail purchasers.

This is a primary system with a clear goal—the production of certain objects of value. And where are the human masters? Removed from the process, of course, monitoring, adjusting, and maintaining.

CHAPTER 9

We Are Project Engineers

Management works in the system; leadership works on the system.

—Stephen Covey

As an ad hoc synopsis—by now you know how much I like to drill home the simple principles from different angles—the essence of the work the system method is to

1. Acquire the mindset; deeply internalize the fundamental perspective. *Get it.*

2. Pinpoint and describe goals for your business, job, and life. Briefly define the general methods you will use to achieve those goals. This is your Strategic Objective.

3. Create your collection of General Operating Principles, your guidelines to decision making.

4. Identify specific processes for improvement, including the ones that exist and the ones you must create. Be ready to discard others. Deal with the most problematic ones first.

5. Dissect each system into its most fundamental components. For your business or your job, describe each on paper in a 1-2-3-step or narrative format.

6. One system at a time, and leaning hard toward stark simplicity, improve the efficiency of the component steps. Change sequences and add or delete steps as necessary. Experiment. Make each of your systems perfect.

7. As an integral part of the system-improvement process, document each process into a Working Procedure in order to ensure continuity.

8. Put the new Working Procedures into play and tend to them on a regular basis, inspecting and tweaking as necessary. Later, this is where you'll spend most of your time.

YOUR PERSONAL ANALOGY

In step one, *getting it* is mandatory. Without this deep-rooted grasp, steps two through eight just won't happen in your real, mechanical world. The strength to take a new direction comes more from a belief lodged in the belly than from something learned in the head.

To truly internalize the perspective, it is useful to create a personal system analogy, a systems template that you find meaningful. Your analogy will illustrate systems methodology to *you*, reminding you of the characteristics that all systems share. In your day-to-day existence, you will keep this analogy in the back of your mind in order to keep your new perspective front and center. A vivid system analogy is the antidote to a too-busy day, a day that ruthlessly attempts to divert your attention from the enhancement process to wasteful acts of fire killing.

Your analogy must be utterly believable, and its mechanical basis must be something you don't question. Also, it is essential to find an analogy that is easy to visualize as separate from its surroundings, one that can stand on its own. You want a closed mechanism.

If you are in medicine, bodily processes and mechanics offer unlimited possibilities. You can draw examples from organ function, skeletal structure, respiratory and circulatory systems, etc.

If you sell cars, consider the conveyor belt of an auto plant, or a car itself with all of its complimentary subsystems, and how they must be monitored and maintained in order to keep it at peak efficiency.

As a firefighter, think about the equipment and procedures that must perform efficiently no matter what.

A pilot has the preflight checklist, which is a terrific example of examining an existing mechanism for flaws while ensuring that all submechanisms are at peak efficiency. A single flight is a great system analogy as the aircraft itself automatically conducts directional micro-adjustments, confirms subsystems are functional, and warns of dysfunction.

Your analogy will keep your energies channeled toward system management as it reminds you that a jumble of fire killing will drag you down. It will be a steady reminder that you are a project engineer who creates and maintains efficient systems, not a fire killer who responds to crisis after crisis.

The analogy will help you enormously at the beginning, and later, after it's hardwired into your psyche, it will be an occasional pleasant reflection of what you believe and how you see things.

As an illustration, here is the analogy I use. As you read, start to think of one that fits your own world. No, you don't have to put it down on paper.

THE NEW-SERVICE FACILITATOR

My analogy is about electricity: how it reaches people in their homes and businesses, and my past role as an electric utility employee.

Power line circuits perfectly illustrate the mechanics of the systems mindset to *me*. I can easily visualize an electricity distribution system as a separate, unique entity and not one on which the surrounding complexities of the world infringe. It's my private, perfect illustration of the mechanics of linear systems everywhere.

When I was twenty-eight, I took a job in the engineering department of a rural electric utility in Central Oregon. The utility is one of the largest Rural Electrification Administration (REA) co-ops in the United States, with thousands of miles of power lines branching throughout the Central and Eastern Oregon regions. It serves tens of thousands of residential, commercial, and agricultural customers.

The co-op's operations staff face extreme environmental, meteorological, and socioeconomic challenges. On the same day, linemen can experience both mountain snowstorms and desert heat; vertical mountain pitches and long river crossings; high-density city construction and extreme remote rural troubleshooting.

For the first half of my seven-year stint with the co-op, my job title was new-service facilitator.

As one of the co-op's four new-service facilitators, I met with contractors and landowners who were about to build homes. My task was to arrange for our construction crews to tap into the nearest existing power line in order to extend new electric service to the customer's construction site. Usually, the distance from the power line to the site was fewer than a hundred yards.

I examined the new home site, found the closest power pole, and wrote up instructions and a list of materials for the construction crews so they could get the electricity delivered to the customer via low voltage overhead and/or underground cable.

My job had little to do with the primary electrical distribution system. My area of responsibility was outside the massive power-generating dams that created the electricity far to the north on the Columbia River, and had nothing to do with the thousands of miles of high-voltage power lines and associated complex equipment that distributes electricity in bulk throughout the region. My simple task was to establish small power line extensions to individual new customers. These low-voltage subsystem extensions were minor additions to my utility's massive electricity distribution network, the primary electrical system.

I filled this position as new-service facilitator for three years, and then I got a promotion. My new responsibility moved me from the periphery of the system to the heart of it, where I would have a much greater impact on the primary network itself and on the many customers it served.

My job title was now project engineer, a perfect description of my new role (and in your new role it will be your title too, so pay attention here). I would be responsible for designing and supervising the construction of large, high-voltage distribution feeders into whole subdivisions, as well as working on complex projects that affected thousands of customers at a time. It was also my job to keep an eye on large segments of the primary electrical system in order to spot problems and to recommend repairs and revisions. There was the necessary overall maintenance, too. System components aged and the environment changed, and it was my task to monitor these variables and submit designs for fixes and upgrades.

In short, my job was to analyze the main electrical distribution system, design improvements, and then pass those improvements on to the construction crews. It was here, in my role as project engineer, that I learned the concept of system improvement.

I put my designs down on paper using a precise format. The goal was to be thorough yet concise; to give the construction crews the information they needed—no more, no less—so they could proceed quickly through the construction work.

Note how the analogy describes my transition from handling small and isolated add-on tasks to large internal system-improvement projects. Also note there were strict design and documentation protocols.

FLIRTING WITH THE NEW PERSPECTIVE

My previous position and my new position had an important commonality. In each case, when I went to work, from the beginning of the day to the end of the day I was focused on the co-op's electrical network. While I was on the job, the system stood separate from the rest of the world. Sure, I took breaks, had lunch, and made a personal phone call now and then, but all in all, the electricity distribution system—the network of poles and wire—was paramount in my consciousness, standing out in my mind as its own entity, separate and distinct from my children, finances, politics, or health. When I was on the job, the electricity distribution system had my focused attention as if nothing else existed. And it was not just separate in my mind, it was that way in reality, an independent mechanism inserted into the world, spreading its tentacles in order to fulfill its singular purpose of delivering electricity to lots of people.

At the end of the day, as I returned home to pay attention to the other systems of my life, I changed my perspective as if I had flipped a switch. At the time, I didn't consciously notice this daily transition, and little did I know that I was quietly internalizing the outside-and-slightly-elevated perspective that would form the basis of this book.

If you are like most people, you have an unconscious tendency to dissect complexities so the exposed elements can be dealt with one at a time. The work the system method will turn that soft, ephemeral proclivity into an assertive, structured quest—an everyday pilgrimage to isolate and then work the systems that compose your world.

SYSTEM MANAGEMENT

With the promotion at the co-op, my role morphed from designing small subsystems for individual customers to improving elements of the primary electrical system that served thousands of customers. Instead of adding to the electrical network in bits and pieces, I was managing large segments to ensure that it continued to provide an uninterrupted supply of electricity to large numbers of customers.

I tweaked the network to keep it strong and efficient.

Notice I was not climbing the poles or stringing the wire. My job was to devise revisions that would make the primary electrical system more robust and then to oversee the implementation of those improvements by other people. It was a strict protocol: as project engineer, I would create the design, but professional linemen would perform the physical work. This is a crucial point of the analogy.

My job was system management. At the time, I was unconsciously *working the system*, and after my awakening, this process would permanently and consciously insert itself into all parts of my life. Today, my former role serves me well as a template for how I want to visualize all aspects of my life. Like my position as project engineer with the electric utility years ago, today I examine, adjust, maintain, and upgrade all the processes of my existence, while I avoid getting caught up in secondary add-ons.

I no longer major in minors. Your own analogy will remind you to avoid that, too.

MAINTENANCE AND 99.9 PERCENT RELIABILITY

Electricity originates from a generating facility, and then power lines carry it to the end user. For the electricity, it's a long, hazard-wrought trip through multiple electrical subsystems and tough terrain. Weather extremes, vandalism, and the incessant ravages of time imperil the electricity's delivery. Yet, interestingly, in checking official statistics at the utility where I used to work, I found that over the last seven years, the average customer's power failed an average of just seventy-three minutes per year. Wow! Think about that. There are 525,600 minutes in a year, which means the average electric utility customer had steady electric power more than 99.9 percent of the time. Does that percentage sound familiar?

In considering a power line's path through hundreds of miles of hostile environment, combined with the volatile high-voltage electricity itself, which is so anxious to escape its confining wire, how does the staff of an electric utility accomplish this astonishing degree of reliability? They do it by viewing their electrical network as a closed mechanical system that must be assertively and relentlessly maintained, not as a conglomeration of poles, wire, and equipment that receives attention only when there are problems. The people employed by the electric company start by designing and installing a robust electrical *machine*, and then, via a corporate-wide systems approach, they pander to it.

In any part of life, in order to avoid system failure and to ensure top efficiency, the performance of regular system maintenance is mandatory: changing the car's oil, conducting staff meetings, watering the houseplants, dinner out with one's spouse, ball games with the kids, bonuses for the best-performing employees, routine visits with customers, record keeping, physical fitness, etc. However, for people in the grip of chaos, skipping these important wheel-greasing chores is the first casualty. In so many life situations that include careers, marriages, friendships, mechanical devices, play, homes, health—all of it—the necessary routine maintenance is skipped because of fire killing, simple laziness, and especially ignorance of the way linear systems proceed in the real, mechanical world.

Without proper recurring attention, outside factors (yes, parasitic outside systems) will cannibalize your efficient processes. Your fine-tuned systems must be kept on track.

An especially satisfying personal maintenance system is the daily half hour I spend at home working my reorganizing system. This is perhaps my simplest system, nothing more than an allocated daily time period dedicated to a narrow purpose: thirty minutes spent reorganizing. It's free-form time used to clean things up—straighten out my office, my closet, the garage, my e-mail in-box. Sometimes it's going outside and pruning the shrubs. It's about putting my individual life-facets in order, and it's the antidote to insidious, looming clutter, both physical and mental.

Another one of my free-form maintenance systems is reading (preferably a book or magazine, not a computer screen). I read daily for at least an hour, usually more. It's therapy, as it removes the mental frenzy that can develop through the day. In the wonderfully profound movie *Joe Versus the Volcano*, the Tom Hanks character is diagnosed with a fake disease called brain cloud. That's a perfect description of my mental state when I don't read for a few days.

WATCH THINGS FROM A DISTANCE

As I visualize an electrical power network as an analogy for all the systems of my life, it is a reminder to avoid being a worker and instead be a project engineer. In your own life, as you apply your analogy to your business or supervisory job, you will find yourself deflecting hands-on work to others or automating or discarding useless systems altogether. Instead of doing the work, you will be creating new systems, devising enhancements for existing ones, and supervising the people who perform the actual work. Of course, if you are a traditional artist or other creator, this will not be entirely true. Yet, whatever your life's role, there is room for significant movement in the work the system direction—a direction that can dramatically improve your life. (I'll discuss more about job and creator aspects in chapter 19.)

In considering your new analogy and via your new posture as a project engineer, you will begin to watch your existence from a distance. The more time you spend seeing your life from this bird's-eye view, the faster you will attain your goals—and the more time you will have to spend on that outside-and-slightly-elevated perch.

It really is this simple: avoid becoming caught up in the work. Instead, step outside, look down, and isolate individual systems in your head and on paper. Then, deciding overall what you want them to accomplish, identify defects as well as outside changing situations. Then, improve the systems while always documenting the revisions. Because you have designed these system-mechanisms to operate without your constant involvement, you can then back off and occasionally (but routinely) monitor and direct.

After just a short while, you're going to get good at this!

I approach all my systems from the project engineer's viewpoint: systems to stay fit, keep in touch with extended family, invest money, maintain computers, and even climb mountains.

In the beginning of my new life posture, I would constantly visualize my electric system analogy and its dictate that I be a project engineer. Now I don't think about it too often because the systems mindset is permanently hard-wired inside my being. In every aspect of my life, I am a project engineer.

What's your analogy? A car, a human body, an airplane, a ship? See the perfection of your encapsulated parallel and apply it to whatever situation you find yourself in. You can do this because all systems everywhere operate in exactly the same way. This is not theory. This is mechanical reality.

 Toilet Paper

This illustration borders on the nonsensical, but it makes two points. First, the systems perspective is not common; second, the perspective will become permanently ingrained once the logic of it is understood.

As an example of systems thinking, and at the risk of making an awful pun, reaching for a piece of toilet paper is the bottom line. Toilet paper is a mandatory accessory. It may be the one material thing that all of us have used daily for all of our adult lives. As an illustration of a system that is ubiquitous, it's perfect.

The act of loading toilet paper on a toilet paper dispenser is a system—a system that proceeds in a linear fashion until the goal is accomplished. Step 1: In the bathroom, approach the sink. Step 2: Open the cabinet door underneath the sink. Step 3: Reach into the cabinet and grasp a roll of toilet paper. Step 4: Take the protective wrapper off the roll. Step 5: Approach the toilet paper dispenser with the roll, etc.

Ask yourself the following question: Right now, in your own house or apartment, is the paper roll loaded on the dispenser with the free end of the paper rolling off the top of the roll where it can be easily grasped? Or is the leading edge rolling off the bottom of the roll and against the wall, where one must awkwardly reach underneath the roll to retrieve it?

With a couple of notable exceptions, paper flowing off the top is most convenient. It's the better way to have it.

For the fun of it, and as a student of human behavior, over the years I've kept an informal tally. Not counting hotels and motels where professional housecleaners have been instructed on the most efficient positioning, it is a nearly 50–50 split with a slight advantage going to those who chose top. This means most people don't think one way or the other about the insertion of the roll in the dispenser. (Or, implausibly, one-half the population is adamant that the roll be inserted one way and the other half of the population the other way.)

Since having the retrieving end of the paper on the top of the roll makes grasping the paper easier, why doesn't everyone load the paper that way every time? Is the task of inserting the roll one way more difficult than inserting it the other way? Not at all. But deciding to always do it one way or the other would require a one-time analysis—in this case it would take just a few seconds of time to establish a permanent methodology—but most people don't spend time considering underlying processes, even ones so innocuous as this one.

Yes, this is a silly illustration, but try to get past that and see this as a lesson for the big picture. See that in considering loading the paper in a different way, you are putting yourself outside and above the act of loading toilet paper. You are deliberately managing the process in order to produce an incrementally better result every single time the toilet paper retrieval process is executed in the future.

There is another, more visceral lesson here, and maybe it's a bit unnerving. Because you have considered this toilet paper question, it may cause you to choose to load your rolls in a more deliberate way, or the contrarian in you may consciously decide not to. Whatever your choice, my prediction is that from now on you will think about the system every single time you replace a toilet paper roll. Like it or not, due to this illustration, there is a small slice of systems methodology that has been permanently embedded in your mind.

Welcome to my world.

For the record, as I was writing this book, I polled my management staff in a staff meeting on how they load their toilet paper at home. I got this response from every single one of them, all in unison: "Pleeeze! Off the top, of course! Duh!" Even in the most mundane tasks, Centratel employees reflexively take a posture of being outside and slightly elevated. Because they have studied and worked with the logic of the methodology, the principles are ingrained permanently. Like my staff at Centratel, the systems mindset will keep you ever alert to small enhancements that can easily be implemented.

The "notable exceptions"? Toddlers and cats are amused by quickly stroking the off-the-top loaded toilet paper roll, thus creating a useless pile of paper on the bathroom floor. The system tweak? Load the paper so it dispenses off the bottom of the roll!

(It's hard to say this delicately, but what the heck: using the toilet has become a powerful recurring reminder—an anchor—for the systems mindset. I'm betting that you will see it this way for yourself, too. Several times every day, the bathroom experience happens out of necessity, and what goes on in there involves several important systems: the human body, with its requirements for fuel, nutrients, and elimination of waste; the freshwater delivery system of the community and then the house; the sewage system, too, where waste is taken away, ultimately to be purified and sent back into the environment. These are critical yet underappreciated systems . . . until one is in the midst of using them, there, quietly in the privacy of the small room.

You will forever use the bathroom with a new thoughtfulness. Each time, this pure, primal system experience will be an anchor, repeatedly driving the systems mindset to the front and center.)

CHAPTER 10

Your Strategic Objective and General Operating Principles

I don't want to be a product of my environment.
I want my environment to be a product of me.

—Frank Costello (Jack Nicholson) from the movie *The Departed*
(Warner Bros. Pictures, 2006)

To REVIEW: the mini-enlightenment arrived because I was under enormous mental and physical pressure. Until that late-night revelation, my strategy was to approach life with a bulldog, damn-the-torpedoes, pound-the-moles, I'm-so-damn-clever persona. It was a toxic brew of arrogance and ignorance—perhaps the most noxious combination of negative human traits. The seething chaos had reared up and was about to crush me for good. Instead, it released me with a flash of insight. I dropped the bulldog routine, adopted a new outside-and-slightly-elevated perspective, and found new confidence. I knew exactly what moves to make and charged out of my self-imposed prison.

Boring but true: to end workplace chaos, get the elements of it down on paper.

First, put together the Strategic Objective. It will require a few hours to develop a draft and a few more hours over another couple of days to get it right. Creating it is pretty much a one-time task, but allow for future minor revisions as the environment changes and new insights arrive. Limit it to one single-spaced printed page.

Second, after you write the Strategic Objective's first draft you will begin work on the General Operating Principles, the contents of which will be accumulated bit by bit and then perfected over a period of a few weeks. Still, the total time invested isn't much. Once completed, this document will also remain relatively static over the years.

Third, you will begin to create a collection of Working Procedures. A Working Procedure is in itself the archetypical system. Products of the system-improvement process, each is an exact guideline for executing the system it describes. (This third document will be addressed in detail in the next chapter.)

Over the long term, you and your staff will spend 99 percent of your documentation time creating new Working Procedures and improving existing ones. Be patient and trust me here: *create your Strategic Objective and Operating Principles first!* They are the foundation of your Working Procedures.

At work, all three documents will remain front and center in your mind. Remember this, and trust me here, too: for every unit of effort and time you expend on the three documents, the return in time and financial freedom will be at least hundredfold. I am not exaggerating, and in fact I am being conservative.

CREATING THE STRATEGIC OBJECTIVE

As I first saw the business from my new outside-and-slightly-elevated vantage point, I realized that Centratel had no objectives and no plan. How could we reach our targets if we didn't have any?

When I bought the ailing Girl Friday Telephone Answering Service twenty-eight years ago, my goal had been to make the company the best in the industry. That mission quickly evaporated as my small staff and I coped with serial fire killing. For fifteen years we thrashed. But in year sixteen, as we began to plow through the systemization process and witnessed immediate increases in quality, my dream of being the best in the U.S. came out from its hiding place to take center stage. We would not just survive. Per verifiable statistics, we would become the best among the two thousand competitors in our industry. This was our first concrete objective.

I dug in and laid out our targets and strategy in a pragmatic one-page document I called our Strategic Objective. The Strategic Objective is the first and most important of the three documents. It gives direction and prevents flailing away. With the Strategic Objective at the forefront, no longer is time and energy squandered in charging down roads that don't contribute to the overall objectives of the business.

The other two documents follow from it.

For Centratel, the ultimate purpose of the Strategic Objective is straightforward, as noted in the use of the present tense in the first line: "We are the highest-quality telephone answering service in the United States." (See appendix A for the complete text of Centratel's Strategic Objective.)

All large and small decisions follow from the Strategic Objective statement. Every ounce of energy is focused on the primary goal. The Strategic Objective is not a nebulous, feel-good mission statement based on self-aggrandized hope; it is not something designed to make the board of directors feel good about themselves or intended to impress stockholders and staff. Instead, it's a concise blueprint in which we acknowledge day-to-day reality in a mechanized, non-wishful-thinking way. Without syrupy excess, it includes a brief narration of what the company does, where it's headed, and how management and staff will get there.

Most business owners have a cursory idea of what success would look like and an inkling of what they have to do to succeed, but because they're hamstrung with fire killing, they don't take time to firmly establish those objectives or to develop specific strategies. *They don't even take the very first mechanical steps necessary to sort things out.* If you can garner the self-discipline to create your Strategic Objective, you will find new strength as you hold the single sheet of paper in your hand. You'll instantly insert yourself into an elite category: literally, you'll be the one in a hundred small-business owners who has a document that outlines company identity and intention. You'll have direction! And once you have this concise, tangible representation of who you are, where you are going, and how you will get there, you will find it uncanny how the physical world will align itself with what you have written down. When you get past the words in this book and the thoughts in your head, and take real-world physical steps—the first of which is the creation of your Strategic Objective—you will know that you do indeed have the strength to pull yourself out of the hole.

CREATING THE GENERAL OPERATING PRINCIPLES

After I completed the first draft of the Strategic Objective I began creating the second critical document, the General Operating Principles. Congruent with the spirit and the specifics of the Strategic Objective, this became a collection of foundational guidelines for making decisions. In the end, it included thirty separate operating principles so we named it simply, "Thirty Principles." You will have your own set, and of course they may number more or fewer than thirty.

I'm jumping ahead just a little here, but note that Centratel's Thirty Principles document is a Working Procedure in itself. (And note that it is a *nonlinear* Working Procedure—a set of components that are not sequentially related, but each of which must be considered across a wide spectrum of decision-making possibilities.) Operating Principles are tried and true, sensible, and simple to understand and remember. They are not flashy, as they lie quietly beneath the events of the day. They change very little with evolving circumstances. Over time they will be adjusted, but their overall immutability is evidence of their soundness.

Think of your Operating Principles as the *guidelines for decision making* for your business or your job. It's helpful to make up a set for your personal life, too. You will find your personal principles resemble the set you put together for your work because they reflect your character and your preferred way of approaching the workings of the world. For whatever roles you're playing, these principles will remain constant in your life.

For an illustration of how the principles can work, consider the following from Centratel's Principle #8: "Just a few services implemented in superb fashion." Ten years ago, this tenet mandated that we stop selling cellular telephones as an add-on service. Because we could not depend on the quality of customer service provided by the cellular company for which we were a reseller, this decision ensured that *all* of our products would be high quality. It also simplified our operation. Had we not written down this principle in tangible form and then abided by it, we would still be selling cellular phones at a considerable detriment to our overall operation.

Another example is Principle #30: "We strive for a social climate that is serious and quiet yet pleasant, serene, light, and friendly." Because this principle is written down, our office is like that: the principle is a hoop through which all decisions must pass. The openness of the physical layout, abundance of live decorative plants, the special full-spectrum lighting, the orderliness and quietness of it all, make Centratel a comfortable place to work.

The General Operating Principles, like the elements of the Strategic Objective, keep us steadily moving in a focused direction whether there's a tendency toward nonaction on the one hand or a momentary burst of impetuousness on the other. We are dogmatic about following our principles.

The Strategic Objective keeps us focused; the Principles document guides our decision making so we are in keeping with the Strategic Objective. Read that again. It's important.

Don't expect your Principles document to be finished in one sitting. Because it was sometimes two minutes here and five minutes there, it took me more than a month to create the rough list, select the proper wording, and polish it. Begin by writing down several principles you already have in mind. Then take notes as additional principles pop into your head in the course of the day. Be sure to seek others' input as you put your list together. (Centratel's Thirty Principles are listed in appendix B. Feel free to plagiarize.)

Why Can't We Find Employees?

It's our greatest challenge: Centratel's pay and benefits are very good, but no matter how aggressively we advertise our positions, we don't have many job applicants. Because we have a hard time finding qualified people, we are fortunate our current staff has little turnover. But the irony of simultaneous recruitment challenges and staff stability is understandable. If one digs a bit, it becomes clear why we have problems finding job applicants—and the good fortune of having high staff stability. It's our drug-testing policy, as posted in the Employee Handbook.

Before we instituted drug testing, we had plenty of job applicants, but there was high staff turnover.

A staff that uses drugs is flighty, and a flighty staff means call-handling expertise achieved through long-term experience and unhampered focus won't happen. People come and go, physically and mentally.

Our brutal judgment is that only a limited number of service-industry job candidates are drug free. It's a painful, almost unbelievable conclusion, but we operate on that basis because the statistics bear it out. The choice seems to be, "I'd rather smoke dope at a minimum wage/no benefits menial job than not smoke dope at a job where I could earn more than double the minimum wage and receive full benefits." Ouch.

Many business owners understand the truth of this so they *don't* require drug testing. Of those who do, it's a gamble. There was a local restaurant that had to close its doors after an impromptu drug screening of all its employees. They had to terminate employment for nine of their twelve people. Another business located in a town near here, a new big-box store, selected twenty people for its automotive department. Sixteen of the twenty failed the subsequent drug testing. (I digress: it seems to me they did the job awarding/drug testing sequence backward.)

At Centratel, did our decision to use drug screening stem from an outside-and-slightly-elevated perspective? There is no question. Per our Strategic Objective, we looked down on our business and decided we couldn't reach our goals without a stable, clear-thinking workforce. We made the decision to trade the chaos of high staff turnover for the staid challenge of finding drug-free people who are steady, superb performers. There really was no other choice.

To be sure, the introduction of a drug-testing policy must be handled with care and supported by a well-thought-out written policy.

CHAPTER 11

Your Working Procedures

Keep your eyes on the road, your hands upon the wheel . . .

—From the song "Roadhouse Blues," written and performed by
The Doors (Elektra/Asylum, 1970)

The quality of execution of a recurring nondocumented system can vary with the time of day, the weather, or the mood of the individual executing the process. In the workplace, salvation lies in making these ubiquitous organic human systems as tangible as the mechanical entities that surround us. Boring but true, we do this with documentation.

At Centratel, we analyze an individual system-process and document it as it is. Then, we find the cause of any inefficiencies, devise fixes for those causes, and then create a prototype written Working Procedure that will include the necessary steps to remove the causes, thus preventing the inefficiencies from returning. We then test the procedure in the real world, tweaking it into a final form that precisely explains the desired execution of the process. The new Working Procedure is released, and Centratel employees follow it exactly as written. (Will staff buy into this rigid protocol? Yes, for several reasons that I will discuss further on in this chapter.)

I want to reiterate something I just said. It's about going to that deeper level: we devise a fix for the *cause* of an inefficiency. We don't just fix the inefficiency.

The Working Procedure makes the system tangible—something to be seen, grasped, understood, perfected, shared, and then applied exactly the same way every time.

The difference between a large successful business and a small struggling one? Documentation.

Know that a this-will-happen-every-single-time protocol won't materialize via mind reading, a one-time conversation, or when it is discussed in a meeting. A system must be set in concrete if it is to be performed perfectly every single time, and this means creating it in hard and/or soft copy, and then ensuring it is implemented.

You who are leaders must consider it your ethical responsibility—not just an efficient way to operate—to provide Working Procedures for your staff. I occasionally remind my employees that it is my personal moral obligation to provide them with the tools to do their jobs. Expecting an employee to be able to read the boss's mind is not just an absurd expectation, it's unfair. I tell them that.

CREATING WORKING PROCEDURES

At Centratel, the same inefficiencies kept cropping up over and over, devouring any bottom-line profit and literally killing me physically. These recurring problems were the natural result of undocumented and therefore undisciplined organic work systems. Now, Working Procedures prevent serial headaches by converting uncontrolled organic work processes into predictable mechanisms. We have approximately three hundred of them. Depending on the task, they can range from the utter simplicity of two short sentences to line after line of detail encompassing twenty pages.

From the overall operation, we isolate systems into small, enclosed *system package units* and then outline each on paper in simple linear, chronological format. (First, this happens; second, that happens; third, ... etc.)

We also have a number of nonlinear Working Procedures that are better explained in either a narrative or bullet-point format.

After documenting a given protocol as it is, we analyze the mechanical process and then develop a streamlined finished product with attending final Working Procedure tweaks.

This is important: *we mentally remove ourselves in order to look down from above* to study the written document. In written form one can grasp an entire system and then, with that overall understanding, make adjustments.

We fine-tune the Working Procedure to make it the best we can, then we implement it. Everyone follows the new procedure exactly as it is written. Over time, we tweak it to perfection as we use it repeatedly. It's a living thing, and we constantly work it to make it better and better.

We follow this routine over and over again, making every individual system perfect.

Note that our Working Procedures often appear in physical hard copy, on paper, but most of the time they exist solely in digital form on a designated drive on our main server. (Drive names include Customer Service, Bookkeeping, HR, etc.)

Feathers in the Wind

Remember, a Working Procedure *must* be in written form. Instructions that are not written down are feathers in the wind. Think of it this way: you can't represent yourself as being a college graduate unless you have the diploma. No diploma, no degree. No exceptions. You are either a college graduate or you are not. Think of your Working Procedures in the same way: if they are not in tangible form, they are not Working Procedures.

FOUR KEY POINTS FOR CREATING WORKING PROCEDURES

Key point number one: Create a formal "bottom-up" corporate expectation whereby line staff is encouraged, and expected, to pass recommendations up to managers. And managers will do the same with their managers, and so on, right on up to the top of the management chain. Bottom-up is the key to both hyper-efficiency and staff buy-in, and yes, it's contrary to traditional pass-down corporate/governmental thinking.

Key point number two for designing, producing, and executing recurring procedures is to use the best solution every single time the process occurs. At Centratel, we collectively decide what works best in the majority of circumstances; we cast the procedure in concrete in written form; then we apply it exactly as written every single time. No matter who applies the protocol, the same best solution will always be applied, and therefore best results will almost always occur.

It's a numbers game, and the enemy is randomness. To create a consistently superb primary system, internal subsystems must execute superbly as often as possible. In the real world, will the Working Procedure provide a perfect result in every situation? Of course not, but results will be perfect *most* of the time, and that will be plenty good enough to ensure the primary system is performing with enormous overall efficiency.

Key point number three is that procedure documentation is not limited to just the obvious problem areas. It applies to all internal systems. Documenting a seemingly flawless system will often reveal small imperfections. It will take awhile to turn every system into a Working Procedure, but the boost in efficiency due to this effort will accumulate geometrically. If a subsystem is already 90 percent effective, yet it can be boosted to a level of 98 percent effectiveness, that's obviously a good thing. What could be better for a primary system than to spend your time incrementally improving its subsystems?

Key point number four is to create your Working Procedure documents for anyone off-the-street. This means that someone who doesn't even work for your organization could perform the process. More on this later.

These days, little goes wrong at Centratel, and what does go wrong is fixed immediately. As fire killing is reduced and more and more processes are automated and delegated, additional free time becomes available. This is the main reason our managers seldom work more than forty hours a week and why my workweek, as company owner and leader, is never more than two hours.

OUR FIRST WORKING PROCEDURE

Coming immediately after my midnight epiphany, our first Working Procedure was the Deposit Procedure, which provided our administrative staff with exact directions for processing the dozens of client payments that arrive by mail in our office each day. This involves more than the actual bank deposit. It also includes physically receiving incoming checks, crediting them to clients' accounts in the receivables software, and cross-checking totals. Years ago, when we created this first Procedure, three management people, including me, were authorized to make a deposit.

Whoever was available on any particular day did it. No written instructions existed.

The reason we focused on the Deposit Procedure first was because it was a critical system and it had deep flaws. It seemed to be our most troublesome system. Without any set-in-writing protocol, and with each of us performing the task in our own unique way, we too often made random mistakes, seldom in Centratel's favor (and if they were in our favor, a client was shortchanged). Sometimes we applied payments to the wrong accounts, and too many times deposit sums were incorrect. One time, a $3,000 deposit was lost by one of our managers, only to be inadvertently discovered weeks later under her car seat.

Of course, any wasted money was subtracted dollar-for-dollar from the bottom line. As we describe in Operating Principle #10, "The money we save or waste is *not* Monopoly money!"

And with all the gyrations and outright errors, the process was taking far too much time, and *that* was a waste. So the three of us put our heads together. After thoroughly interviewing my managers, this first Working Procedure took me four hours to compose. Then, to make it perfect, it took maybe three more hours spread over a couple more days.

This first Deposit Procedure contained *fifty-three* individual steps. Here is how it went:

Step 1: "Put the envelopes in a stack in front of you on the desk and open all the envelopes. (Do not yet take the contents out of the envelopes.) Leave them in a stack."

Step 2: "Open the receivables software and go to the deposit module."

Step 3, etc. progressed through the procedure, up through the last step. step 53 ("Place the deposit printout in the daily deposit file in the receivables file cabinet in the CFO's office").

We agreed that if any one of us saw room for betterment in the procedure, we would collaborate on the spot. If we were convinced the change would improve the process, we would instantly update the Working Procedure—and just as quickly implement the revised version.

This is important: *a published procedure itself is inflexible, yet we will immediately change the construction of the procedure if the change will improve it*. (This "change it immediately" parameter is exactly congruent with per our do-it-now Operating Principle #14.)

We put the Deposit Procedure into play. From then on, no matter who performed it, the deposit process proceeded the same way every single time. Over time, we improved it even more, and each time we improved it the procedure became more efficient. We built double checks into it so we knew for certain the payments were tallied correctly, and we added steps to ensure that the deposits made it to the bank.

Because we put the procedure together in a simple 1-2-3, off-the-street format, anyone within the company could make a deposit. As a result, I didn't make deposits anymore. All these years later I recall the moment I physically handed the brand new written Working Procedure to someone else. I remember wondering happily, *is it really possible I am doing this?* And I also remember realizing that because of the written procedure's simplicity, I didn't have to take time to train this staff member on how to execute the task. I just physically handed over the Working Procedure and walked away! It was a profound moment in time that I will never forget, and that was the point when I knew we would document every system in the company

Completing that first Working Procedure reduced my personal workload by at least two hours each week. That's two hours per week over twelve years. Do the math: that's the equivalent of more than seven months of full forty-hour workweeks completely eliminated. Yeah, man!

In its own way that first procedure was a tiny masterpiece, and yet we continue to polish it to even greater effectiveness. Since we started using it, there has been only one small, easily corrected error. Of course, repairing that particular error meant yet another small enhancement in the written procedure. Today, the Deposit Procedure is down to merely twenty-three steps because of better software and my staff's learned ability to simplify, streamline, and economize. We still work it, and recently added a bank-provided check reader that allows Teresa, our accounts receivable manager, to make deposits without physically leaving the office. This means fewer steps, more time savings, and greater security in making deposits. Per William of Ockham, simplicity is indeed evidence a solution is sound.

Even though we put that first procedure together so long ago, I remember this vividly: it was satisfying beyond words to know the deposit processing was finally stable and efficient and that satisfaction has not decreased over time.

The Working Procedure, a mandatory element of the system-improvement process, is not theory or feel-good fluff. Rather, it's a mechanical tool that is down-and-dirty *useful* in the real-time world. This reminds me of the title of a short story by Raymond Carver: "A Small, Good Thing." That's what a Working Procedure is. A small, good thing. The idea is to make your business and your life a huge accumulation of small, good things.

A Structure of Steel, Cast in Concrete

Yes, the work the system Working Procedure is inflexible: the Procedure is to be executed *exactly* as described. For staff or even outsiders, this intense regimentation can be off-putting at first. However, there is a critical counterbalance to that regimentation. If a staff member recommends a change, and affiliated staff and direct management concurs, the change will be made instantly.

A WORK IN PROGRESS

What was our second Working Procedure? We analyzed, dissected, and set in stone the methodology the telephone service representatives (TSRs) use to process incoming calls.

Our TSRs have executed this Working Procedure thousands of times *every day* since we put it into place over a decade ago. Precisely following this procedure is the ticket to relaxing and enjoying their work. For example, if there is an error in delivering a message, the TSR holds no blame as long as he or she followed the message delivery procedure exactly. The vast majority of message relay problems are due to system error, not TSR error.

Because our TSRs follow written procedures exactly, a majority of errors are traced back to clients who have not informed us of changes—changes that invalidate the previous, on-record Working Procedure for that client. The procedural system was at fault, not the employee. The cure is to make an immediate mechanical update in that client's Message-Relay Working Procedure, not chew someone out. This lack of finger-pointing contributes much to the level of serenity within the office.

We were jazzed. In the months after instituting the Deposit and TSR Answering Procedures, we hammered hard, working our systems, analyzing and streamlining scores of other recurring systems, including how to put together the staffing schedule, how to streamline collections, and how to pay the bills. We created procedures for performing the monthly customer invoicing, ensuring various housekeeping tasks were done on a regular basis, and for making the most effective sales presentation.

For some undocumented processes, our analysis suggested that creating a Working Procedure wasn't necessary, and in fact we had been wasting our time performing the process at all! Eliminating the system of storing paper records of customer contacts was a good example of this purging action. In analyzing the system from outside and slightly above, we discovered that after years of carefully storing hard-copy evidence of every client interaction, no staff member had ever gone back to those files for information!

When these obsolete systems occasionally appeared, we dumped them with a flourish, a collective grin on our faces. It's curious: in reinventing Centratel, there was nothing more satisfying than discovering and then discarding useless processes.

For other less-than-efficient tasks, we found ourselves devising radically altered protocols, with final versions unrecognizable from the originals. The assertive effort to root out and improve every single system led us to these unexpected deletions and substitutions. It was a cleansing process and as we dug in even further, it became contagious; a self-sustaining "positive obsession."

Centratel became dramatically more efficient. Our focus had shifted from killing fires to improving and documenting system after system. Interestingly, there were rarely relationships among the procedures we created or revised. The sore spots we tackled were unrelated, but we had a methodology for setting priorities: we straightened out the weightiest problems first.

Yes, as we worked up the new procedures and released them as official, I delegated more and more tasks that had been my individual responsibility. I simply handed a completed Working Procedure over to the appropriate employee and walked away. I was steadily gaining additional time to reinvest in tackling more problem areas. It was the same situation for my managers as they delegated tasks down the chain of command. Through all this, the number of incoming problems and complaints plummeted.

And it wasn't just the delegation of tasks that saved time. We ruthlessly automated processes whenever possible. Having a machine do the work instead of a human is the consummate act of delegation.

Although the original, one-time heavy lifting—the documentation of all of our procedures in one gigantic effort—ended years ago, we continue to assertively apply the system-improvement methodology on a moment-to-moment basis. We spend the majority of our time coddling our machinery so that it creates the results we want. We spend very little time coping with bad results because we just don't have many.

The Test of Time

Regarding the Strategic Objective and the Operating Principles, know that an endorsement of their viability is the test of time. If you are truly using them and they change little over the months and years, this is confirmation they are sound. On the other hand, Working Procedures should constantly evolve, and that evolution is confirmation *they* are valid.

JUST WRITE IT DOWN

Note that the very beginning stage of documentation is where the ball can be dropped—where a massive error of omission can occur—not just because this is all new, but also because the penchant for fire killing is still in full force, still poised to haul you back into serial mole whacking.

This is inevitable: I promise you that at first it will seem as if you don't have the spare time to work through the Working Procedures process. Know that this is wrongheaded because if you think creating procedures is a spare-time task, the process will take a backseat to the crisis du jour.

Procedure documentation must go to the top of your priority list or the process won't start, or it will be derailed in a week or two. You will fail. For your business or job, raise the importance level of writing procedures to the number one position, even above some of the fire killing of the day. Forget about finding spare time to do this work. Don't derail yourself by starting on that premise. *There is no such thing as spare time.*

So, although it might take an hour or two a day to write up and then institute new procedures, do it. Time savings will begin immediately upon implementation of your first Working Procedures, and when you observe this, you will have all the proof you need to dig in even deeper. Soon you will crave spending time on your quest to document your entire operation, and the fire killing that used to give you morbid satisfaction will become simply morbid. As the same old fires crop up, one by one you will douse them forever.

Remember, the litmus test for simplicity is that anyone from outside the company, off-the-street, would be able to perform the procedure. Of course, depending on your business or job, this simplicity might have to be more specific. For example, writing an electrical engineering procedure for an off-the-street layperson is not going to work. But writing an electrical engineering procedure for an off-the-street electrical engineer makes perfect sense.

I touched on this already, but for the record: with off-the-street Working Procedures, you will save enormous time in training people to full effectiveness. An employee who doesn't know the ropes of a particular task will simply read the procedure and then get the job done without assistance from other staff members. There will be no belabored, error-prone learning by osmosis.

Note that first-timers are a terrific source for gathering new information for moving a procedure toward perfection. Someone using the procedure for the first time has fresh eyes and is not jaded by an insider's can't-see-the-forest-for-the-trees limited vision. Have the new staff member execute the procedure and then ask what can be improved to make it truly off-the-street.

And of course, for yourself and for your staff, the extra time saved is used for improving systems even more. It's the cycle of increasing returns.

Here's another large plus: with written Working Procedures in place, your operation will become more professional. Your people will recognize this and raise their expectations for themselves and for their company. Your staff's pride and enthusiasm will shine brightly as they know your operation is in the one in one-hundred category.

A MACHINE TO IMPLEMENT TASKS

Our point-of-sale internal communications hinge on Microsoft Outlook, which keeps us organized through its standard calendar, task list, and contact information sections. For Centratel's leadership team, the most important part of the software is the tasking feature. In a moment's notice, the manager can direct a task to a staff member that includes precise instruction as well as a completion deadline date. The task doesn't disappear from the manager's task list until it is completed. Outlook also prompts for regular updates.

Of course, there are other platforms that perform the same functions. Whatever the method, the key is to keep the uncompleted task front and center, and to have the person who delegates the task be the same person who confirms the task is completed. The most important point here is that there should be a full-circle conclusion to the process.

A PROCEDURE TO CREATE PROCEDURES

As we first began creating Working Procedures at Centratel, I felt compelled to do much of the documentation myself. It took me months to see this was unnecessary, and I caution you not to fall into the same trap.

There is a system for everything, so certainly there is one that will oversee the creation of procedures by people other than you—a Procedure for Procedures. This master Working Procedure lays out the format and tone you want staff to use in creating everyday Working Procedures! Once complete, you will train your people to use it exactly. (Centratel's Procedure for Procedures is listed in appendix H.)

Whenever I mention the Procedure for Procedures to a group, I hear some "aha!" chuckles. This is not because "Procedure for Procedures" sounds silly; it's because it is so profoundly logical and, in a nutshell, it illustrates the essence of how to create a self-sustaining machine, a machine that can operate itself.

The core of management staff training is the Procedure for Procedures itself. And when I say train, I mean *train*. Set aside group classes that will be uninterrupted. You will be the teacher, and your managers will be the students (they should study this book). Note: A quiz for testing comprehension of the work the system principles is available at workthesystem.com/quiz.

Having your staff create the Working Procedures ensures they will buy into the methodology. They will see the beauty of it firsthand, from the bottom-up. However, be relentless in examining the procedures they create. You want to know what's happening, and certainly your input will be useful.

Again, it is the leader's job to make sure staff members have exact guidelines for each task they perform. Then it is the employee's job to follow the instructions precisely, yet assertively offer suggestions for improvement.

Will Staff Buy into the Working Procedure Rigidity?

On this point I am adamant: it is the staff member's first responsibility to implement a procedure *exactly* as written. There is no latitude here. There must be strict adherence. Do my staff members comply? Yes, for four reasons, a couple of which I have already mentioned: first, simple logic. Because the written procedure methodology works, they buy into it 100 percent. Second, they are involved with the creation and the approval of nearly all procedures, so they are fully vested in them. (In fact, Centratel's staff write 98 percent of all procedures and have a heavy hand in the other 2 percent that I create on my own.) Third, if an employee has a good idea for improving a procedure, we will make an instant modification—with no bureaucratic hang-ups. No one wades through the procedure process grumbling about how intractable it is. Fourth, staff appreciates that if a procedure is followed and something goes wrong, he or she is not at fault. It is the procedure that is in error.

Ruthlessness and Flexibility

Point number three in the previous paragraph merits repeating. Yes, be ruthless in insisting that your staff follow procedures exactly, but balance this strict rule with the understanding that if a procedure can be improved, it will be improved instantly. The procedure itself is rock solid and inflexible until the moment your management people agree that changes are necessary. At Centratel, we make the decision to modify a procedure *right now*, in an ad hoc meeting any time, any place. We modify the procedure in that moment, and in the next moment the adjusted procedure will be distributed to all parties affected. The entire enhancement, including the documentation modification, can happen literally within five minutes. Unwieldy bureaucracy is the enemy, and like a virus it infects most organizations. Each time one of us at Centratel witnesses slow-moving decision making in other businesses, we cringe.

The perfect example of bureaucratic paralysis is, of course, government—the quintessential nonprofit organization that is in business to spend other people's money on other people. Government has given written procedures a bad name. If there is a ubiquitous generalization about the nightmare of paperwork and bureaucracy, one can say thank you to the overabundance of governmental organizations that surround and engulf us. And I'll add this here: *government is a system* and it has a penchant for preying on the efficient business and cultural systems that are the foundations of any healthy society. Some functions of it are necessary, of course, but in the United States, for example, local, state, and federal governments now eat up over 40 percent of GDP. It's worse in other Western countries, particularly in Europe. Government systems are too often parasites, justifying their own growth by referring to themselves as benevolent entities while voraciously eating up the resources of those who create and build.

The Centratel Staff Is Paid to Tweak

We pay TSRs a bonus of up to 30 percent of their previous months' wages based on their personal performance in the current month. However, in order to qualify for the bonus, each month a TSR must submit at least twelve recommendations for improvement of the main customer information database—the same database TSRs use to process client calls. This database for our one thousand clients is massive, and errors or less-than-perfect descriptions/instructions can occur as they get lost in the sheer immensity of available information. However, this enormous database is constantly utilized by TSRs, therefore making them the best source of recommendations for system improvement. They know the database system intimately. TSR submissions may be as minor as a missing comma or as large as a recommendation for a new message relay protocol. Via e-mail, each suggested revision is submitted by a TSR to a supervisor. The supervisor examines the suggestion, and if it's viable, instantly makes the database revision. This is how we keep the information system that is the heart of our operation superbly accurate: by paying our people to aggressively search out imperfections and then eliminate them.

Your Competitors Don't Do This

I used to be involved with answering-service trade groups. I've served as president of two national associations and was a board member for a couple of others. I became knowledgeable about the politics of my industry and enjoyed communicating with my peers.

Twelve years ago, I gave a presentation to sixty answering-service owners in Las Vegas. The topic was "Procedures and Their Importance." At the beginning of the one-hour session, I asked the group, "How many of you have written procedures for your operation?" *No one raised a hand!* I am still shocked to think of that moment, of the sudden realization that the vast majority of small businesses operate without any written guidelines.

A majority of small-business owners are looking for answers to their chaos problems in the wrong places because they have not gone through the dissection process that thorough documentation demands. They don't have goals, and they don't see the internal inefficiencies of their systems, so they seek spur-of-the-moment global solutions: some quick fix—a magic pill—that in one fell swoop will make everything better.

Often, the magic pill they seek is a God-like new employee, a mind reader and fortune-teller, an extraordinary human being who will flawlessly oversee the business and, with little guidance, take it to its deserved success. Of course, on planet earth, these people don't exist.

Here's the curious fact that most small-business owners don't get: terrific employees are out there, but in a nondocumented business, none can function anywhere near their potential because mind reading and fortune telling are not things humans can do, no matter how advanced their IQ or educational pedigree. (See appendix G for a trade publication essay I wrote about leadership and employees.)

At the risk of appearing impudent, I ask, is it any wonder that Centratel can advertise itself as the highest-quality telephone answering service in the United States? Our people know exactly what to do and exactly how to do it. Errors seldom occur because we relentlessly manipulate internal mechanisms to perfection. And when there is an error, that error spurs us to devise an even better mechanical process for the future.

Again: We don't spend our time coping with random bad results that are the products of neglected systems. We're down in the basement, working our systems so random bad results don't happen!

It's elementary: *if each component of an organization is nearly flawless, the organization as a whole will be nearly flawless,* as evidenced by profitability, net worth, customer-reported error rate, client longevity, staff longevity, reputation, etc.

Centratel's seven managers are tenacious in applying the work the system strategy. They assertively search for inefficiencies, revel in devising enhancements, and enthusiastically create Working Procedures to make those more efficient systems permanently efficient. Their individual reward includes reasonable-length workweeks, individual freedom with lots of room for creativity, and intense pride in what they do and where they work. Also, they are highly paid.

Systems, systems, systems!

It all adds up to supreme satisfaction for staff, beyond-compare quality for customers, and solid profits for my partner and me. Further tangible evidence of our efficiency: in our TSR quality statistics for 2011, we averaged one client-reported error for every 11,501 messages processed. (One TSR, Mandy, made not even a single error in the more than thirty thousand messages she processed.)

Our service rates? Depending on the type of account, they are sometimes higher than the competition's—but not by much—because our
systems methodology has eliminated waste and therefore generated tremendous cost-savings efficiency. Our customers? Successful in their own
businesses, they are happy with the arrangement with Centratel as illustrated by our average client tenure, which approaches seven years (keep in
mind that the average new business has an 80 percent chance of failing in
its first five years).

How about your small business, or you and your position in the company where you work? Attain the systems-perspective epiphany and then
buckle down to start the documentation. The day you begin you will be
in select company, way out in front of 98 percent of your small-business
competitors (or, if you work for someone else, your coworkers).

Note that written Working Procedures are not necessary for your
personal life. Why? First (and forgive my firm grasp of the obvious), it's
just silly to write down how you will maintain the car, work on the details
of your marriage, stay in shape, pay bills, or develop a system for staying
in touch with friends. With your new vision ingrained, you'll handle these
processes methodically without having to write them down.

Second, a primary reason for creating Working Procedures is to make
sure that the people you supervise are handling details just as you would
handle them. Since you are the only one operating your own life, it is
good enough to mentally internalize your personal Working Procedures.
The exceptions? Travel itineraries, shopping and to-do lists, and intricate
technical instructions, perhaps for complex in-home electronic devices. I
have a working procedure for precisely mounting the bicycle rack on the
top of the car.

(Note: You can find several of Centratel's Working Procedures in
appendix C.)

I'll reiterate this here: You are not documenting processes and then
filing the documents. You are creating exact step-by-step instructions for
completing everyday tasks in real time. The word "working" in the term
"working procedures" suggests movement. Constantly keep them in the
middle of things; on the front burner!

A Summary of Procedure Documentation

1. At work, every recurring process requires a Working Procedure. The procedure will precisely define the best method of performing the action, handling the situation, or answering the question.

2. A problem is a good thing when your staff takes it as a cue for the creation or modification of a Working Procedure.

3. Do not create an unwieldy bureaucracy by writing up procedures to handle problems that are random or seldom occurring—problems that have little chance of resurfacing. There is a danger of being inundated with a massive conglomeration of rarely used procedures, thus creating complexity due to the sheer volume of instruction. Solving infrequent problems requires just a bit of common sense based on the guidelines provided by the Strategic Objective and General Operating Principles documents.

4. Be sure your staff is involved in creating the new procedures. In fact, relentlessly delegate. It's bottom-up!

5. By making procedures identical in presentation, their individual instructions will come through loud and clear without becoming confused by various style or tone variations. This is where you as the leader come in. It's up to you to keep affairs simple and consistent. (See our Business Documentation Product, Appendix J.)

6. Without exception, test every new procedure. Before releasing it, give it to a staff member who will carefully go through the steps to spot glitches. Take this stance: in a new or revamped procedure, glitches will *always* occur.

7. As the leader, sign off on major procedures yourself. Make sure they are congruent with your overall vision. Always keep your operation in line with your Strategic Objective and Operating Principles. That's your job.

One more thing: Yes, links, photos, and videos can be incorporated into Working Procedures. We like video-based Camtasia, especially for computer applications. And for still shots, there's Snagit. I've kept this chapter simple, to better explain things, but once you understand the principles of what is necessary for effective working procedures, I encourage you to create them to fit your personal desired format. (In the consulting arm of our business, one on one with the client, we go deep into this particular customization. See Appendix F.)

Frank Zappa's System-Improvement Strategy

Frank Zappa (1940–1993) was one of the most brilliant avant-garde rock artists of the '70s and '80s. He scored each note of every song and required 100 percent performance accuracy from his band members. After a concert, when most of his contemporaries would likely be attending a post-performance party, Frank would be conducting a mandatory-attendance postmortem with his backup band.

During these performance autopsies, individual players were assessed a $50 fine for each and every note missed. New band members were quick to challenge Zappa's recollection of the score and their individual performances; more-experienced members knew better. Frank's perfect recall of the performance was easy enough to verify. The evening's audio recordings would confirm what Frank already knew, and the fines would stand. Band members who were penalized were not likely to forget to rehearse their parts before the next performance. Frank set the bar high, and his success is rock music history.

Does this attention to detail seem persnickety? If so, prepare to change your ways: your challenge is to embrace this level of attention rather than be repelled by it. The end result? Less work. More time. More money.

By the way, Frank Zappa never used drugs and was quite the family man.

PART THREE

SO SAY WE ALL
(FURTHER CONSIDERATIONS)

CHAPTER 12

Good Enough

*A good plan violently executed right now is far better than
a perfect plan executed next week.*

—George S. Patton

To PREFACE THIS DISCUSSION, understand this is about work, not about relaxing or some combination of the two. If you own a business your mission is to work hard but not long, to reduce the workweek significantly, and to earn more money than you require. If you have a job, the goal is to use your forty-hour workweek to produce large quantities of superior output in order to quickly ascend the corporate ladder so you are earning serious money and can call your own shots.

This needs to be said, and it's a good time to say it: if you are going to work, then work! Kill the Facebook/Twitter routine, get your feet off the desk, stop the pointless babbling with coworkers, and put your head down. *Get in, do the work, and get out.*

If you're a flower smeller, sniff the flowers later when you can give them proper attention. Combining working and relaxing will result in frustration in both areas: in your work, long hours spent in a mishmash of unsatisfying mediocrity, and in your leisure, an unsettled persona.

LESS-THAN-PERFECT PERFORMANCE IS OK

Here's my definition of perfect, as noted in the work the system glossary in the Introduction: *In the work the system world, 98 percent accuracy is perfect because trying to achieve that additional 2 percent demands too much additional output. It's the law of diminishing returns in action, and it's a catch-22: the enormous energy required for this tiny betterment is in itself imperfection because that energy could have been put to much better use elsewhere.*

So, here it is: getting circumstances *too* perfect is shortsighted and counterproductive. The following story from my background illustrates that more than good enough can be a horrible waste of time and money.

When I was twenty-four years old and studying land surveying in technical school, our instructor told our class a story at the beginning of the term to prep us for the curriculum lessons that would follow. The story setting was the early '70s, when the typical survey crew consisted of a party chief, who was responsible for supervising the actual in-the-field survey work, and three additional crew members.

The party chief was given a project, and it was up to him (in those days, it was almost always a "him") to take the crew into the field, do the job, and report back to the owner of the surveying company with accurate and usable notes so a map of the surveyed land could be created. With the notes and the map, the landowner's questions of property size, boundary lines, and future development possibilities could be answered.

A survey project is a linear, encapsulated process—yes, a system—and a project begins when the survey-company owner tells the party chief, in not so many words, "Here's the job. I presume you can handle it. Be quick and accurate according to the specifications I give you, then come back and give me your field notes so the draftsman can make a map of the property. Then I can get paid by the land owner."

BEN AND JOHN

This scenario is about a surveying company and two of the half dozen survey crews it employs. The party chiefs and their respective crews are to survey the boundaries of two parcels of land. The land owner wants the surveys performed in order to get a general feel for where the property lines and property corners are located.

The owner of the survey firm assigns the first parcel to one crew (with Ben as the party chief), and the second parcel to another crew (with John as the party chief).

The owner provides Ben and John with brief yet thorough verbal instructions about what is required. As in any survey project, the crews must measure the distances and angles of the property boundaries quickly, efficiently, and with suitable accuracy. The degree of accuracy depends on the reason for the survey, and of course higher degrees of accuracy require more crew time and therefore are more expensive. In survey work it's a balancing act between speed and accuracy as a crew moves along, physically marking property corners and providing distance and angle statistics to the party chief, who takes notes.

Time is always of the essence to the survey-company owner because he pays his crews by the hour but receives a flat fee from the client. In this story, time is even more critical because the property owner has a deadline to meet. The crews must get to work immediately and finish the two surveys promptly.

The surveying will be challenging. Each parcel is wooded and undulating and has irregular perimeters. Each is similar in size—several miles in circumference. Based on the survey-company owner's verbal briefing, each party chief makes a determination of how much accuracy is required to survey his particular parcel.

The next day, the two crews separately gather the necessary materials and equipment and head off to their assigned projects. Both crews go to work.

Ben decides his survey requires measurement to the nearest one hundredth of a foot—a high level of accuracy. Using a theodolite (a sophisticated tripod-mounted instrument for measuring precise angles) and a steel tape measure for calculating near-exact distances, his crew slowly and methodically works through their parcel, carefully marking the physical property corners, exactly measuring distances and angles, checking and double-checking their work. Ben takes careful notes in his field book. The four are focused and fastidious, their work exact.

It takes the crew four days to complete the survey at a total cost of $800 to their boss, the owner of the survey company. Their work is perfect; the submitted survey notes are neat and concise, especially because Ben took an additional half day to review them.

In the meantime, John determined that his crew would survey their parcel with less accuracy, measuring only to the nearest whole foot, thus allowing his crew to finish the job quickly. Using much less sophisticated equipment for the angles than Ben's crew, a compass instead of a theodolite, and not taking time to measure distances and angles precisely, the crew moves at full tilt. They mark approximate property corners while rapidly taking angle and distance measurements. John takes quick notes, double-checking as he goes.

They complete the survey in just two days. John immediately submits his work, telling the survey-company owner that the measured distances and angles are not precise. The submitted notes are smudged and wrinkled, evidence of a quick-moving crew that is not concerned with appearances. The total cost for John's two-day survey is $400.

The owner of the survey company reviews the notes of each party chief and . . . *fires* Ben!

The party chief who took so much care and produced such accurate work is *fired?* Why?

In land surveyor parlance, Ben committed a "blunder." The survey didn't require measurements to one-hundredth of a foot, so the additional time expended to provide that level of accuracy was an utter waste. In his original briefing to each party chief, the survey-company owner had explained that the property owner wanted only a general idea of where the property lines and property corners were located. Ben had not listened carefully, self-enamored with his ability to produce tremendous accuracy. In his zeal for precision he wasted two days and $400 by providing a huge amount of super-accurate but useless information.

It was a blunder based on arrogance and narrow vision. Precision that is produced but not required is often just that.

98 PERCENT PERFECTION

Time and money wasted is time and money gone forever. And a waste of time and money means some other positive thing that could have happened, didn't.

The Good Enough rule is especially applicable to Working Procedures. A 100 percent perfect document that took forever to create carries imperfection because the extra time spent creating the masterpiece is lost forever; the finished product carries an embedded taint, and it can never be called "perfect."

So make your procedures detailed but don't make them *too* detailed. They should be good enough so the desired results are consistently produced and so someone off-the-street can execute them, but no more. See it this way: in putting your procedures together accurately enough, you are reaching a kind of perfection—the perfection of a useful product created without waste.

Throughout this book I have asserted that you must tweak your procedures to perfection. Now you better understand why my definition of perfection is 98 percent, not 100 percent.

Regarding the work the system process, are there exceptions to the rule? Yes, there are two. Both your Strategic Objective and General Operating Principles should be as close to 100 percent perfect as possible, despite the additional time it takes to get there. These documents are your guiding lights for today and tomorrow. They are short and you and your people will read them repeatedly. Imperfections will stand out, overshadowing the message. The Strategic Objective and the Operating Principles documents are the brief summations of everything you are and how you will proceed, so yes, spend good time on them.

Beware Useless Information and Whining

Guard your consciousness and your focus. Don't waste time on useless information or complain about what you can't influence. With the people and events around you, be militant about relegating unimportant media- and advertisement-driven trivia to the mental trash pile. Don't let zero-value details poison what is important to your life, no matter how dogged the encroachment. Do you get caught up with what is not fair in the world? That's an utter waste of time if you can't accomplish something tangible to fix the unfairness (and whining and complaining don't count as accomplishments).

Choose your battles.

This Is Not a (Expletive) Clock

I was a construction inspector working with line crews that build over-head electric power transmission lines. Following written construction designs, the crews use massive crane trucks to insert enormous seventy-to eighty-foot wood poles in the ground. Then they go back to string heavy-gauge conductor (wire) between them. It's tough, dirty, and some-times dangerous work.

The men on these crews are weather-beaten, hard-living, all-American linemen. Good men, straight out of the union hall, they have the surly countenance of loggers and roughnecks and are not apt to suffer fools gladly. These men do not practice yoga and burn incense.

I was working with such a crew in the hot, windswept backcountry of Eastern Oregon when I found fault with the work they had just com-pleted. In sighting down a half-mile-long line stretch of six poles, one pole was clearly out of spec, two to three feet out of alignment with the others.

I pointed out the problem to the crusty foreman. To correct the error, he would have to order his men to go back with the heavy equipment, remove the poorly placed pole from the ground, fill in the old hole, drill a new hole, and then reset the pole in the proper alignment. My foreman was not pleased. Nobody likes to do the same job twice, especially when there is a degree of humiliation attached.

I will never forget his grizzled scowl and clear disdain for college boy inspectors like me as he spit on the ground, glared at me, and growled, "We're building a (expletive) power line, not a (expletive) *clock*!"

Well, the pole *was* out of alignment, and his crew did go back to reset it properly, but his power line/clock analogy has stuck with me through the years. That cut-to-the-bone comment, however off-target in that par-ticular circumstance, is an enduring reminder that the quality of work must not exceed the required result.

CHAPTER 13

Errors of Omission

We do not so much look at things as overlook them.

—Zen proverb

It's an interesting exercise to look back and ask, "In descending order of impact, what have been the top five mistakes of my life?" When I propose this question to friends, they chide me about dwelling on the past and focusing on the negative. Yes, I understand all that, but if one spends some time summarizing, a commonality will surface, one that can be useful for future decision making.

It's important to approach the task with an objective and detached persona. Take time to think it out carefully from different angles, get it down on paper and the list will stand the test of time. That's how it has been for me. My top-five list has remained unchanged for twenty-four years.

On my list—and I'll bet yours, too—the largest errors were not the result of overt mistakes; they were the outcome of failing to take steps that should have been taken. These are errors of omission. The large errors of omission are bad enough, but numerous small ones will add up to an equally dire end.

Is there a primary cause for errors of omission? Yes. Too often it's procrastination, or what I call a lack of quiet courage. (I discuss quiet courage in the next chapter.)

CHRONIC, COVERT, AND INSIDIOUS

A list of a life's five largest mistakes could include not finishing college, not heeding that stop sign just before the traffic accident, or not starting that savings account way back in the teen years. What about not keeping one's mouth shut at a crucial moment, or not doing the little things that could have saved a marriage? Or maybe not bothering to apologize when it was the perfect time to do so? Other errors of omission: failing to get enough sleep, forgetting to lock the door of the car, and not submitting tax payments on time. You've already guessed the one I'm going to mention now: not taking the time to establish direction or to define the systems of your business or job.

Not taking action is the physical manifestation of any error of omission.

What Haven't You Done?

The errors-of-omission principle is a simple enough concept, but it lies buried beneath the jumble of life's demands. As usual, recognition is 90 percent of the solution, and that recognition is vivid once the systems mindset takes hold. And just as the outside-and-slightly-elevated perspective provides a better vantage point for observation of life's hard and cold mechanics, internalizing the errors-of-omission principle gives you a better foundational stance from which to deal with your own natural inclinations.

What follows are still more errors of omission. Think of examples in your own life. Failure to

- exercise leads to a lethargic energy level and an unhealthy mind/body;
- recognize birthdays, anniversaries, and holidays contributes to the transformation of a friendship into an acquaintance;
- pay a bill leads to late charges;
- watch what you eat/drink leads to a less-than-productive next day;
- make the phone call, close the sale, smooth out the misunderstanding, or ask for help contributes to a less-than-desirable outcome;
- clean the house contributes to an underlying sense of confusion;
- admit a mistake leads to the end of a business relationship.

The errors-of-omission principle works hand-in-hand with the axiom, "What you say or think is irrelevant; it's what you *do* that counts." Nike's simple "Just Do It" credo, which is as metaphysical and profound as a dictum can be (and is perhaps the most recognizable three-word sequence in the English language), confirms Ockham's admonition for "parsimony in scientific explanation."

Inaction Is Action

In any context, an omission is something left out, something not done. Here's the rub: it is a *choice* not to do something that should be done. Laziness and procrastination are choices, therefore *not taking action is a choice!* No matter what we do or don't do, we are always making choices.

When we do nothing, we continue to have an impact on our environment. Sitting on a couch and not moving a muscle is a *choice*. At a minimum, we take up physical space, absorb energy, and create waste, so it makes sense to get off the couch, take that body that is already using up resources, and do something constructive with it.

It boils down to the usual flat-out simple logic: since you are making choices all the time anyway, focus on making more active choices and fewer inactive choices.

Does your body—the physical mechanism that carries you around—need attention? Then mentally segregate it into easily understandable subsystems and then take a first step toward improving them one by one. Does your disorganized home system require attention? Acknowledge the disorder and begin to organize it, one room at a time.

Don't just sit there!

What Am I Not Doing Right Now?

How can you begin to apply this action principle in your daily life, business, or job? Stand apart and watch the events of your day as they occur, and while they are occurring, ask, "What am I *not* doing right now that is holding me back?" Should I stop and buy a small gift for the person I love? Should I find a way to exercise for an hour? Should I have a chat with a certain employee who seems a bit disconsolate lately? Shall I start, right this minute, to read that book I bought two months ago? Today, will I make an active effort to get a grip on my life by writing a first draft of my Strategic Objective?

Of course, you know this approach is in perfect alignment with the systems mindset. Your new life will be on the offense, not the defense.

 ## The Power Is Out

Late in the afternoon on July 3, 2006, the electricity in Bend, Oregon, failed. A lightning strike had disabled a main transformer at the electric company substation on the edge of town. We were 160 miles to the north at a family Fourth of July celebration in Portland when Andi called to say that half of the city was without electricity, including Centratel. Losing power to our answering service operation is not an option as we promise our clients 24/7/365 fail-safe emergency message processing.

A rare event, the power outage did not present an immediate problem because Centratel's internal battery backup mechanism automatically took over, keeping all telephone answering service computers operational.

But the backup system has only a three-hour capacity, so while the electricity was out we held our collective breath in Bend and Portland, hoping the power company crews would fix the problem quickly. They did, replacing the main transformer in just over two hours.

Over the years, it had been our experience that the infrequent power outages had been brief, and in this case, although the outage lasted longer than usual, our backup system yet again covered it perfectly. Without a hitch, our TSRs continued to process emergency calls during the outage.

But because of an aspect of our documented methodology, this was not the end of the story. Principle #7 of our Thirty Principles document says: "Problems are gifts that inspire us to action. A problem prompts the act of creating or improving a system or procedure. We don't want setbacks, but when one occurs, we think, 'thank you for this wake-up call,' and take assertive system-improvement action to prevent the setback from happening again."

Yes, our internal backup mechanism worked flawlessly, but per that principle, we didn't just breathe a sigh of relief and then move on. Instead, we asked this question: "If we have only three hours of battery backup, what would happen in a worst-case scenario? What if the electricity was out for more than that, maybe an entire day, or longer?" That condition had not occurred in Central Oregon in more than forty years because devastating storms and earthquakes are rare in our region. But nonetheless, what if this outside system—the electric company that is not under our control—experiences a catastrophic long-term failure?

We concluded that the possibility of an extended outage was real enough, and for the welfare of our clients and the viability of the company itself, we had to consider the worst-case scenario. So we took the incident as a warning shot and decided we could no longer rely 100 percent on the electric company. We had to be able to process calls without interruption, with or without externally supplied electricity.

The system solution? We purchased an on-site generator. The installation was a long, drawn-out, and expensive process with numerous complications, including structural challenges, permits from city government, and finding the right people to do the work. But the new generator, which operates on either natural gas or propane, ensures that should a catastrophic power outage occur, we will be able to continue to process calls indefinitely. (Power outages don't typically cause telephone service to fail because telephone companies have their own backup generators.)

Per a recurring Microsoft Outlook task, one of our staff tests the generator once a month. With off-the-street simplicity, our managers have documented every single step of the generator activation process, and we always use that exact documentation in our testing exercises. (It's interesting that with each monthly test, invariably there are incremental revisions made in the lengthy written procedure. The Power Outage Working Procedure is a living thing, conforming to a changing environment and the tester's additional ideas for making the process better.)

And how does this installation conform to the work the system dictate of posturing ourselves outside and slightly elevated above Centratel? Perfectly. We inserted a generator between the outside electric grid and Centratel, creating an alternative power source for ourselves. No longer must we rely on a critical system that is outside our circle of influence.

CHAPTER 14

Quiet Courage

People with courage and character always seem sinister to the rest.

—HERMANN HESSE

ALTHOUGH THERE ARE MANY POSSIBLE technical excuses for failure, it is a lack of what I call quiet courage that often precedes a downfall.

What is quiet courage? Quiet courage is unadorned action and is the opposite of procrastination. A lack of quiet courage incites an error of omission. Quiet courage resides deep inside and causes one to buck up to do what needs to be done whether one wants to or not. Founded on internal fortitude, it is made real by self-discipline.

Yes, for certain it's there inside you, but sometimes it might go into hiding.

Understanding the quiet courage concept is, no surprise, just a matter of digging a little deeper. Here are some demonstrations of quiet courage:

- Facing a misbehaving child in the evening with the same fairness and respect that was given to the child in the morning when the parent was rested and fresh.
- Going to work on a day when one just doesn't want to go to work.
- Facing up to a dead-end situation and taking action to address it once and for all.
- Exercising on a regular basis.
- Apologizing.

- Taking on a long-term, frustrating project, finding it even more draining than expected, but carrying on to finish anyway.

- Walking away from an argument with someone who is unreasonable.

- Living up to an agreement when it is more convenient to make excuses not to.

- Taking extra time to train an employee when the day is busy.

- Making an organizational change when sitting still would be more acceptable to everyone else around you.

- You knew this was coming: taking the time to create a Strategic Objective and a set of General Operating Principles, not to mention starting to put together a collection of Working Procedures.

The quiet-courage scenarios that escape notice are in contrast to the occasional overt gallant acts that earn instant recognition, such as challenging the boss with a delicate subject, approaching a neighbor with a legitimate but inflammatory complaint, or removing the delinquent young adult from the house.

Don't get me wrong: I'm a big fan of overt courageous acts. The more, the better. But never underestimate the damage caused by timorous, under-the-radar avoidance and procrastination.

Steady doses of quiet courage, combined with the step-by-step system-improvement methodology, will take you where you want to go.

ONE CAN'T MEASURE BAD EVENTS THAT NEVER OCCUR

Problems that will never happen can't sap your time and energy; they can't hold you back. Therefore, problems that will never occur have tangible value. But how can we measure future problems that won't happen—problems we prevent before they become reality? The answer is, it can't be done.

Measurement and stark objectivity are important, but an inability to measure should not stymie efforts to invest resources. This is where one must summon common sense as well as courage.

Here is an example of action based on—and in spite of—something that was unmeasurable. At Centratel, the staff wage scale is close to 100 percent higher than our competitors' compensation. How do we measure whether this elevated pay scale is a smart thing to do? That's an easy question to answer: we don't measure it because we can't measure it. Too many variables and too much subjectivity preclude analysis. Instead, we pay high wages because we have enough quiet courage to believe the extra cost is a good investment, not a waste of money.

At the beginning, it was tough to take this expensive subjective stance when a hard objective statistic—the total payroll dollars we paid out every two weeks—screamed for *lower* wages. An escalating payroll is easy to measure, but the benefits of the additional expenditure are impossible to pin down in hard numbers.

For instance, our high wages engender low staff turnover, which means less hiring and training. In dollars and cents, how does one measure the savings of the training costs that don't happen? Additionally, because of our superior quality staff, some quantity of error won't ever occur. How do we measure the benefits of that?

And how does one gauge the value of customers *not* lost due to the poor quality of service that *didn't* occur? How many customers remain with us today who otherwise would have gone elsewhere? Impossible to say.

So we invest time and money to prevent unmeasurable negative events that won't happen and to foster equally unmeasurable positive events that *will* happen. This is quiet courage.

Yes, when it is possible and appropriate, we should measure.

PROCRASTINATION IS THE EVIL ONE

At Centratel and at home, the quiet courage posture is easy for us because it aligns with the rest of the work the system philosophy. It's a learned habit, ingrained by simple Pavlovian positive reinforcement. It works, so we do it.

When Centratel was just moments away from collapse, finding the wherewithal to summon up quiet and not-so-quiet courage was not a problem because there was a gun to my head. The loss of everything was a vision right in front of my face, and I exhibited the same visceral pro-tective reaction I would display if someone were to physically push me toward the edge of a cliff. With an almost cavalier attitude, I thought *my business is ruined if I don't do something, so what do I have to lose?* As Henry Ford put it, "The greatest inspiration is often born of desperation."

But without the presence of a gun-to-the-head motivator, and when making excuses is enticing, quiet courage's number one nemesis, procras-tination, is at work once again. (An antidote is the point-of-sale action posture. We'll talk about that in the next chapter.)

Here are two other cognitive strategies for when the internal battle rages.

The first tactic is to mentally rise above it and visualize laziness as an object, something tangible that is outside of you and perched on your shoulder, like a small bird. Once the mechanical laziness is observed—most often it is temporary indolence cloaked by some lame excuse, such as "I'm too busy right now" or "I'm too tired"—just brush off the external seduction and get moving without a second thought.

As the excuses line themselves up, the second approach is to ask, "Why am I being cowardly in this moment? Why am I being a *sissy*?" It's a bit of twisted psychology that rattles the cage and inspires passionate reaction. Of all human failures, cowardice is perhaps the most abhorred. Procrasti-nation—that is, the lack of quiet courage—will ruin your life if you let it.

 You Will Begin Now

Here is a real-time, outside-and-slightly-elevated exercise. It's about what is happening right *now*. Here, *you* are the story.

Anyone can read a book, but it's a courageous act to shift in a new direction. Clearly, because you have read this far, implementing the work the system method is a new life trajectory you are considering.

How do you get to the point of actually beginning the process without relegating it to some future date when spare time might become available? Here's how: right now—*this* second—put this book down—yes, right now, *this* second. Find a blank piece of paper and write "Strategic Objective" at the top. You can do all of this within sixty seconds.

Do it.

Now, place the paper in a location where you will easily find it later so it will serve as a reminder to get on the computer and actually hash it out. Putting your Strategic Objective together won't take much time—it's just a page long—and I promise you'll be happy with yourself.

Congratulations! Your pilgrimage has begun!

CHAPTER 15

Point-of-Sale Thinking

Why? Because I'm the mommy, and I said so.

—ANONYMOUS MOMMY

DO IT NOW AND LET'S GET ON WITH WHATEVER IS NEXT!

Point of sale is a phrase taken from the cash register industry. It describes action where (and when) the purchase takes place.

Consider the cash register, which instantly updates inventory and orders new product. Before the customer walks away from the till, a replacement for the purchased item has been ordered, internal accounting is completed, and the commission is tallied. The concept is described in our Operating Principles document, Principle #14: "Do it NOW. All actions build on 'point-of-sale' theory. We don't delay an action if it can be done immediately. Just like any major retail outlet, we 'update databases and inventories and tally commissions at the exact time the transaction takes place.'"

At Centratel, there is no paperwork floating around the office after a physical transaction. We ask, "How can we complete the task *now* so we don't have to deal with lingering details later?"

The aim of point-of-sale processing is to gobble up details as they arise. Accomplishing this is the antithesis of fire killing. Point of sale means being in the offense, eyes open, ready to handle whatever comes up, instead of defensively looking backward, burning up precious time sorting through old details.

For both your business and your personal life, the point-of-sale posture allows you to focus on the path ahead while your other systems strategies prevent problems that try so hard to sneak up from behind. Wear the point-of-sale banner on your sleeve and you will experience robust confidence, the opposite of being overwhelmed. The excuses "I don't have enough time" and "I've been too busy" will disappear from your life.

In a nutshell, here are two point-of-sale strategies that will make your life simple and clean. The first is to reject procrastination. Get tasks out of the way now by immediately doing them, delegating them, or discarding them. *Make it your quest to knock off tasks as they appear.* The second strategy is to eliminate the requirement for action by automating tasks. By making events happen automatically, the do-it-now goal is achieved without any effort at all.

Here's an additional benefit of the point-of-sale stance: you will be in an assertive posture, prepared to handle the inevitable body slams that are part of living a life.

Your Conga Line Dance Leadership

Embracing the point-of-sale stance makes you the first person in the systems mindset conga line. You're the one determining the line's direction and speed. The dozens of followers just shadow your movements. The conga line goes where you want it to go despite the disparity in shape, size, and finesse of the dancers who follow. You are the leader, forging the path ahead while those gyrating behind sort themselves out on their own. The simple task for those following behind? To keep their hands on the hips of the preceding dancer and to stay in step. Of course, this conga dance analogy is about your organization's incorporation of the systems mindset.

IT'S JUST THE WAY WE DO THINGS AROUND HERE

When the "Shall I do it now or later?" question comes up for a new Centratel staff member, their not-yet-disciplined internal dialogue goes something like this: *"What's the difference if I do this task now or later? I just don't feel like doing it right now. I'll do it later because my guess is I will feel more like doing it then."* A variation is: *"I function better under pressure. I need an imminent deadline to force me to take action, so I'll do this task next week when that deadline arrives . . . or, maybe the task will miraculously disappear by then."* Sound familiar?

We ask the new staff member to change that internal self-talk to "I'll do it *now* because that is how things are done at Centratel."

Our experienced managers embrace the do-it-now credo not just because it's our policy but because it is so potently effective. The rule is, "Do it now and then get on with the day!"

Yes, this because-I-said-so dictate may grate a bit, especially in the milieu of independence and freedom we Westerners take for granted. We don't like arbitrary rules imposed by others, but in a business setting an employee has the freedom to quit if the rules don't seem reasonable. In the free world, anyone can leave a job to go to work for someone else, start a new business, or sit on the couch and do nothing.

But for the new Centratel employee, once he or she tests a concept and its workability is proven, it's a no-brainer. It's logic: consistently superior end results are justification for a cast-in-concrete methodology.

Of course, the point-of-sale concept also spills over into personal decisions, too. Here's an oversimplification, but it captures the point: "I'm shopping for clothes. While I'm out, should I make one more stop to buy groceries for tomorrow?" The answer, of course, is "Yes!"

Multitasking Is for Machines

The goal of the point-of-sale strategy is to foster super-efficient primary systems. However, it is important to remember that in a point-of-sale cash register, the all-at-the-same-time tasks are *automated*. Multitasking—many systems executing at the same time—is a perfect application for a computer, not a human being. Let your Mac or PC do the multitasking. In fact, a tenet of Centratel's philosophy is that our staff members do *not* multitask. Rather, they "give full attention . . . to the detail at hand" (Principle #27). This means proceeding in a single sequential, linear format.

THE WORKWEEK IS FORTY HOURS LONG

The systems mindset approach naturally devises strategies that save time, and there is no question that point-of-sale thinking has much to do with keeping our salaried staff's workweek to a reasonable length. My partner and I say to our employees, "Here's the deal: if you give us 100 percent, we will compensate you well." Yes, it's a generalized promise, but nonetheless it is our guarantee to staff that when they work hard *and* produce, we will provide them a healthy wage, great benefits, generous bonuses, and a workweek of reasonable length.

Because of our efficient procedure-driven, point-of-sale methodology, our people do not see the fifty- to sixty-hour (or more) workweeks that are common in small- to medium-size service businesses like ours. Also, my partner and I require that well-paid, salaried employees work no more than forty hours a week because, first, on a personal level, we want them to have a life outside the business. And second, when they have time to unwind, they are fresh and spunky when they return to work, able to give the required 100 percent that is part of the deal.

COMMUNICATIONS AND POINT OF SALE

Point-of-sale methodology is at the heart of our communications strategy, too. Fine ideas have a way of passing quickly through the thought process without being captured. One might be driving, talking to a colleague, lying in bed, riding a bicycle, or traveling cross-country when a great idea arrives out of nowhere only to depart in the next instant. That's why I rely on the digital voice recorder in my smart phone. If a great idea pops up out of nowhere, I immediately record it. And I like the voice-to-text-to-e-mail messaging app for simple thoughts that are better shared instantly. Also, on my iPhone, I like the "Say it & Mail it" app. Fleeting as they tend to be, creative ideas are too valuable to lose because of a lack of mechanical means of capturing them. We have also configured our office voice mail system so voice messages can be easily sent to the entire staff. Yes, of course we use e-mail and instant messaging, but for some subjects a voice message explains a situation faster and with a more nuanced subtlety. (See appendix I for an overview of Centratel's communication strategy.)

Being Cold-Blooded About What Really Matters

In your business or job, or in your personal life, how much of what you do *really* matters? This is not a loaded question; it's one of enormous pragmatic consideration. Be ruthless in examining your situation and eliminating the thoughts, data, and preoccupations that have no value. Also look hard at the information that is of *some* value. See if it serves *enough* value to make its existence worthwhile. If any information you receive is not used, or is of marginal use, categorize it for what it is—a waste of time, energy, and/or money—and then dismiss it from your life.

What will you do with the time, energy, and money you save? You'll expend these precious resources on things that matter.

STRENGTHENING THE HABIT

Procrastination (here it is again!) most often appears in the low times, the times when willpower is weak because of stress, fatigue, problems, and distractions. Failing to carry through with the point-of-sale philosophy is often the first casualty. You think, "Yes, point-of-sale is a good concept, but this afternoon I'm tired and there is always tomorrow."

You are probably right. More often than not, a task *can* happen tomorrow. The danger is that when you compromise a habit, the habit becomes weaker. But when an excuse to put something off arrives and you do it anyway, the do-it-now habit becomes incrementally stronger.

Point-of-sale actions are about self-discipline and the willingness to stretch into uncomfortable territory. Just do it!

SLOW DOWN; GET ORGANIZED

Too many people live in chaos because they fail to slow down enough to set goals and determine sensible strategies to reach those goals. Mindless rushing too often prevails when one should instead be calmly making system adjustments, which would prevent recurring problems from recurring.

Yes, the key phrase is *slow down* and—let me guess—slowing down is what you are struggling with right now as you work your way through this book.

If slowing down doesn't feel right at first, that's normal. Be patient.

I had my first clue to this quietly potent mindset on my high school ski team while training for slalom, a discipline that requires forethought, fast reflexes, strength, and balance. I used to slam through the bamboo gates with abandon, powering down the course off balance, my arms and legs flailing. I was giving it everything, but my race results were mediocre, and too often I crashed and didn't finish the race at all. It was because of what I couldn't detect on my own: multiple errors and inefficiencies generated by my brute-force, hell-bent approach.

My aggressiveness concealed my inefficiency.

Then one day, Otto Frei, my coach, told me to relax; to think "smooth and slow" instead of "power." At first it felt wrong and it was frustrating because it seemed to me I was not trying hard enough. But I forced myself to hold back, to ski slowly and smoothly. My results instantly and dramatically improved. From then on, including two years on a college team, I seldom failed to finish a race and consistently ranked well. But that lesson at sixteen years of age was just a lone clue to a more effective way of handling things, and it affected only my skiing. It would be decades before the slow-down-and-be-smooth lesson spilled over into the rest of my life.

 ## Measure Your Body

I mentioned this earlier, but I want to go into more detail here. Twelve years ago, in the depths of my workplace chaos, I was also dealing with a sick body and an exhausted mind. I was delirious during the day and couldn't sleep at night. My doctor had me on antidepressants, then Ritalin, convinced I was depressed—my hundred-hour workweeks notwithstanding!

But as a result of my mini-enlightenment regarding the systems of my business, I knew that my body was likewise a collection of systems. I asked myself, "*What is my physical body made of?*" It was obvious. The human body is composed of chemicals. Armed with this realization, I asked my doctor to give me a wide range of blood tests. Convinced of my depression, at first he balked at the idea but then he conceded.

The blood analysis showed that my adrenal glands had shut down and so the master hormone, DHEA, was not in evidence. The stress hormone, cortisol, was in the stratosphere, another important hormone was deficient, and I was chronically dehydrated.

My task was to work on each of the systems individually and one by one bring each back to normalcy. Once I got all five dysfunctional systems back to efficiency, I would have a balanced, holistic body and an alert mind. How could it be otherwise?

For the next two years, I took blood tests repeatedly while I faithfully took supplements and modified my lifestyle, bringing my various chemical systems back into balance. At the end of that time period, I was physically strong and my thinking was clear.

Was it that simple? Yes and no. On the one hand, the road to recovery was obvious—*what* I had to do was clear. On the other hand, it was sometimes a struggle to be self-disciplined enough to do what needed to be done. I stumbled once in a while, but I succeeded enough to improve circumstances dramatically. Do I still stumble? Yes!

How about you? Are you sure the chemicals that compose your body are OK? If they aren't, could this be negatively affecting your physical and mental performance; your happiness? Consider taking your health into your own hands by directing your doctor to perform full-screen blood tests. Then again, your solution may not require a doctor. Maybe you just need to get regular exercise, eat better, and go to bed earlier.

A final thought about measuring your body. If you are addicted to a substance, however benign, an imbalance exists. Any foreign substance throws your systems off, so a good starting point is to quit those substances and face the world cold turkey. It may not be easy, but if you can pull it off you'll be in select company.

There is no better place than one's body to start getting matters straightened out. Using systems strategy to analyze the physical body— the vehicle that holds and transports individual consciousness—is perhaps the most outside-and-slightly-elevated position you can take.

CHAPTER 16

Extraordinary Systems Operated
by Great People

Start with good people, lay out the rules, communicate with your employees,
motivate them and reward them. If you do all those things effectively, you can't miss.

—Lee Iacocca

I'VE TALKED ABOUT THE IMPORTANCE of creating carefully documented systems but have not sufficiently addressed a prime benefit: they are for regular people like you and me, people who do not have superpowers.

Acquaintances have said to me, "I'm sure you are successful because you've been lucky enough to find very good people to work for you." Translation: "You just stumbled into finding people who respect you, know your every thought, and willingly perform your every wish . . . and who work their tails off. You lucky guy!"

The idea that one must find the right people is a pervasive misconception. It is not that the statement isn't true; it's that the inference is backward. At Centratel, we *do* have an extraordinary staff from top to bottom, but that is not because of dumb luck. It's because we attract and keep quality people due to the great work situation we offer. The great situation *attracts* the great people. We just need to have enough sense to recognize them when they come in the front door.

Plenty disciplined, hardworking, honest people are out there, quietly looking for a fair shake so they can put themselves on the line to show what they can do. And when they perform well, they want to be rewarded.

All you have to do is find these people and then give them black-and-white instruction, good pay, and the promise of a bright future. As always, it's just simple mechanics.

Seeking the perfect employee who will solve all problems—a from-the-top-down solution—is not systems thinking. In the work the system business, your job as a leader is to provide an exceptional business machine that will cultivate a hardworking, loyal, and long-term staff—a bottom-up solution.

So these great people *become* great employees. You make it possible for them to shine by providing a forum for their innate skills and high motivation. You listen attentively to their recommendations. You give them opportunity and turn them loose.

Assertively Apply the Guidelines

Help your staff avoid the danger of becoming bogged down in the pros and cons of a decision. Accomplish this by encouraging them to assertively apply the guidelines of the three critical documents without always double-checking with you. Tell them it's better to make mistakes than to hem and haw or wait for approval.

At Centratel, I like it when a new employee mentions that he or she is taking a certain action simply because it is congruent with a guideline within the Strategic Objective, the Operating Principles document, or a particular Working Procedure. I like it even more when they have a recommendation to improve one of these documents.

TO THESE PEOPLE YOU OWE YOUR BEST

You want smart, honest, clean-living, and enthusiastic people who will believe in what you have created; individuals who become intrigued with your vision and who will want to continue into the future with you—at least for a while. These good people are the bedrock of your future. To them you owe the best—and the best's centerpiece is the carefully constructed, system-based business mechanism you provide. Then, if you teach them well and your people grow with your company, it will be a compliment to you if someday they go out and start their own businesses. On the other hand, it will be the supreme compliment if they choose to stay with you over the long term.

Is the Focus on the Product or the System?

It seems logical that a leader should hyperfocus on producing the product and finding customers. But this is the problem! Exclusively concentrating on these tasks without an overall strategy of system improvement of the product and its delivery ultimately leads to dysfunction because the roots of events aren't being addressed.

Failure to adopt an outside-and-slightly-elevated perspective is the primary reason only one business out of one hundred will survive fifteen years.

Here's good news: the bulk of those one in one-hundred survivors are doing very well indeed. Albeit morbid, here's more good news for you personally: the vast majority of your new competitors are doomed.

Understand what large successful businesses have in common: the leader's largest time expenditure is *not* in coordinating big deals and pleasing the board of directors. Instead, the leader is spending most of his or her time supervising adjustments of the system mechanisms that produce and sell the product.

GETTING YOUR STAFF TO BUY INTO THE METHOD

We discuss this climb-on-board aspect in depth in our Work the System Academy training program (see appendix D). There are staff-empowering subtleties that must be built into your new machine. For instance, employees should not just be empowered to create new Working Procedures, they should be encouraged to make suggestions about improving existing ones. (This is a key element in our Business Documentation Software, see appendix J.) Also, as previously discussed, a staff member's suggestion should be considered and decided upon as quickly as possible (see chapter 11, "Your Working Procedures").

There are many other subtleties regarding staff interaction that will naturally evolve out of your first two primary documents, the Strategic Objective and your Operating Principles. And be sure to look hard at finding a way to reward employees for great individual performance (see chapter 11 for the explanation of how Centratel employees are paid to tweak). Another salient point is that you are not turning your business into a democracy. You are the leader, and that's OK! It's what you want, and it's what your staff wants. I wrote a trade journal article quite a while back that gives a sense of how management should consider staff (see appendix G).

The key here is in getting the new mindset. Once that happens and the business is seen as the machine that it is, the subtleties of how to treat staff and provide guidance comes naturally. Once staff is properly empowered as a part of the primary system that is your operation, you won't have the attitude problems that plague so many businesses. It's an amazing transformation to witness, but it's completely logical: treat your employees as adults and as the important part of the operation that they are, and they will climb on board.

EVALUATING PEOPLE

Your team must see the operation in the same way you do. If you are going to be in control, you are going to have to be in charge of your staff, and that means you will have to remove people who can't or won't deal with your vision. (Sorry about that.) You will replace them with new people who share your systems mindset.

In our search for system-oriented personalities at Centratel, here are a few hoops that job applicants must negotiate. Note that clear-headedness and self-discipline are common threads. Did the applicant:

1. Show up for the interview on time?

2. Achieve the minimum required score on the aptitude test?

3. Know about the business? Did he or she check out the website before applying for the position? Are there questions about what goes on, or is the applicant just looking for *any* job? Is advancement important?

4. Smile? Seem happy? Generally, did he or she seem to be self-disciplined?

5. *Listen* to you, or were your words sliding by unheard as he or she waited for the next opportunity to pitch his or her expertise?

6. Carry on a reasonable conversation? Did he or she look you in the eye when speaking?

7. Appear to be literate? How does the resume and any written work performed as part of the interview process look? How did the applicant verbally express himself/herself (too many "yeahs" and "ya knows")?

8. Convey taking care of herself or himself? If not, the raw truth is that in most cases of personal neglect, there is a corresponding lack of self-discipline.

9. Previously bounce from job to job?

10. Pass the drug test?

11. Pass the criminal background check?

12. Have solid references?

By breaking down the subjective interview process into bite-sized component parts, we transform it into an objective, black-and-white test. Yes, intuition can be important, but it should never override your guidelines. Don't confuse feelings with logic; subjectivity with objectivity. However compassionate, the "this person needs a break" gut feeling is too often a mistake. *Use gut feelings to disqualify rather than to qualify people.* (That's a useful rule to follow elsewhere in life, too.)

At Centratel, it is critical the job applicant passes through all of the aforementioned hoops. If he or she fails just one, we won't offer the position because that one negative indicator probably points to a problem that can't be neutralized even by all the other positive attributes added together. We are hard-hearted about this and don't make exceptions.

College education? We don't worry too much about that, although a college degree is sometimes evidence of someone who can stick through long-term challenges to reach a goal and who has learned to mentally focus. Unfortunately, a college degree is no longer a reliable barometer of literate capability or of a reasonable mindset. Only one of our eight managers has a four-year college degree (and that degree is in political science).

You know this already: hiring and then firing someone is not just a bad investment for the company, it's an intense personal blow to the employee. For the job prospect, it's infinitely less painful to not get the job in the first place. Be compassionate by creating a thoughtful (and, of course, documented) hiring procedure.

KILL THE MOLES, COMMAND THE FLEET

And what about the leader of a typical large, successful company? Most times, these people are not innately special. Beyond an adequate degree of intelligence and their willingness to work hard, their leg-up is that they naturally operate from a systems perspective—while the huge majority of people do not. These leaders are heavyweights because they understand that moles must be eliminated, not repeatedly whacked.

I mentioned this already but it's worth saying again: The systems perspective is permanently ingrained in those who direct large, successful organizations, but despite the fact that it is such a simple precept, many of the people who execute it can't describe it, much less pinpoint it as the critical factor of their success.

Via managers who understand the process, the large-business leader focuses on perfecting systems and keeping them that way, constantly making efficiency adjustments while simultaneously keeping up with trends and market permutations. It must be the same for you if you are to climb out of the morass within which 95 percent of the population struggles.

For your business, you must find and keep employees and suppliers, supervise the creation and sales of your product, make payroll, pay taxes, and steer the whole enterprise toward a profit. If you are to leap ahead, what you sell must be consistently superior, and that can't happen if your people don't hyperfocus on the underlying machinery.

In the short term, you must concentrate on creating extraordinary, well-defined systems. In the long term, you and your staff must relentlessly tweak and maintain them. The by-product will be an exceptional service or product that people want.

Know this: *all* the ships in your fleet must be traveling at full speed, so you will want to ensure that *all* your people are on board with your new methodology. One slow boat will hold back the entire flotilla. You'll want everyone in your organization working at peak capacity, creating, adjusting and repairing. The fleet must move forward full steam, directly toward the common goal, and it is your job to make sure that happens. This is called being a leader.

If you hold a job and your goal is to advance, you have equal challenges. To win in the long term you must be more efficient than your peers, and you can't accomplish that by winging it, depending on good looks and magnetic charm, or by performing like everyone else.

 ## A Super Market

A bonus of the systems mindset is the ability to instinctively distinguish the efficient from the inefficient.

In southern California there is a certain grocery store chain that passionately ensures that all of its stores are precisely organized and customer-centered. The rows of goods are full. Everything is clean and polished. In fact, the people who work there are clean and polished! Walk the aisles and catch the eye of a clerk. You can feel the pride.

Each store is assertively systematic. I don't know the top people, but it's obvious: here is a perfect model of thought-out and documented systems strategy, directed from the top of the organization down to the customer-contact level.

Of course, other businesses just like this one exist. They are not common, but you will find them. When you do, spend time there and think about the system mechanisms that are behind the efficiencies. Watch and learn.

It's easy to find floundering businesses. You can't help spending time in them because they are everywhere. In visiting such businesses there is also much to learn. Note the lack of attention, the lack of detail oversight. Feel the chaos. This is the antithesis of what you want for your work and your life.

CHAPTER 17

Consistency and Cold Coffee

My goal in sailing isn't to be brilliant or flashy in individual races,
just to be consistent over the long run.

—Dennis Conner

In the Pacific Northwest, the coffee kiosk is pervasive. Often smaller than a hundred square feet in size, these tiny portable buildings inhabit parking lots adjacent to busy intersections and high-traffic streets. Typically operated by perky, bright-eyed baristas, the kiosks are convenient for the drive-up-on-a-whim coffee drinker. The concoctions they serve run the gauntlet of complexity and can cost as much as $8. Although the kiosks offer every coffee drink imaginable, I don't often use them. The infrequent times I drink coffee, I go out of my way to buy it at either a national franchise (guess who?) downtown or a locally operated shop, with a preference for the local shop (because, well, it's local).

A long time ago, in the midst of my eighty-hour workweeks, I experimented with patronizing a new kiosk near my home. On the way to work early one morning I pulled over, desperate for a cup of strong, hot black coffee.

The barista reached down to my car window and served it to me in a paper cup. I set the cup in the holder, negotiated my car back onto the busy street and was again on my way to the office. I was so ready for that first sip and . . . Yeck! It was tepid, thin, and tasteless. Arrggghhh! I instantly ratcheted to ten on the frustration level—and have always remembered the intensity of my annoyance with that particular cup of coffee.

Going out of my way, I drove downtown to one of my standby shops, and with a ceremonial flourish, dumped the still-full kiosk cup in the trash bin outside. I stepped inside and bought another cup.

As was usual for this shop, the coffee was hot and strong. And to this day I remember my satisfaction with *that* particular cup.

Here's the aftermath that still surprises me: I shy away from buying coffee at a kiosk. Why? Am I being too critical, too unforgiving? Neither—it's more self-serving than that. It's because I don't want to deal with the inconvenience again, and especially I don't want to feel like a fool for making the same mistake twice.

So after all these years, my first impulse is to avoid patronizing a kiosk if one of my regular coffee shops is within five miles. And for various other reasons, I have this same aversion to a number of other local establishments too, including half a dozen restaurants, as many retail stores, and more than one gas station. To be sure, my gut-level judgments are not completely fair or entirely rational, but they are real.

Centratel is a pure service operation, so judging quality of service is my natural focus everywhere I go. When out and about I find myself evaluating the service quality of restaurants, sandwich shops, retail stores, movie theaters, bed and breakfasts, public transportation services, etc. It's an unconscious analysis until I encounter superb service or especially poor service, at which point I instantly get conscious. On the spot, I have offered jobs to upbeat servers or cashiers who can't keep smiles off their faces. Then there are the other times when someone with a lousy attitude forever alienates me from that establishment.

Outside of work, Centratel managers naturally do this evaluation, too. Once the systems mindset takes hold, it's impossible to ignore. There's no going back!

In fairness to kiosk operators, several years ago just before the second edition of this book was published, Hollee, our TAS manager, informed me that Centratel's Latte Monday drinks (we buy coffee or cocoa drinks for everyone on busy Monday mornings) were being provided by a kiosk, not one of the local shops as had been our tradition. Our staff members said the kiosk drinks were consistently superb. Could it be this particular kiosk had something special going on? Could it be it was being operated differently than the cold-cup kiosk of so many years ago? The answer to both questions is obviously yes. Interestingly, this kiosk was sold for a profit a short time ago.

Why was the coffee so poor at the cold cup kiosk? The proprietor had no procedures installed to ensure consistent quality. She had no clue that one had to consciously manage systems in order to keep customers, and further she had no idea of the enormous negative impact of one bad cup of coffee. I am sure she winged it every day, hoping for the best and hitting and missing, depending on her emotions, the attitude of her customers, or even the weather. The result? That particular kiosk went out of business after just a short time.

WATCHING YOURSELF CLOSELY

In observing my own overreaction to that single cup of cold coffee, I learned something: the success of Centratel was going to depend on our ability to provide *consistent* high quality.

What if you work for someone else? That's easy and here's the mantra: "My boss is my primary customer. At work, my number one task is to avoid letting my boss down." (Of course, if the boss is impossible, or the position is dead-end, exiting the situation is probably a better strategy.)

I mentioned this earlier: in our culture and despite the universe's propensity for efficiency, service quality is too often poor, mostly because of the human tendency to neglect the systems that produce the service. But the good news is that it's easy to provide superb service if the focus is on creating and maintaining systems that will ensure consistent quality.

Here it is yet again: creation, maintenance, and enhancement of internal systems must be the manager's main objective.

The following is a not so tongue-in-cheek example. You don't want a customer treated badly by an employee who has a hangover. What you want is a system that will cover the bases for someone who is having a bad day (presuming this someone is not a chronic problem employee). You can't stop the person's headache, but you can create solid, fluid, and sensible procedures that will get them through the shift without alienating customers. Not providing guidance and leaving affairs totally up to your not-doing-so-well-today employee is a losing bet—the numbers do not bode well for you, the business owner, or the department manager.

And what if *you* have a hangover? If you have sufficiently worked your systems, sit back for a day or so, stay out of the way without gumming up the works with your sour disposition, and let your systems carry the load.

It's a powerful human idiosyncrasy, this willingness to make snap yet irreversible negative decisions based on one-time bad experiences. So beware: when customers are disappointed in service, they will have a predilection to go elsewhere next time and never return. Your best bet is to not fail them in the first place.

The Tip System

Consider this anecdote about tipping as it relates to our discussion of refining a process. Serving customers is a recurring process that can be honed into a fluid machine that will produce huge tips. Or not. (For the record, and per Linda who was a waitperson for many years and who sits across the table from me at 90 percent of the meals I eat, I'm a generous tipper.)

We sit down for a meal in a restaurant. At this point, before even saying a word, the waitperson, in this case a female, has earned a 25 percent tip. It can be downhill from this point forward. If she greets us with "How are you *guys* today?" there is an immediate 5 percent deduction in the tip for offhandedly referring to Linda as a guy. Now the tip can be no more than 20 percent. If the waitperson delivers the food and walks away with a semipretentious, airheaded "enjoy," there is another 5 percent discount. If she delivers the check along with the food (workingman's diners excepted), there's another 5 percent off the top. If she checks to see how we are doing at midmeal and blatantly interrupts one of us midsentence, yes, there is another 5 percent deduction. Now we're approaching no tip at all.

Although I don't sit there consciously tallying a waitperson's performance, and seldom does one go without being tipped, the essence of my thinking process is in this formula. It is systems thinking both at its best and at its most ridiculous.

How does this relate? If I were the owner of a restaurant, understanding that serving food is a system that repeats itself, I would be watching my own reactions while dining at someone else's restaurant. I'd take notes. In my own restaurant, I would produce a Working Procedure of "never-use phrases and actions" and then would make sure every single one of my servers knew it by heart. It would be called the Forbidden Phrases and Actions Working Procedure. (Yes, really. That is exactly what I would call it.) The Procedure would be my obsession and my staff's center of attention. Together, we would continuously update it, using my own judgment as well as feedback from customers, open-eyed staff, or whoever. Only one or two pages in length, it would be alive; the continuous centerpiece of discussion and action, a document that old-hands and new people would study, discuss, and adjust. With everyone's input it would improve steadily over time. Together, all of us would relentlessly work the system to higher and higher potency.

I would post it prominently in the kitchen, in my back office, and the lounge. I might even frame it and hang it near the front door where customers could see it.

For the owner of a restaurant, how much work does this entail? A simple Working Procedure could quickly take a restaurant's service quality from mediocre to superb—an incredible payback for a tiny investment of time and effort.

WE WATCH AND LEARN

At Centratel, we watch and learn and we use that information in our work and in our personal lives. We try hard to avoid foul-ups, but when we do commit an error we are finicky about fixing it. We bombard the unhappy customer with tender loving care to the point where he or she is happier after the error than before it. (Via our Complaint Procedure, we call the customer back a minimum of four times, at prescribed intervals of one day, three days, ten days, and thirty days, to make sure the error has not repeated itself.) Also, two staff members call customers on a regular basis, just to see if everything is OK and to update their account information.

Our Complaint Procedure doesn't end there. We also inform the *entire* staff of *every* complaint, as well as the steps taken to remedy less-than-perfect situations.

What if you don't operate a business? If you are someone's employee and your position has potential, apply these principles creatively and watch your rapid ascent of the corporate ladder.

TWEAKING AND MAINTAINING

So the primary commonality among successful businesses is the concerted effort to maintain consistency in product and service quality. This means that in a prosperous business the leader spends most of his or her time supervising the adjustment and maintenance of subsystems. The more successful a business is in gaining and retaining customers, the more one can be sure that whoever runs the business is focusing on a strict set of methodical guidelines for quality assurance and customer service. And yes, for the successful employee aiming to climb the corporate ladder, this system-improvement process is also the center of attention (although confined to one's area of responsibility rather than to an entire company).

Just how hard can I beat this concept to death? It's all about perfecting systems and then maintaining that perfection!

What about your personal life? It's what mom told you: always return a friend's phone call promptly. Say thank you whenever you can. Pay your bills on time. To loved ones, observe holidays and don't forget birthdays. To anyone, if you promise something make sure you do it no matter how trivial. Be very ready to apologize.

Do this consistently and people will trust you. They will know you are open and dependable and will want to spend time with you.

A PLACE FOR EVERYTHING AND EVERYTHING IN ITS PLACE

You must develop the habit of consistency, the child of character and self-discipline. Consistency is not a hand tool one picks up to use only when needed; it's a trait to pack around everywhere, permanently embedded in the fiber of your being.

To cultivate this habit, the largest challenge is to fight the old habits of laziness and procrastination. By paying attention, good results come quickly, and with those successes you'll find that consistency soon becomes effortless and backtracking into old habits dissatisfying.

It is no good to set up a highly-tuned organization at work and then return home to chaos. It doesn't pay off to exercise a few days of the month, be nice to your spouse most of the time, or to apply the work the system principles sporadically. If life is to be efficient, being organized is a full-time job.

Over fifty years ago, my grandfather told me, "Sam, there is a place for everything and everything in its place." I was eight years old then and I wondered how Grandpa knew his favorite platitude was true and why he seemed so caught up in the idea. Was there *proof* this was a good idea?

His simple explanation was *it's just true that being organized is worthwhile*. At first, if you must, take it on faith that being organized is something good. Then find time tomorrow to clean that top drawer in your desk, and this weekend go out to the garage and start the cleanup. Do some organizing every day, even if it's just for fifteen minutes each time. Work on the old clutter but also avoid creating new clutter as you move through the day. Accomplish this cleanup and then step back and ask yourself how you feel. There will be intense satisfaction, and the great thing is, this satisfaction is addicting; you'll want to feel it again and again. Keep at it and soon disorder will bother you. You'll become a fanatic about organization and systems thinking as you discover that your world is becoming smooth and efficient.

And yet, you'll see disorganization in the people and places around you—disorganization you can't fix—and you will shake your head as you understand the waste of it. Plow through the disorder in your existence and you'll find the process is perfectly congruent with the other aspects of the work the system method. Will your new orderliness make you an uptight control freak? No. On the contrary, you'll find yourself loosened up and relaxed. You'll be a smooth operator with time and energy to spare.

Breaking the Rules and Job Security

The following narrative has nothing to do with employee discipline or conflict resolution. Simply, it has to do with thorough documentation and staff buy-in that will circumvent those grim management entanglements. With clear-cut rules, no gray areas exist to cause uncertainty and anxiety.

Five years ago we had problems with two Centratel employees. The first one's work was very good, but he failed a random drug test. The second one's work quality was also exceptional, but she violated our computer privacy policy. Both instances were serious breaches of the company's written guidelines.

What to do? It crossed our minds that we could sweep these major offenses under the carpet in order to spare unpleasantness and eliminate a time-consuming search for replacements. But we had to ask, if we keep employees who violate policy, wouldn't this render our policies impotent?

The system solution? We spell out rules, regulations, and guidelines in our Employee Handbook, viewing this collection of policies as a primary system in itself—a giant Working Procedure. (You can find the entire thirty-five-thousand-word document at centratel.com, under Resources.) All employees are required to understand the company's policies and sign a statement showing that they accept them as a condition of employment.

Per the handbook, these serious violations were cause for employment termination. And that's what happened. We ended their employment on the spot. There was no arbitrary, manipulative corporate judgment call. We simply followed the conditions of the employment mechanism that had been set up in advance.

Our Employee Handbook allows leadership to be objective, remaining outside of any emotional or manipulative positioning. It exactly spells out our policies, explaining the ramifications of not following them (albeit most violations don't result in employment termination). These two employees knew they were gambling. They lost their respective gambles and their departures were simple and clean. Parties on both sides—and our remaining staff—understood why these terminations occurred.

Because we follow policies exactly, Centratel employees know that a deliberate act of crossing the line will not be met with wishy-washy "don't let it happen again" platitudes or interminable second chances. After a serious violation, do employees deserve a second chance? Well, actually, no, as a matter of policy they don't. But because of this intractable position, policy violations seldom arise, and we are not often faced with letting someone go.

Employees want rules to be consistent and fair. In contrast to some conventional corporate wisdom, my partner and I believe that when we let someone go for assertively violating clear-cut policy, our remaining employees feel *more* secure in their jobs, not less. Yes, we lost two valuable people, but for the company the losses were outweighed by the positive, long-term effects on the remaining rule-abiding staff who always understand where things stand and that management is fair.

There is an important subtlety here that I want to clarify: did we terminate the employment of these two individuals to set an example? No. We fired them because that's the deal. If an example was set, it was a by-product of the action.

CHAPTER 18

Communication: Grease for the Wheels

The quality of your communication equals the quality of your life.

—ANTHONY ROBBINS

IT SEEMS SENSIBLE THAT A DISCUSSION of communication would parallel other work the system protocols, protocols that dictate that quality supersedes quantity. I, however, disagree with this. The sense I have developed over the years is that *quantity* of communication is a direct determinant of the *quality* of communication. I am referring here to sensible discourse between two parties. It's no good if one party spews enormous gobs of useless information while ignoring what the other side has to say. Is one person talking and the other one listening? Or is there silence? Simply looking at global affairs confirms that between nations, the degree of cooperation is in direct proportion to the *amount* of two-way communication that occurs. Paranoia ensues if exchange is limited.

Quantity of communication connects directly to any success or failure. It's this way everywhere. More communication leads to better efficiency, stronger cooperation, and deeper trust. Between two people—or between two nations—if silence reigns, problems will arise in the relationship or there will be no relationship at all. Of course, if one party is crazy, communicating can become worse than a waste of time; it can be damaging.

Clicking Communications?

Are there social situations where it seems communications don't click? For instance, have you inadvertently disrupted a conversation, which in itself was a kind of virtual system between two other people? How does it feel to be distracted with extraneous stimuli when you are deeply involved in a private process, such as a phone conversation, book, or some complex detail of your work?

If lots of communication occurs, the quality will take care of itself.

Because our regular communication at Centratel is hyperthorough, I am sometimes at a loss for agenda topics for our weekly staff meetings. Nevertheless, we meet once each week even if it's just to chat about an upcoming wedding or someone's birthday. It keeps us in touch and we feel like a team. We laugh, and that alone is worth it. But we keep the meetings short because we have work to do.

As the leader, I have ad hoc get-togethers now and then—in person, by Skype, or by phone—with my two senior managers, Andi and Hollee, who have the deepest understanding of the company's overall systems strategy. These meetings get to the root of things. Our discussions are fluid and concise, and in very few minutes we discuss a variety of issues. My partner Sam and I have occasional quick check-in chats too, pointed and brief.

There's a caveat (it seems there's always a caveat) to the idea that quantity trumps quality: communication with oneself—one's own self-talk. In Western culture, excessive internal communication is a problem. We examine, reexamine, dissect, and massage our thoughts, endlessly wondering, *What is the problem? Is he (or she) angry with me? Did I say something wrong? Did I do enough? Do I need medication? Counseling? Am I a good person?* Arrghhh!

We could do well to act more and self-ruminate less.

Do What You Say You Will Do

Keeping promises is a system in itself, one that maintains personal self-respect as it engenders solid relationships.

Don't distinguish between large promises and small promises. Keep them all. Keep them to everybody you make them to, including yourself. Keeping promises will set you apart from the crowd. Think about it. In your experience, how many times have people failed to do what they said they would do, especially relating to the classic assurances "I'll call you next week" and "I'll take care of that right away!"

What if you become 100 percent reliable among your friends, family, and work associates? What if you dogmatically keep the promises you make, rather than leaning on them as manipulations intended to change the topic or exit the dialogue? What if people don't have to prod you into action? What if you do what you say you will do, exactly as promised and on time? The short answer is that the people around you will hold you in high esteem as someone with high integrity; someone who can be counted on.

COMMUNICATION MECHANICS

Discussing communication mechanics can be a monstrous proposition, so let's boil it down. This is basic stuff:

- If there is a problem with someone, have a meeting immediately. Talk it out one-on-one. If silence ensues, do something to promote dialogue. But be careful. If emotions are running high, put point-of-sale aside and wait for the situation to calm down.

- Be accessible. Give people an opportunity to leave a private message if you are not available. Can the people who are important to you reach you readily, or are there mechanical, bureaucratic, and/or psychological barriers?

- Promote fluid discourse by making communication tools available to your staff and by providing various meeting opportunities for one-on-one conversation. Scheduled group meetings are prime tools that provide everyone a forum for communicating. But keep meetings brief.

- Can your staff, clients, and potential clients find out more about you through a website or social media? Do you talk about yourself to the people around you, or do you stay on the sidelines? Mysterious people typically don't do well in business or friendship.

- Yes, it's important to keep lines of communication open, but are you going back and forth with a person who routinely works against you? This could be in a family or friend relationship, or with an employee or client. If the other party's intentions are systematically contrarian or malevolent, it's irrational to continue to communicate. End the relationship. You are not in the business of defending yourself or being coerced. Do you have a close family member who is on the attack or is a crazy-maker? If so, I sympathize. That's a tough one.

- Get to the point. Unless you are at a barbecue on a Saturday afternoon, cut yourself and those around you a break by getting on with things.

- Be cordial and friendly, but don't overdo it.

- Never bash others behind their backs. It's low class, and any employee, client, or relative who has any degree of sophistication will consciously or subconsciously devalue *you*. Talk up to people if that is the context. Your client, who is paying you, wants the bottom line—your personal friendship or clever witticisms are not part of the deal. Likewise, with your boss, while you take direction and provide information, be cordial but not too cordial.

- Speak authoritatively and clearly to the people you supervise. What they want from you is concise direction, respect, and paychecks that arrive on time.

- You aren't pals with your child, you're the parent. Act like one. Don't try to be some kid down the block, or Santa Claus. Be the adult/parent template he or she requires. It's disturbing to see a father down on all fours, goo-gooing with an infant; yet on the other hand, it's equally unnerving to see a father speaking man to man with his four-year-old, reasoning and explaining as if the child were an adult.

In perfecting the primary communication mechanism for staff at Centratel, we didn't limit ourselves to subsystem devices, methods, and policies. Here's an example: our physical office is part of our communications strategy. Burning up time looking for each other is utterly wasteful so we provide a subsystem to prevent it: glass walls between offices. Each administrative office has them on three sides so staff can always see one another. To determine the availability of another manager, all we do is raise our heads to see whether the person we need is busy talking to another staff member or whether he or she is on the phone. There is no need to call or get up in order to investigate availability.

The TAS operations department—the heart of the service we provide—is in the center of the office space, with the previously-described
administrative offices around the edges of the room. It's a psychological
reminder for everyone that the main purpose of our business is to take and
deliver messages.

Our office is an energizing space, too. Open and bright, it promotes
positive group chemistry as each of us sees the rest of the team quietly
hammering away. *We're all in this together!*

Yet, Linda and I do our part of management without having to be
in the office. Our in-office capabilities are available anywhere we travel
because we have access to all files and we can videoconference with our
iPads. With no fuss, I've led staff meetings from all over the world. Even
today, as I work on this third edition, it's early morning on April 2, 2011,
and we're in Paris, and it seems we're just as close to the operation as if we
were home in Oregon.

Intense management of communications systems delivers freedom.
(See appendix I for Centratel's System for Communication.)

Gone Missing

Several years ago we had our house remodeled. Immediately after, we
flipped another house. In both cases, numerous subcontractors, both
experienced and inexperienced, did the work.

Linda was the interior designer. I was the general contractor.

In this world of framers, plumbers, electricians, roofers, and concrete
specialists, there is an interesting commonality among the inexperienced:
it is difficult to communicate with them. Phones go unanswered, voice
mail boxes are full, or messages are left with no return calls forthcoming.
The subcontractor has gone missing.

One has to wonder how these people stay in business (and it's my
guess that most of them don't).

The dysfunctional communication system is a reflection of the new
subcontractor's chaotic business methodology in which he or she is so

wrapped up in reactionary fire killing and doing the work that insidious inefficiency goes undetected as it devours the bottom line. It's a profound error of omission in which silenced customers are relegated to the bottom of the priority list.

CHAPTER 19

Prime Time

*It has been my observation that most people get ahead
during the time that others waste time.*

—Henry Ford

PRIME TIME IS ABOUT MAXIMIZING PRODUCTIVITY when brainpower is at
peak capacity. The approach aims at the most fundamental of systems: our
own actions. Here is the opportunity to exert tight governance over the
most potent primary system at your disposal—yourself.

There are two components. The first has to do with your most effective time of day due to biological makeup. Let's call it *Biological Prime
Time*, or BPT. The other component has to do with *what* you do with your
time. This is *Mechanical Prime Time*, or MPT.

The prime-time concept is mind-numbingly elementary and has
everything to do with Ockham's foundational premise that the "simplest
solution is invariably the correct solution." Like all systems mindset fundamentals, the unadorned logic makes it easy to understand.

THE EPHEMERAL NATURE OF BIOLOGICAL PRIME TIME

First, let's talk about Biological Prime Time. We function at maximum
effectiveness just a few hours within a twenty-four-hour day. It is important to take advantage of this interesting facet of human performance. To
illustrate, I am a morning person, and over a period of two years, six days a
week, I wrote 95 percent of this book between the hours of 5:00 a.m. and

11:00 a.m. I write at this time because my energy level is at a peak and my thinking is sharp. But that's me. Your BPT could occur later in the day.

Because my BPT quality and speed are never better than during early and midmorning, I avoid squandering it during this period on television news, exercise, or reading. I spend it only on my most important projects—the projects that promote freedom and peace. By noon, my critical thinking ability is declining and my energy slumps. By 2:00 p.m., it's hard for me to keep my eyes open.

If I miss or squander my daily six hours of BPT, that's a full day's peak creative allotment wasted.

In the early to midafternoon I tend to nonessential or less mind-intensive activities. I humbly accept my afternoon downturn because it's just a mechanical phenomenon—a sine wave low point—a decreased performance period that has nothing to do with my overall intelligence or worth. Because my car is out of gas does not mean it needs repair.

If a peak performance is required during my low-ebb period, I exercise or find some other nonchemical way to stay in gear. I get a second wind at about 4:00 p.m. It lasts a few hours but is not as potent as my early morning session.

Certainly, these ebbs and flows are genetic. Both my mother and my father share the same pattern.

Linda's BPT lags behind mine by about four hours. She is devastatingly effective from 9:00 a.m. to 3:00 p.m., but she's a zombie (her words) at 6:00 a.m. Her second wind comes in the evening around 8:00 p.m. and lasts three hours or so. As the two of us go through the day, there's an overlap. It can be amusing as our individual highs and lows overlay each other. For the one bottoming out, it's an exercise in humility; for the one reaching peak, it's a demonstration of mental incisiveness. We joke about it.

When Is Your BPT?

Analyzing the *why* of BPT is not important. What is vital is to know *when* it occurs.

If you are a night person, you'll slowly wake up in the morning, cruise gently into the day, and gradually work up your head of steam. If this is you, zealously protect those midday and evening BPT hours because, unlike people whose BPT is in the early morning, you will be challenged by the world's demands and distractions. Events of the day will be in your face, making it a chore for you to concentrate unless you take preemptive defensive steps. Turn the smart phone off and shut the door, or disappear in a library or obscure coffee shop. Protect yourself.

So, what *is* your BPT? Stand outside yourself and observe your energy levels over the course of a week or so. Note when you are most motivated, positive, and energized—and when you do little more than stumble around. (The downturns are the easiest to pinpoint; they can hit like a hammer.) You must be rested, relaxed, and healthy when you do this.

You'll figure it out with no problem unless you are a habitual user of mood adjusters, such as coffee, alcohol, antidepressants, or other legal or illegal state-of-mind modifiers. Morning coffee, for instance, thoroughly masks the BPT energy cycle. If you are addicted to caffeine and wish to stop drinking it in order to pinpoint your BPT—you know this already—expect some mental depression.

My experience with caffeine is that it is a sixteen-hour, top-to-bottom drug. People who are mildly addicted need it in the morning to counteract the withdrawal symptoms of the previous day's indulgence, but after their morning dose they can get through the afternoon and evening without it. Removing 90 percent of the withdrawal effects of mild addiction takes three to four weeks of total abstinence. If you are a heavy caffeine drinker—you drink it all day—my condolences because quitting is going to be tough.

There is another benefit to getting through the day without dependence on a state-of-mind adjuster: personal pride in facing the world cold turkey. (In *my* life, am I completely clean? No. I enjoy a cup of coffee now and then, and during my long-haul trips overseas to the U.K. to meet with my business partner, or to Pakistan for NGO work—a jet-lag body slam of twelve time zones—a small dose of Valium helps me sleep properly until my body adjusts.)

Managing Your BPT

BPT is when you should create your Strategic Objective, General Operating Principles, and Working Procedures. It's also the right time to sit with your staff to explain your new strategy.

Of course, there are other aspects of your day besides work in which you need to be sharp, and BPT will be there for whatever requires focus. You will learn to cherish these golden hours as a commodity to be carefully parsed; never wasted.

After your peak, remaining non-BPT hours are available for taking care of less demanding activities and for recharging the biological, psychological, and social batteries. These are the hours for napping, iPods, periodicals, movies, yard work, exercise, and time with friends.

The non-prime-time hours are a reward for the prime-time hours that were well spent. Both periods are equally gratifying.

One-Day Chunks of Life

If you are going to break complexity into workable components, it makes sense to reduce time into one-day manageable chunks. *It is easier to master one day at a time.* Plan each day carefully, pay attention to linear sequences, and watch the hours quickly pass as you work toward your goals, riding the ebb and flow of your energy cycle. At the end of the day, look back and evaluate your accomplishments. Take what you learned, good or bad, and apply it in your next day-chunk.

IS THIS YOU?

For too many, this is the twenty-four-hour cycle: upon waking, external demands of work and family kick in. A dose of caffeine generates an artificial morning prime time no matter the natural BPT cycle. The day's fray begins and the fire killing takes over. The mindset is, *"There aren't enough hours to do what must be done!"* The day is spent whacking moles, and any plans for making things better remain amorphous and ill defined. *There is so much to do and so little time to do it!*

In the evening, the caffeine buzz has transmuted into nervousness, and alcohol is applied to forcibly calm down. That night, deep sleep suffers because of the lingering effects of the day's mood adjusters. (This is a serious consideration because every night a minimum quantity of deep sleep is necessary for solid mental and physical functioning the next day. As time goes on, sleep debt increases, and until it is paid back hour-for-hour, performance and mood suffer.)

The next morning the repercussions of long-term sleep deprivation, combined with alcohol and caffeine withdrawal, begin anew, and another caffeine pick-me-up is mandatory if anything is to be accomplished. It goes on and on, day after day, and . . . whew! The result is a nervous and exhausted treadmill human being, just another rat in the rat race.

It is understandable why many Western adults take yet another step, trying to find peace in antidepressants. But here is where things can really begin to get shaky. Notwithstanding sleep deprivation, how can anyone be cutting-edge effective with caffeine, alcohol, *and* antidepressants circulating in the body?

Within this mood-adjustment cycle, is there any hope for an unadulterated BPT focus each day? In the majority of cases, not without some serious effort. So for most, the magical BPT hours remain a mystery, muddled by unpredictable external demands, exhaustion, and mood-altering substances.

But not for you! If you don't want it to be that way, you can clean things up. Discover when your BPT occurs and then discipline yourself to use it judiciously. Never waste your Biological Prime Time!

Universal Ups and Downs

For the population as a whole, and despite individual variations, a general surge of energy occurs during two periods of the day. The first is in the morning around 8:00 a.m. and extends maybe another five hours. The early- to mid-afternoon hours are low key (which is the reason much of the world takes a nap after lunch). Around 5:00 p.m., energy picks up again and a secondary surge begins that usually lasts several hours. At around 9:00 p.m., mental sharpness begins to decline one last time for the day, and it's time to get ready for bed. This universal cycle is part of human biology, and whether you are a morning person or a night person, your individual sine wave peaks and lows will intermingle with the universal pattern.

MECHANICAL PRIME TIME AND THE REAL BUSINESS

Mechanical Prime Time has to do with *what* you do with your time. It's the time spent building primary systems such as a business or a career and, with some notable exceptions that I will discuss, it is not the time spent doing a job for money or mechanically producing the product or service.

Whatever you do, if you wish to create freedom and prosperity, maximizing your MPT is critical.

Unlike BPT, which happens automatically whether we are ready to take advantage of it or not, MPT exists only if we create it. Many people never experience MPT because they don't know what it is, or if they do, they are too busy killing fires to go there. Most just stumble into it occasionally. Your task is to identify exactly what it is for you, and then spend as much time there as possible.

Let's define MPT through the back door by discussing my rather strict definition of a real business. This interpretation presumes there are but two positions in life: either one is the boss or one isn't the boss. One either owns the enterprise or one works for the enterprise. The obligatory caveat: can a person be both? Sort of. We'll get to that.

In a real business, the owner is not the one physically generating the product or service. This can be a bitter pill to swallow, but it is difficult to dispute that if you are the one doing the work of creating the actual product or service, you're working a job. You own a job, not a business. Yes, even with attendant high income and prestige, doctors, attorneys, consultants, celebrities, and professional athletes have *jobs*, not businesses. (Don't get me wrong here. A job is not a bad thing, and offers some real advantages over my rigid definition of a business. We'll get to that soon, too.)

The key indicator of a job is that one *has* to show up. Not so with a business. A true business operates with cursory supervision from the owner, churning out profits as its own primary machine—its own organism, self-sufficient and independent. Think this good thought: "Money keeps materializing in my bank account while I'm elsewhere."

MPT is time spent doing the creative work of building a business in order to achieve the above. It is not the time spent working in the business, or dealing with everyday business affairs.

If you are a professional and have other professionals working *for* you—and without your direct moment-to-moment input they are accomplishing goals you have set out for them—this portion of your life is a business, and the cursory time you spend dealing with it is MPT. In contrast, the ongoing time spent with patients or clients is production work, so that part of what you do is a job, not MPT. If you *must* trot out into left field at specific dates and times as a New York Yankee, or be on location as the star of a feature film, that's a job—albeit a very good job!

Here's another example of a job versus a real business: real estate sales. If the real estate professional is selling property and living on the income, that's a job. However, if some time is spent allocating some of those commissions into investments in rental properties or bare lots, that is a business. MPT is the time spent doing the legwork of acquiring and managing personal portfolio property, not time spent showing up to list or sell property.

The Defining Question

As you analyze your actions, know it is the moment-to-moment mindset that matters most. During the workday, no matter what you are doing, look at each action you take and ask yourself if it is contributing to making more and working less. The day you *get it* and switch your focus to the blow-by-blow mechanics while leaving aside theory and wishful thinking, freedom and wealth will begin to materialize. You've attained the systems mindset.

IT'S YOUR JOB *AND* YOUR BUSINESS

If you are a creative person making a living in art or performing—for example, a professional athlete, a writer, an artist, or an independent consultant—or you are the centerpiece in some endeavor or another, yes, you have a job, but you also have a business. *You* are the business and you carry *you* everywhere. Yours is a unique skill that is a blessing—you are a creator—but as you create you must deal with the showing-up challenges of managing the day-to-day gyrations of the enterprise.

You not only must do what you do as a creator, you must also preside over accounting, purchasing, accounts receivable, advertising, customer service, public relations, and so on. And if you make your living as a celebrity, there is also the extra notoriety baggage that comes along with the package. This is the reason why, in an enterprise where the creator is doing the production *and* managing the details, life can be exhausting at the least and nightmarish at the worst. The goal is to use the MPT mindset to find ways to minimize the day-to-day administrative burdens so focus can remain on creative efforts.

Mental Positioning

If you are a charter boat captain taking fishermen out on the ocean every day, while every night you must hunker down to do the books, recognize that you have a job. And if this job makes you unhappy because you feel a lack of freedom, then only by taking an outside-and-slightly-elevated vantage point will you be able to devise a future in which others are piloting the boat and doing the books. Your new posture will allow you to visualize assembling the pieces in a way that will remove you from the production and secure the peace and prosperity you want.

The Beauty of Holding a Traditional Job

Most people have jobs, and as of this writing there is not a general revolt against the concept! A job is a revered enterprise in any society, as it carries a certain "it's a good feeling to be part of the team" camaraderie. It's understood in democratic and socialist states alike that the people who are out there working jobs are the bedrock of the society. They keep the wheels turning.

For you, having a traditional job is ideal if any one or more of the following are of the highest importance:

- It is a relief to be able to leave the job at the end of the day and not have a single work-related worry on your mind.
- You are put off by the idea of managing the extra degree of financial risk, uncertainty, and headaches that can come with a business.
- You are doing what you love and feel a high sense of self-esteem, and simply don't want that to change.
- You are building something of value, and the future looks bright.
- It is the only way you can obtain the necessary resources to do the things you truly love (flying a jet or participating in politics, etc.).
- You value the social aspect of being surrounded by peer employees.
- For the moment, you must survive as you prepare for independence down the line.
- You are making more money than you require, creating a future of freedom just from the assets you are stashing away.
- With your skill set, because of your physical location, or for whatever reason, there is no opportunity elsewhere.
- You crave the security of dependable benefits: insurance, retirement fund, savings plan, steady paycheck, etc.

If you enjoy your job and don't want to be on your own, know that the MPT mindset is a tremendous asset. It will provide you with a better understanding of the big picture of the organization, and with a clear vision of where the organization is headed, you can make a more potent contribution. If advancement is your goal and there is a ladder to climb, the MPT mindset will energize the process.

Beware Falling Off the Roof

Presume you are the sole proprietor of a chimney sweep company, and every day you climb up on a different roof. This makes you an integral component of the chimney sweep business system. You're the employer *and* the employee, and, bad news, you're gambling with the long term because when you least expect it you may fall off the roof and be seriously injured. Since you are the employee, who will perform the production work when you are out of commission? Your time on the roof is not MPT. Your time up there is a job, and a dangerous job at that.

MPT is the time you spend finding someone else to climb up there on those roofs to clean chimneys; it's the time you spend thinking about how to extricate yourself from the mechanism so you have time to build it and make it self-sufficient.

A Self-Contained Entity of Worth

Here's the great thing about owning a real business: someday it can be sold as a packaged entity, a self-contained primary system.

The ability of a business to generate income without the owner doing the actual production work is what endows a business with enduring value beyond everyday cash flow. If you are a critical element in the generation of the product or service, the need for your presence is going to be a problem when you want to sell what you've built. If you are a service provider and wish to retire with just a customer list to sell as an asset and no one to perform the production of the service, how much is *that* worth? Unquestionably, much less than you want it to be.

But if you have people doing the production work and the organization cranks out a good bottom line without moment-to-moment input from you, your business will have tangible worth to someone else. It will be a money machine for you while you own it—and for someone else who buys it later.

The ability to churn out a black-ink bottom line without the owner's immediate contribution means the business is its own organism, separate from the owner, with tangible worth as an independent entity.

No, this doesn't mean you will create a business that won't need you. You will have to keep it pointed in the right direction and continuously muster its growth.

CREATING MPT

At the root of MPT, the leader must spend the majority of time focused on driving the business to self-sufficiency and making it grow. The charter boat captain or the chimney sweep *can* turn eighty-hour workweeks into forty-hour workweeks, and then into two-hour workweeks. Proper use of MPT gets one out of the boat—or off the roof—and turns a job into a business, a stand-alone money machine that has intrinsic value.

For those in corporate leadership positions, the same MPT strategy accelerates the ladder-climb.

Remember this: *executing production is a distraction from what must be done to achieve freedom and control.*

To maintain MPT throughout the day, ask the following question repeatedly: for the efforts required to create my product or do my job, how can I delegate or automate those efforts so they are still performed with maximum efficiency?

STEERING THE SHIP WITH BPT AND MPT

Now, in my business, I simply steer the ship. There is great income, and the asset base grows steadily. My BPT is carefully allocated to the actions that are most important for long-term gain—MPT tasks—which include reviewing and suggesting refinements, occasional brief meetings with staff to provide whatever guidance or input they need, and envisioning and planning.

My non-MPT tasks include handling payables (because overseeing expenditures is the smart thing for me to do) and maintaining our website and blog (because I enjoy doing it and because I am the best one to keep the marketing message congruent with what I think and believe).

Of the brief time I spend on business issues, most of it is MPT, and no, I don't answer the phones or take deposits to the bank anymore.

When you are *not* in BPT, if you feel like it, it's OK to focus on MPT tasks—the tasks that have to do with improving and growing your business and your life. High energy or low energy, keep your work activities pointed toward primary business-building or career-advancing activities per your critical documents. In your day, stay in MPT as long as possible, but remember, you must be balanced in order to avoid burnout. Have a life outside your work.

Once you begin to see a reduction in time demands, you will be inspired to use BPT and MPT even more efficiently. It's that cycle of increasing returns. Later, maybe it will be your choice to write a book or to get that easel out and paint again. You will have lots of time to do those kinds of things.

In This Moment, Be Wary

Once there is some progress there will be no going back to the old ways. You will see that *you* are in charge; *you* are building something good. Never again will you be the victim of unpredictable circumstance!

Nevertheless, in *this* moment, be wary. You have not yet developed new, good habits, and you are still prone to old bad habits. If the "my life is composed of systems!" lightning bolt hasn't struck yet, all you have right now is feel-good theory. If this is the case, maybe go back and read the chapters in part one again.

Even after the aha! strikes, you will sometimes have to muscle your way through the initial documentation, especially when your energy levels are low. It takes maybe eight weeks to form a new habit, so give yourself time. But then again, positive results will probably come sooner, and then your motivation will be powered by plain common sense, the most powerful motivator there is.

A POINT-OF-SALE APPRECIATION OF LIFE

I sit here writing these particular words on a Wednesday in November. It's noon, and I have been on-task for eight hours and I am still at maximum throttle. It's one of those rare and exquisite maximum-BPT days (perhaps because that is my topic today). I will work for a while more and then plug into my iPod and rake the lawn because that is both relaxing and satisfying.

After that, Linda and I will go for a walk in the neighborhood. Then we'll see a movie. After the movie, we'll have dinner out.

There is a Zen proverb: "Before enlightenment, chop wood, carry water. After enlightenment, chop wood, carry water." It's perfect, really, as we immerse ourselves in the simple mechanics of what needs to be done *right now*: creating, adjusting, and maintaining systems.

Chop wood, carry water.

Sometimes we say to each other, "*This* is it!" It's a simple, happy way to remind ourselves *this* is the existence we've envisioned, and there is no need to pine for anything different. Life is as tangible as it can be when we just acknowledge it in the moment and agree it is good. No matter where we are or what we're doing, this instant in time—this right now—*is it!* Any other time is not real; either memory or conjecture.

For fleeting moments in the middle of working our systems, we withdraw a bit in order to celebrate the only true reality there is—this *right now*—and we're grateful.

PTO and POS

In the systems revision discussed here, we altogether eliminated a complex system (as always, a delightful event) and replaced it with an automatic point-of-sale mechanism.

We went back to a premise: paid time off (PTO) is an employee benefit intended to help keep staff satisfied and happy, but most of all it's a perk that will encourage them to continue working for Centratel—and working means showing up for work!

There was a problem with our paid-by-the-hour staff's PTO arrangement. In theory, it sounded great when we first offered the benefit, but in the real-world application it was terrible.

First, it was a pain to calculate and administrate. Did our managers do their weekly job of tallying all eligible employee PTO hours and then submit those hours to bookkeeping? Did a TSR report his absence yesterday as PTO time, and beyond that, just how many hours are still available for him to use? Did the books accurately accumulate the new sales person's

PTO after her ninety-day probation was finished? In any case, our PTO system consumed too much administrative and record-keeping time.

Second, our people used PTO hours in ways we did not intend. We had designed it for employees to get away from work once or twice a year in a way we could plan and schedule around. And our intent was that it would also be available to use for occasional sick days or appointments. But for many staff members, PTO was used as soon as it was accumulated and with short notice—a few hours here, a few hours there.

Many times, it was an excuse to be absent from work under the pretense of "I don't feel good today and I think I have accumulated enough PTO to take the day off, so I am going to call in sick." It turned out that too often the hourly-paid TSR did *not* have enough PTO accumulated to take a full day off and so did not work the usual weekly forty hours. For the staff member, this resulted in a smaller paycheck than expected. And no small thing, Centratel was understaffed.

Third, errors in the complex administrative processing invariably led to the granting of too much paid PTO, and over the years this had been a substantial loss to the company's bottom line.

What should we do?

We dropped the old process altogether, adopting another much simpler one. Our point-of-sale Principle was key in developing the new policy: we stopped the long-term accumulation of PTO. Instead, on each paycheck, we pay it as it is earned.

Based on the number of hours worked in a given pay period, our accounting system automatically determines the paycheck's PTO amount and includes it as a line item disbursement. There is no more manual record keeping, and the employee knows where he or she stands at all times.

Can employees take vacations? Yes, they can take time off as they wish, but they know the time off has been paid in advance and there will be no money earned while they are gone.

Now, since employees earn their pay only when they work, unwarranted absenteeism has been reduced by literally 90 percent, manual administrative paperwork is eliminated, and there is no confusion.

An outside-and-slightly-elevated solution? Absolutely.

CHAPTER 20

The Traffic Circles of Pakistan

Confusion is a word we have invented for an order which is not yet understood.

—Henry Miller

In Lahore, Pakistan, the traffic circle is the epicenter of the driving experience. Like traffic circles everywhere, the Pakistani version absorbs vehicles from various points and then spews them out at other points. However, these circles differentiate themselves from the more civilized circles of the West, with each Pakistani driver's unspoken proclamation, "Enter here but beware! I do not care what you want. Your existence is an obstacle to me! May the best man win, and know that that man is me!"

The driving is instinctual and primal.

The circles are beautiful, really: raw, closed, no-nonsense hell-bent-for-leather systems in which an observer can generalize about how other third-world social mechanisms operate. My favorite circle is huge, with five concentric lanes of traffic, each with vehicles wildly careening around and around the potholed pavement.

A DEARTH OF GUIDELINES

In the Pakistani traffic circle there are three rules: go clockwise, go as fast as possible, and avoid colliding with other vehicles. That's it. It's every man for himself (in Pakistan, for cultural reasons, seldom is a woman behind the wheel), with the whole system being propelled by an invisible frenzy of mocking desperation. A Westerner standing on the sidelines understands that for every driver it's clearly a matter of life and death; each must reach his destination just a bit sooner than is humanly possible. Within the seething circle—indeed, a living organism—there is no rule for which vehicle has the right of way, unless one considers intimidation a rule.

It's amazing. There is no agreement on protocol beyond the three rules previously noted; in fact, the opposite of what one might expect can take precedence. For example, more often than not, the vehicles entering the circle have the right of way over the cars already within.

The drivers revel in the silent pact that no organizing guidelines shall interfere. It is similar to most third-world gatherings of people: queuing into a single-file line just doesn't happen because everyone silently agrees that survival of the fittest is the single rule for securing whatever is to be had. In the Pakistani traffic circle, no one is insulted or irritated by the hyperassertive jostling and the line crashing. It's the nature of the game, and within the circle you will cut me off while blowing hard on your horn—and that's OK!

The traffic rages, with all participants frustrated that the general vehicle velocity isn't faster than it is. Competing for space are fragile donkey carts, huge ornately decorated trucks, tiny Chinese cars, cantankerous bicycles, and hordes of darting, weaving motor scooters. When a car or truck breaks down, the driver simply stops his vehicle without any attempt to pull over to get out of the way. He nonchalantly lies down on his back under the disabled vehicle and makes repairs. Nobody cares or pays attention to the driver, who escapes being crushed through no act of his own.

Within the circle there is no cooperation or consideration, and everyone agrees that's fine.

COOPERATE OR CHALLENGE?

Comparing the traffic circles of Pakistan to those in the West reveals a stunning contrast.

To flatten the playing field for my forthcoming theory, I am presuming all drivers everywhere share the same desire—to travel without physical damage from point A to point B in a minimum amount of time.

Here's the question: to get what one wants—in this case, traveling from one place to another as rapidly and as unscathed as possible—shall it be by independent, single-minded challenges to one another (a rudimentary, free-for-all system) or shall it be by group cooperation (an intricate and formal system)?

In Bend, Oregon, one follows many rules of the road. If not, there *will* be problems. For instance, the cars already within the traffic circle unquestionably have the right of way. Incoming drivers rarely violate this rule, but if they do, a physical altercation could ensue, with the vehicles pulled over and the drivers making fools of themselves by the side of the road. The Western right-of-way rule is ironclad, and 99.99 percent of drivers follow the rule exactly. Of course, there are also other Western rules that have to do with speed and signaling and protocol. No one would ever dream of changing a tire anywhere near a traffic circle, and horns are rarely heard as they are an in-your-face semi-insult. Drivers work hard not to impede traffic or challenge one another. The mindset is on the rights of the other drivers.

One does not see this oh-so-sensitive driver persona in Lahore, where one driver does not consider the other driver, each charging into the fray without forethought or consideration.

At the risk of being culturally judgmental, it is my contention that in getting from point A to point B, cooperation is more efficient than a competitive free-for-all. My guess is that despite the Pakistani hyperfrenzy, more traffic flows through the staid Bend traffic circle than flows through the equal-size Lahore traffic circle. It's also my bet that there are fewer accidents in the Western traffic circle.

So again, at the risk of making a stupid, bellicose East-West judgment, it is obvious to me that if the goal is to move huge volumes of traffic from point A to point B, the cooperative social agreement of a rigid-rule traffic circle beats the chaos of a no-holds-barred, noncooperative traffic circle. The West's higher-capacity circle is an illustration of the importance of mutual consideration, as well as efficiency enhancing rules that participants understand and agree upon. And away from the traffic circles, in societal processes, it is more productive for each participant to consider the welfare of other participants and to follow simple rules that deal with common contingencies. For traffic, and for the culture as a whole, it just works better. It's a matter of mechanical efficiency.

But there is more to this than efficiency. Ignoring the mechanical aspect, which traffic circle is the most creative and fun? The most innovative and free-form? Clearly, it's the Pakistani circle. The flair and competitiveness in Pakistani streets is a remarkable thing, with a colorful, good-natured jostling that is fascinating to watch. For a Westerner on the periphery looking in, it's a spectator sport in direct contrast to the uptight, boring military orderliness of the streets of the West. When I'm in Pakistan, I just stand there on the edge of the madness, fascinated. It makes me feel alive.

These people are not just going somewhere; they're free-form artists, creating and surviving and having a hell of a good time doing it. They're living moment to moment. We Westerners could learn something from that.

FROM THIS RIGID FRAMEWORK, TAKE YOUR RISKS

The drivers in Lahore, Pakistan, and Bend, Oregon, *do* ultimately arrive at their respective destinations. Like any business or any life—with individual comportment and social expectation being major influences—strategies for making those journeys range from pedantic rule-following to vainglorious self-interest.

The two cultures' traffic circles beautifully illustrate the extremes of how one can go about getting what one wants. But is there a middle ground? In life outside of the traffic circles, could it be that a staid, conservative foundation could be the launching pad for surges of innovation and leaps of faith?

Think about traffic circles as you make a plan for getting yourself through the day. And consider the circles as you contemplate creating a thoughtful, planned framework—a framework that is a safe harbor for later, off-the-wall new ideas that will further propel you into the life you want.

Today, slow down and begin to create order and structure. Later, from this framework, take your risks.

CHAPTER 21

System Improvement as a Way of Life

Dogs bark, but the caravan moves on.

—ARABIAN PROVERB

FOR A GIVEN PRIMARY SYSTEM, to ensure desired results occur over and over again, the task is to adjust subsystems so the correct components are being used and they are sequenced properly.

It's about preparation. If you pay attention to the mechanical details of your world and make proper manipulations to the key systems that compose it, you will construct a life that is unencumbered with fire killing, and seldom dictated by urgency. Flexible, strong, and resilient, it's a life of smooth, calm days—days that have lots of room for thinking and planning, for building and creating, for friends and family, and for just being yourself. It's a life that encounters road bumps, but seldom earthquakes.

Whatever your station in life, if your days are frustrating—crammed to the max—and you're not getting ahead, know that things can be fixed if you focus on system improvement.

You will gain a deeper understanding of the mechanics of how this material world functions and then apply this understanding in every instance. The systems mindset will be so ingrained that it will modify even the smallest decision of the day. It will be part of you.

Following is a final summary of work the system mechanics.

A Summary of the
Work the System Methodology

1. It starts with your change in perspective, the aha! insight arriving in a moment of time. Deep down, you permanently internalize your new vision. You see each life event as the product of the mechanisms that engendered it, not as an isolated happening, a product of luck, fate, God's justice, karma, the stars, or the benevolence or wrath of someone else. When the insight arrives, the next mechanical moves are obvious.

2. You establish your goals and strategy through the creation of the Strategic Objective and General Operating Principles. You do this to establish firm direction and so there is continuity in your goals and efforts.

3. You examine the mechanics of the subsystems that make up your business, job, health, and relationships. You analyze them one by one, looking for opportunities for enhancement. Sometimes you add new ones. Sometimes you discard useless ones.

4. You make the revisions, moving each subsystem to peak efficiency. If you are in a business or a job environment, for permanence you carefully create documented Working Procedures to describe the protocols. You create this documentation from scratch. Then, when you're done, you incessantly coddle your systems and the documentation, always tweaking to perfection. From now on, you and your people spend the majority of time in system improvement.

5. A more positive attitude comes naturally because you have developed a solid faith in the reliability of the systems that are at work everywhere. You are powerful and serene because you have successfully harnessed your systems, directing them to do what you want them to do. With subsystems isolated, perfected, and then combined together again, you preside over stunningly efficient primary systems—your business, job, relationships . . . *you*. At the gut level, without putting your

head in the sand regarding the many things that are not perfect in this world, you grasp the great truth that 99.9 percent
of everything works just fine.

SINGLES AND DOUBLES

Forget about making mighty home-run swings that will win the game.
The numbers are more than a little against you, and your big swings will
be a distraction. Instead, hunker down, preserve what you have, and go
for the surefire, incremental system-improvement advances: the singles
and doubles. Go slowly at first. Be patient. Relish the small yet permanent
betterments that will add up to something big down the line.

It's the small details that add up.

Focus on the mechanical systems that produce the results, not the
other way around, and never doubt that a superb collection of subsystems
will produce a superb primary system.

Maintain a positive regard for those around you and do what you say
you will do. Demonstrate quality and do it consistently. Keep your goals
in mind and relentlessly work toward them through thick and thin. Don't
try to fool yourself or others around you. Start and finish tasks on time.
Don't complain. Your job is to lead the caravan and leave the barking dogs
behind. Your life will get better sooner than you think.

The reality is that most people look for better results without considering the mechanisms that would produce those results. They don't understand the system-improvement concept. In thinking locally, this gives you
a great advantage. Thinking globally, you know there are a whole lot of
people out there not getting what they want.

Remember that your body and mind compose the primary system that
is your life. Fortunately, these two major components are the ones you can
most easily adjust. Improve your systems at every opportunity; maintain
them always, keep them strong.

In everything you do, focus hard on the pragmatic details and perform
the basics well. Keep things simple but be cautious of shortcuts.

With finesse, take life as it comes.

The largest problem with swinging for the home run is that all those hammer swings will cause you to strike out too often. And all those strike-outs added together will make life a struggle or take you down altogether.

Instead, slow down and focus on each separate pitch. Relax, keep your eye on the ball, and make contact. Your steady swing, combined with the right pitch, will send the ball over the fence when you least expect it and more often than you could predict.

See that each swing is a closed entity unto itself; each has the singular goal of making contact with the ball. When you miss the ball, and of course you sometimes will, calmly accept it as a natural outcome in the numbers game of life and then, undistracted, give 100 percent focus to the next swing.

One last time, I remind you that the mandatory adjustment is in your moment-to-moment perception of the world. All your actions stem from this new, outside-and-slightly-elevated vision: your world is composed of mechanics that function flawlessly 99.9 percent of the time. All you need to do is see this and then climb on board!

Every day has its flavor, its tone. Work with your individual day-chunks and savor them as they slide by.

Stay off the circular track. Know it is the climbing you want.

Understand that most people wake up in the morning with only a vague sense of their ultimate, primary goals. Events quickly peel back the layers of control and the day becomes a Whac-A-Mole epic that dictates stumbling reaction to bad results while disallowing efforts at system improvement.

In contrast, you *carve* through the hours as you direct subsystems with confidence and precision, constructing the primary systems you desire. You remember that control is a good thing, and you seek it.

You see the machinery. You work it so it produces the exact results you desire. In your life, no longer will invisible systems produce random bad results.

By filling your days with accomplishment, the negatives that previously dragged you down will no longer factor into who you are and what you do. They will just annoy you occasionally.

Will you become blind to the dysfunction around you? Not a chance. In fact, you'll be in a position to do something about dysfunction as it comes within your ever-growing circle of influence.

The work the system mindset is focused, deliberate, and organized. It's about action, not reaction.

A VISION TO CULTIVATE

Most of us have at least one process in which we excel. For you, what is it, and why are you good at it? It's probable that when you are in the midst of performing this process, you experience a delicious taste of precision and confidence. You bask in the flow of it. What you do well is your passion, and you take every opportunity to repeat it. It's a positive obsession.

You ask, for this thing I do well, do I love doing it because I am good at it, or am I good at it because I love doing it? The black-or-white answer is elusive, but consider a third possibility: do the two go together without distinction?

Again, what do you do well? What makes you passionate? Leaving aside the chicken-or-the-egg question, and while continuing to hone your particular passion, extend that fire to the perfection of the mechanical workings of the other facets of your existence. Get visceral about it. Wallow in it.

Be outside the events of your day and treat those events as elements of an overall game, a game that your proper engineering will make perfect. That game, of course, is your life.

Few people understand the magnificence of the systems around them—but now you do. From this point forward you will reject escapism as you appreciate the here and now for the miracle it is—the miracle that was always right there in front of you, but which you didn't see.

Now you will find command and freedom because you understand the mechanisms that determine the events of your life.

You will never go back.

EPILOGUE

It's 3:00 p.m. on March 17, 2011. We're in England, in a cottage in the tiny rural coastal town of Sidmouth, and while we travel I'm working on the final rewrite of this third edition. We sit at the dining room table with spring in full flush outside. The sun is hot; the birds are chirping. I walked in the moors and forests early this morning while Linda slept. In my hiking gear, I returned through town and was met with smiles at every turn. At a pastry shop I bought two strudels and arrived back at the cottage exactly at noon to make coffee for the two of us and to share the pastries. Here we sit.

I'm a writer now, and here I am in an English country cottage with my beautiful wife across the table, busy with her own work. *This* is what I want. I thank God for allowing me to live this life, and for giving me the power to make it what I've always wanted it to be.

APPENDIX A

Centratel's Strategic Objective

NOTE TO STAFF: *The Centratel Strategic Objective is the basis for all corporate and individual decision making.*

Trite mission statements that declare "We want to be the best and we want our customers to be happy" don't provide meaningful direction and do little more than make company stockholders feel good for the moment. And voluminous multiyear work plans can't account for the day-by-day changes in our industry.

Instead, the Strategic Objective precisely describes our market and direction, as well as who we are and how we function. It reminds us of what is most important and it gives us an overview of general strategy. By following its guidelines, growth and success will take care of themselves. In the spirit of simplicity, we limit the length of the Strategic Objective to one page. We've modified it through the years, but the fundamentals have never changed.

We are the highest-quality telephone answering service in the United States.

Our fundamental strategy is to relentlessly "work" the systems of the business to perfection.

Our guiding documents are the Strategic Objective, Thirty Principles, and the collection of Working Procedures.

Centratel's primary offering is 24/7/365 telephone answering service for business and professional offices throughout the United States. Peripheral services are voice mail and paging for the Central Oregon region only.

Through intense commitment to our employees, we will contribute to the success of our clients. The consequence of having loyal, smart, hard-working, long-term, and well-compensated staff is superb quality service to customers.

Our business is complex, with many human, mechanical, and computer systems in simultaneous motion. Success depends on refined communication and organizational processes, dedicated staff, documented point-of-sale procedures, first-class office space and equipment, rigorous quality assurance with continuous measurement, assertive innovation, intense planned maintenance/system improvement, aggressive and measured marketing, and relentless attention to detail in every nook and cranny.

Competitive advantages include a near-flawless level of message processing accuracy, products designed around the unique needs of the customer, thoughtful customer service that is immediate and consistent, the latest high-tech equipment, and personal/corporate integrity. We use extraordinarily efficient communication tools and protocols. We constantly refine and improve all internal systems and mechanisms.

To grow, we proceed with an "if we build it, they will come" philosophy, juxtaposed with assertive marketing efforts.

Although we tightly direct Centratel's operation through guiding documentation, we will modify that documentation immediately if an enhancement can be made: "Our operational framework is rigid, but that framework can be modified instantly."

We segment responsibilities into specialized "expert compartments" with appropriate cross-training among departments. We have backup personnel for all positions.

Primary vertical markets include medical, veterinary, home health/hospice, funeral home, HVAC, property management, hi-tech, 24/7 on-call, front office/virtual receptionist, and utility.

APPENDIX B
Centratel's Thirty Principles

1. Company decisions must conform to the Strategic Objective, Thirty Principles, and Working Procedures documents.

2. We are the highest-quality answering service in the United States. We do whatever it takes to ensure the quality of service to our clients is unmatched anywhere.

3. We draw solid lines, thus providing an exact status of where things stand. Documented procedures are the main defense against gray-area problems.

4. "Get the job done." Can the employee *do* his or her job, or is there always a complication of one kind or another? This ability to "get the job done quickly and accurately without excuses or complications" is the most valuable trait an employee can possess.

5. Employees come first. We employ people who have an innate desire to perform at 100 percent. We reward them accordingly. The natural outcome is we serve our clients well.

6. We are not fire killers. We are fire prevention specialists. We don't manage problems; we work on system enhancement and system maintenance in order to prevent problems from happening in the first place.

7. Problems are gifts that inspire us to action. A problem prompts the act of creating or improving a system or procedure. We don't want setbacks, but when one occurs, we think, "thank you for this wake-up call," and take system-improvement action to prevent the setback from happening again.

8. We focus on just a few manageable services. Although we watch for new opportunities, in the end we provide "just a few services implemented in superb fashion," rather than a complex array of average-quality offerings.

9. We find the simplest solution. Ockham's Law, also called the Law of Economy, states, "Entities are not to be multiplied beyond necessity . . . the simplest solution is invariably the correct solution."

10. The money we save or waste is not Monopoly money! We are careful not to devalue the worth of a dollar just because it has to do with the business.

11. We operate the company via documented procedures and systems. "Any recurring problem can be solved with a system." We take the necessary time to create and implement systems and procedures, and in the end, it is well worth it. If there is a recurring problem, a written procedure is created in order to prevent the problem from happening again. On the other hand, we don't bog down the organization with processes and procedures that target once-in-a-while situations. Sometimes we elect to *not* create a procedure.

12. "Just *don't* do it." Eliminate the unnecessary. Many times, elimination of a system, protocol, or potential project is a very good thing. Think simplicity. Automate. Refine to the smallest amount of steps or discard altogether. Would a simple "no" save time, energy, and/or money?

13. Our documented systems, procedures, and functions are "off-the-street." This means anyone with normal intelligence can perform procedures unassisted. The real-world evidence of this is we can hire an individual "off-the-street" who has good typing skills and have him or her processing calls within three days. For this result, protocols have to be efficient, simple, and thoroughly documented. (Before we implemented our systemized training protocol, it would take six weeks to train a TSR.)

14. Do it NOW. All actions build on "point-of-sale" theory. We don't delay an action if it can be done immediately. Just like any major retail outlet, we "update inventories and databases at the exact

time the transaction takes place." There is no paperwork floating around the office after a physical transaction. We ask, "How can we perform the task NOW without creating lingering details that we must clean up later?"

15. We glean the Centratel mindset from Stephen Covey's books, including *The 7 Habits of Highly Successful People, First Things First,* and *The 8th Habit.* As well, we consider *Good to Great* by Jim Collins; *The E-Myth Revisited* by Michael Gerber; and *Awaken the Giant Within* by Anthony Robbins.

16. We pattern individual organization upon Franklin-Covey theory. We use organizing mechanisms that are always at hand. We prioritize, schedule, and document. The system is always up-to-date and we use it all the time. (For Centratel, this is Microsoft Outlook.)

17. Sequence and priority are critical. We work on the most important tasks first. We spend maximum time on "non-urgent/important" tasks via Stephen Covey's time-matrix philosophy.

18. We double-check everything before release. If a penchant for double-checking is not an innate personal habit, then it must be cultivated. Double-checking is a conscious step in every task, performed either by the individual managing the task, or someone else.

19. Our environment is spotless: clean and ordered, simple, efficient, functional. No "rat's nests," literally or figuratively.

20. Employee training is structured, scheduled, and thorough. Assertive client contact is also structured, scheduled, and thorough.

21. We are deadline-obsessed. If someone in the organization says he/she will be finished with a task or project by a certain date and time, then he or she commits to finishing by that deadline (or, if legitimate delays intrude, he or she advises coworkers well in advance the deadline is impossible).

22. We maintain equipment and keep it 100 percent functional at all times. If something is not working as it should, fix it now—fix it now even if it's not necessary to fix it now. It's a matter of good

housekeeping and of maintaining good habits. This is just the way we do things.

23. Mastery of the English language is critical. We are aware of how we sound and what we write. We do whatever we can to improve. We are patient as a coworker corrects us.

24. We study to increase our skills. A steady diet of reading and contemplation is vital to personal development. It is a matter of self-discipline.

25. As opposed to "doing the work," the department manager's job is to create, monitor, and document systems (which consist of people, equipment, procedures, and maintenance schedules).

26. The CEO/GM oversees department heads and overall systems. It is the CEO/GM's job to direct, coordinate, and monitor managers.

27. We avoid multitasking activities. When communicating with someone else, we are 100 percent present. We give full attention to the person in front of us (or to the task at hand). We focus on listening and understanding. Read the classic *Treating Type A Behavior and Your Heart* by Meyer Friedman. "Mindfulness" is paying complete attention to one thing at a time: read *Full Catastrophe Living* by Jon Kabat-Zinn.

28. When in the office, we work hard on Centratel business. We keep our heads down; we focus, and in turn the company pays very well. That's "the deal." The workweek rarely exceeds forty hours.

29. Complete means "complete." Almost or tomorrow is not "complete." In particular, this is germane to administration staff's use of Outlook task functions.

30. We strive for a social climate that is serious and quiet yet pleasant, serene, light, and friendly. Centratel is a nice place to work.

APPENDIX C

Sample Working Procedures

Here are several sample Working Procedures from Centratel, exactly as we use them as of the date of this printing. Note that the format of all Working Procedures should be the same, so it is important to establish a set template for all to use. We provide a software platform that has set parameters for all three primary documents, ensuring consistency, privacy, and protection of all documents. See appendix J.

E-mail Signature Procedure

4/08/11

Your signature on your e-mails should conform to the following standards. Use 10- or 12-point type in your choice of Arial, Times New Roman, Verdana, Tahoma, or Garamond typefaces. You may do it in black or dark blue. List your information as follows:

1. Your name
2. Your title
3. Centratel
4. Telephone numbers
5. Fax numbers
6. Website address

   Example:
   Jim Jones
   Telephone Service Representative
   Centratel

Tel: 541-385-2616 or 888-482-4393

Fax: 541-388-2351 or 800-330-7303

www.centratel.com

To create your e-mail signature in Outlook:

1. Open Microsoft Outlook

2. Click on "Tools"

3. Click on "Options"

4. Click on the "Mail Format" tab

5. Click the "Signatures" button

6. To create a new signature click "New," or to edit an existing signature click "Edit"

7. Enter the information as listed above

8. Click "OK"

9. Click "OK"

10. Click "Apply"

TSRs: Bidding on Shift Blocks

3/3/08

This is the protocol for filling an empty shift block. Also, it is an opportunity for any TSR to indicate a preferred schedule block, even if their desired block is currently filled.

1. A new shift block opening will be announced by e-mail to all TSRs. If a TSR is on vacation, management will make every attempt to reach the TSR, informing them of the new shift block availability.

2. There will only be one bidding period and it will be at least 48 hours in duration. A deadline date/time will be given.

3. To apply for a shift block, a bid must be submitted by e-mail to the Call Center manager within the bidding period. No late bids will be accepted.

4. If a TSR bids on a new block and is ultimately awarded that block, their old block will become available. So, for any TSRs who would

like a different block, even if that block is currently filled, he or she should indicate their preference so that if their desired block becomes available in the bidding process, they will be considered for it.

5. A TSR's current schedule block will not change unless he or she bids on another block. In other words, TSRs who are happy in their existing schedule block do not have to do anything during the bidding process: TSRs who do not bid will not, under any circumstances, be changed to another block. In doing nothing, a TSR's block is absolutely secure.

6. TSRs should not consider their bid officially accepted until he or she receives notice from the Call Center manger that it has been received.

7. If two or more TSRs bid on the same block, the block will be awarded based on seniority.

8. If there is still an open block after the bidding deadline has passed, we will look outside the company for a new employee to fill that block.

9. In accepting a new shift block, a TSR will be ineligible to bid on another shift block for a period of three months.

NOTE TO READER: The following Daily Deposit Procedure was at twenty-three steps for a number of years, but in April 2011 we added a check reader so our receivables manager would no longer have to physically deliver checks to the bank. This latest system improvement also adds up the checks into a total amount, saving additional time. With this additional subsystem, the procedure is now at thirty-two steps, with a general bullet point added at the end. So, with this system improvement, there are more steps in the working procedure but lots of saved time for our AR manager (approximately three hours total time per week). Also, there is less liability for all concerned as there is no longer any street time involved in making the deposit. It took a total of four hours to install and debug the check-reader system and tweak the working procedure. Yeah!

Daily Deposit

4/14/11

To process the deposit each day into TBS for any VM, Paging, or TAS Account.

1. In TBS under Activities menu, select "Enter Payments."

2. Select "Direct Entry."

3. Select the hand to the left of the "Cust Ref" box and toggle until you find "Account."

4. For each separate payment, enter the four-digit account number and the account will automatically be pulled up.

5. Enter the amount of the payment in the "Payment Amount" box, using the decimal point. (Verify that the amount is paying the account balance or invoice balance. If not, keep track of those accounts so they may be reviewed later for discrepancies.)

6. Tab once to the "Check Number" field and type in the check number (if there is an excessively long check number, only enter the last five digits).

7. In the "Payment Type" field, select appropriate payment method. If it is a money order, enter "M.O." Note: If payment is in the form of cash, type the word "Cash" in the Check Number field.

8. Click the "Post" box to apply the payment. Once posted, it will clear the screen so the next payment may be entered.

9. Continue until all payments have been entered.

10. Double-check that each check has not been postdated and has a signature.

11. When all payments have been entered, select "Payment Register." This will show all payments entered on this deposit transaction.

12. Open Internet Explorer and click on bookmark tab "Daily Deposit Deployment."

13. Click on "Smart Client."

14. Log in with your User ID and Password assigned by the bank; this will bring up CSB Daily Deposit screen (maximize it).

15. Click on "New Deposit" and Create New Deposit screen will pop up.

16. Verify that Colejenn Checking is listed for primary account.

17. Enter the deposit total from TBS Payment Register.

18. Place the batch of checks into the check scanner facing the window in the right side holder and click on "Capture Items." The machine will then scan the batch. (Don't panic about checks in red on your screen saying "failed"; you will be prompted to modify when finished.)

19. Once scan is finished, click "Next" and remove checks from machine.

20. If any checks have failed, a Scanning in Progress box will pop up saying, "There are still items remaining in scanner. Stop scanning now." Click "yes." The checks will come up one by one for you to enter in the amount and click "accept."

21. Deposit corrected box comes up saying "items are correct"; click "OK" to proceed to balance. (If balance isn't correct, check to make sure all checks were scanned; some of them may have been missed. Put missing ones back in scanner and click capture items again.)

22. When "Deposit Ready" comes up, compare the amount with TBS and make sure they match and click "Transmit now."

23. In Transmission summary box, click "View Deposit Receipt" and print, then click close and close summary box. Exit out of the program and scanner will shut off automatically.

24. In TBS, under "Payment Register," select "Bank Deposit."

25. Verify the deposit date in the window. Click the green check mark. A window will open. For the Title, type in "Deposit" and the deposit "date."

26. PRINT THIS DOCUMENT!! This is the best print of this document. However, if you don't print it for any reason, you can print any

day's deposit record, although you need to print two reports—one gives you the detail per customer and one gives you the total—the two should match. To print those reports—in TBS under "Miscellaneous"—Payment Register Summary (click detail for account names).

27. After printing the document, close the window. It will ask "O.K. to deposit this payment batch?" Select "Yes."

28. Attach both printed reports together and highlight totals.

29. In the bottom left-hand drawer are slips of paper; write date and total of deposit and attach to the checks. File the batch in the box.

30. Have someone verify that the printed deposit report amounts match. They should initial by the total deposit amount on the TBS deposit report.

31. Enter the amount of deposit in "Daily Receivables Journal." I:\Daily Receivables (password is "cash").

32. File the initialed report in the appropriate folder for the month and year of the day's deposit. File cabinet is in the automated service manager's office in the top drawer.

  • Most "General Receivables" may be processed with the normal deposit for the day. However, sometimes Sam may indicate, if the amount is large, to do a separate deposit for certain items. Check with him in these circumstances.

Filming an Interview

NOTE TO READER: Here is a working procedure that we created just before publication of the third edition. It's rough, as I put it together in a matter of just a few minutes as we began to create marketing elements for our new Work the System Academy product. Clearly there is more work to do to make this procedure more comprehensive and understandable. I add this rough-hewn draft to show that it is not necessary to be an experienced professional in a given endeavor in order to produce a procedure that will be entirely useful.

Three Cameras: Basic Setup

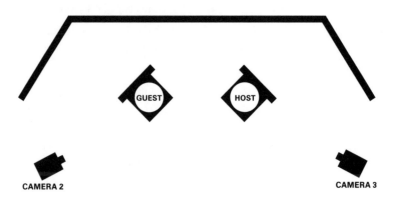

1. At the site, allow at least one hour for setting up.

2. Camera 2 has host audio. Camera 3 has guest audio.

3. Use two light umbrellas: one between camera 1 and camera 2, and the other between camera 1 and camera 3.

4. Cameras are to be set up out of harm's way so they can be easily monitored from behind.

5. Host framing (camera 2): vertical second button down/slight space overhead, with horizontal spacing at 60 percent left/40 percent right. Can be framed to shoot slightly upward.

6. Guest framing (camera 3): vertical second button down/slight space overhead, with horizontal spacing at 60 percent right/40 percent left. Can be framed to shoot slightly downward.

7. Camera 3 option: include back shoulder of host.

8. Carefully gauge backdrop so there is no vertical line converging with the host's or guest's heads. Is anything else distracting in the background?

9. Do the cameras have fresh batteries (transceiver and receiver for each camera)? It is the director's job to make sure all batteries are fresh. The major danger is losing audio.

10. Do a sound check.

11. All cameras should be connected to AC power, if available.

12. All cameras operate unattended. Do *not* adjust zoom. Do *not* touch. Do *not* walk in front of running cameras.

13. The guest and host should remain in the same position in their chairs for the duration of the interview.

14. The guest and host should not slump back in their chairs. They should stay upright or slightly forward. (A fish-eye lens makes whatever is closer look bigger.)

15. Turn *all* cell phones off (if there are any landlines, their ringers should also be turned off).

16. All three people must start the cameras at the same time.

17. Use 1-2-3 countdown to simultaneously start cameras.

18. Each operator must confirm that camera startup was successful.

19. The director steps between the host and guest and does a single hand clap to sync the audio.

20. The host and guest must not speak (make sounds of agreement, laughing, etc.) while the other is talking.

21. In an informal setting, the production people are not to drink alcohol. (Perhaps it is OK for the guest.)

22. The production people are not to do anything that interrupts the flow of the host/guest dialog. They should keep their movements and chatter to a minimum; each should sit down, relax, and quietly monitor their own camera.

APPENDIX D
The Work the System Academy

MY ASSOCIATE, MIKE GILES, refers to the Work the System Academy as "the framework on which every business should be built where the business owner has a primary objective to work less and earn more."

Businesses have their various departments, of course, including sales, IT, operations, accounting, etc., but too often they lack an efficient, mechanical underlying structure. It's a little like building a skyscraper without the steel framework. The Academy is designed for businesses that got started too quickly and went for growth while brushing structure, systems, and processes to one side. The good news is that it's never too late to rebuild the framework. The Academy provides the business owner and his or her staff with a simple and fast bolt-on installation of the method, which will bring about stability and control and thus cause super-high efficiency. Of course, super-high efficiency means more bottom-line profit for the business and more free time for the owner: *making more and working less*.

I never intended for my book to be feel-good entertainment. I wanted to go deeper and really help my readers by providing a set of clear, tangible instructions to follow. But a book is a static object and can't force anyone to *do* anything that he or she is resistant to doing.

My aim in sharing the work the system methodology is not to help the reader experience a short-term high and then return to self-defeating ingrained habits within a few days of reading the book, having failed to follow the action steps. Instead, I want to see people *do* something to fix their less-than-satisfactory situations because I know firsthand the extraordinary difference it can make in a life. For some, the book is not enough, and for these readers we created the Academy.

Over the past four years I've been asked the following questions, and they are what I address in the program:

1. I don't have time to do this because I'm too busy, so how can I get the work the system method installed in my business?

2. How can I get motivated enough to make sure I actually follow through?

3. How do I get my staff to buy into the work the system method?

4. What are the organizational changes that I must make? How do I implement them?

5. What is the format of the documentation? How can I be sure I include all necessary content?

I understand that many people will struggle to take action and implement the work the system method in their own lives and businesses. This is just human nature. It's also true that making a half-attempt at implementing the work the system method is not the way to do it, although it is better than doing nothing. More than a few people I've talked to want to do the work but need some kind of catalyst to spark them into actual action, and I've had numerous requests over the years to create something that would enable business owners to break out of their state of entanglement and fully reengineer their lives and businesses over a short period of time. Many of the requests have been from people who want hand-holding through the process, with every step explained in three-dimensional detail, making it impossible for them to go wrong.

There also have been questions about what it takes to get staff to climb on board and questions suggesting there is fear that there will be a mutiny or serious blowback from staff about the method. (It pains me to hear this because, truth is, the work the system method energizes and motivates staff.) The great thing about the work the system method is that it provides fast results. No delayed gratification. And, the process is believable and logical. Your staff will be excited to be involved if you explain the changes properly and include them in the process. You'll find there is not one segment of the Academy program that must be held back from staff. There's no mystery or special secret here, nothing that can't be shared.

The heart of the Academy product is the detailed video training in which the explanation of the method is done personally by me, with Mike's assistance. We train you and your management staff *directly*. This way, nothing is left to chance or question, and the burden of teaching much of the information is removed from your shoulders. Clearly though, you, as business owner, will play the lead role in creating a proper environment for your staff to learn the method, and of course you will be ultimately responsible for making sure the work is done. We recommend that you and your management staff watch the specifically employee-targeted video sessions together as a team. This way you will have company-wide buy in, and the compound impact of your entire team working with you on this will be far reaching. The employee's role is to make his or her domain vastly more efficient, which will in turn have a dramatic impact on the overall operation. If you have no staff, the work the system method still applies. Once you create a solid framework of systems and procedures, you will establish a foundation for growing your business. Most single-proprietor businesses remain without staff because they can't figure out how to scale their operation.

Then there are questions about documentation. Mostly they are about what format to use and exactly what information to include. I can understand this. At first, I struggled with that, too. But now, we've customized a software package to make things simple (see appendix J).

Mike and I have spent a huge amount of time designing this program, which goes way beyond the book in scope. It's a one- to three-month program (the time necessary to complete it depends on the complexity of your business and your readiness to make changes).

In the Academy, we provide all the templates, software, and step-by-step video training required for you to make a shift in the way your world functions—and, in short, to help you get what you want in your business and in your life. You get everything you need to implement highly efficient systems and processes in your business with the aim of freeing up more time and making more money.

The information is presented in a logical, methodical order so you can permanently rid yourself of chaos and disorder. It's about helping you find real freedom by paying attention to the simple mechanics of your business and your life.

For up-to-date information, go to workthesystemacademy.com.

We also plan to release an enhanced program designed to train independent business consultants specializing in the work the system strategy. Must one already be a business consultant in order to develop this business? No. You must simply have a passion for helping others get what they want in life. See appendix E and go to workthesystemconsultants.com for more information. Or, do you need a work the system consultant to help you get your business smoothed out? See appendix F and go to findworkthesystemconsultants.com.

APPENDIX E

Become a Work the System Consultant

The Work the System Consultant Business Opportunity is designed for the individual who is passionate about helping others make more money and work fewer hours, and who desires to operate his or her own operation. This is an in-depth training program in which we teach you how to operate a lucrative consultancy practice based on the work the system methodology. We provide all the tools, templates, and software required to help your clients master the systems mindset. As part of the program, there is a live, multiday training session that I, most times, will attend and help conduct.

You will typically attract clients who need a full handholding service and don't feel they have the time to manage the implementation of the methodology themselves. A tremendously rewarding endeavor of your own, it's an opportunity to earn a full-time income working part-time hours. For more details, go to workthesystemconsultants.com.

APPENDIX F

Find a Consultant

WE OFFER WORK THE SYSTEM CONSULTING PROGRAM FOR BUSINESS owners who don't have the time or inclination to implement the work the system methodology in their business and life and need help managing the process. The Work the System Consultant Program is a fully tailored service that includes face-to-face training and support over a three- to six-month period for you and your staff. It is important that you and your team do the work of creating the documentation so that the systems mindset becomes embedded deep within the internal structure of your operation. The key factor here is that your staff does it *with* you to ensure that creating robust systems and processes occur properly and that you complete the work across every area of your business. Your consultant will guide and energize this process. For more details, go to findworkthesystemconsultants.com or call us at 800-664-8351.

APPENDIX G

Ockham's Razor and the TSR

NOTE TO THE READER: *I originally wrote this article in 2002 for a telephone answering service trade journal. It was directed to answering service owners, but the message is simple and is applicable to any business with employees. I have updated it slightly for this book.*

Ockham's razor is a principle attributed to the fourteenth-century English philosopher William of Ockham. It states that "entities should not be multiplied beyond necessity; that one should choose the simplest explanation, the one requiring the fewest assumptions and principles."

OCKHAM'S LAW AND THE LONG-TERM EMPLOYEE

Exactly *what* is the problem?

What attributes do telephone answering service (TAS) owners seek in their telephone service representatives (TSRs)? The short list includes cheerful and constructive attitudes, high-quality performance, and long-term employment.

Employee performance and turnover are *the* major topics in our trade meeting get-togethers, both in general sessions and in one-on-one discussions. In our industry, it's a fact that most TSRs don't stick around for the long term, and for those who do, there are sometimes "negative comportment" problems.

Why is there such tumult within answering service operations departments? Why are owners constantly trading tips and secrets in an attempt to stem the tide of incessant staff turnover, and why do these owners berate themselves, their employees, and the telecom industry in general?

The problem is not due to unqualified job applicants or a general lack of work ethic. Instead, it's the owner's failure to address the real-life requirements of staff, proffering instead gimmicky and manipulative incentives and/or punishments.

I once knew an answering service owner who claimed that staff turnover was *not* his greatest problem (although it was his number two problem). He argued that the greatest challenge was the state government's mandated increases in the minimum wage. He complained, "It keeps going up!"

There was another owner who had a well-thought-out, documented employee punishment procedure for nonperformance and "bad attitude." (The floggings will continue until morale improves!) And here's a comment I overheard from a TAS operations manager: "We can't do drug testing. I would have to fire everyone and then there would be no one to answer the phones!"

None of those three people is in the industry anymore—and all three of the businesses they operated are defunct.

Let's start with the topic of wages. What about TSR compensation? Here's the ubiquitous industry rationale for offering meager pay: "You just don't understand. This is a competitive, cutthroat, low-income industry and we *can't* pay a better wage. A telephone answering service sells a commodity, and although quality is important, in the end, success is more a function of low price. If we raise our service rates, we'll lose our customers."

Of course, client service rates are a factor, but what if we could pay our TSRs more while making their work environment more stable and logical? If this produced a long-term staff that provided better service quality, could we charge clients more?

So why is there so much staff turnover? What are the root no-frills, no-cover-up, no-Band-Aid causes of the problem? The causes *are* simple and, in their simplicity, they expose unsuccessful attempts to cultivate stability for what they are—smoke screens that offer initial intrigue but have nothing to do with a TSR's fundamental needs.

I will interject a simple yet vital concept here. Long ago, when I had just started in the business, the owner of a large and successful TAS in

Portland, Oregon, told me: "Your TSRs *want* to do a good job. It is your job to make that easy for them. Don't ever second-guess their motivation. *They want to do a good job!*"

If an owner or manager begins with the premise "all employees are lazy" or "there is no work ethic anymore" or "I can't pay enough to find and hold quality people," where will that lead?

If these are your fundamental beliefs, you must change them. If you don't, you are doomed.

Here are the three primary reasons why most answering services can't keep people long term. They are disarming in their simplicity. First, employees aren't getting what they want in terms of pay and benefits. Big surprise. Second, they don't know what ownership expects of them. They have to be mind readers in order to stay out of trouble. Third, with knee-jerk irregularity, owners manipulate TSRs in subtle and not-so-subtle ways, while seldom acknowledging their good work.

In other words, the money is not good, requirements for performance are mysterious, and childish reward and punishment schemes erupt sporadically while good work goes unnoticed.

A PHILOSOPHY AND A SYSTEM OF EMPLOYMENT

Develop a philosophy of employment that will address the true needs of your employees. If you worked for someone, would you want it any other way? Could anything be more simple?

Remember this: there are no superhuman people out there, but there are plenty of great people who are looking for solid opportunities.

You need stable employees; ones who are reliable, honest, and hardworking. There are lots of people out there like that, and if you do things right, they will find their way to you, be committed, perform superbly, and stay long term. All you must do is satisfy people's reasonable needs and not ask them to be mind readers. Tell them exactly what you want them to do, and treat them like the adults they are. If you do this, you will have an extraordinary employment system: one that acknowledges your TSRs' worth as it fulfills their personal requirements.

Be crystal clear about the employer-employee arrangement without being afraid to throw in a challenge that says "this is the deal" between the employer and the employee. At Centratel, the deal we offer TSRs is simple: "We will pay you very well if you give us 100 percent."

You must put your extraordinary employment system down on paper so your people know what it is. It will take time to do this, but so what? You are already breaking your back dealing with chronic staff turnover. Isn't *that* hard work? Doesn't *that* take time? Just channel the same time and energy and money in this different direction. Swallow the pill: sensible documentation is a prerequisite for long-term staff stability; if you create it, stability is what you will have.

WHAT TO LEAVE OUT

Incentive plans that don't address the fundamental needs of employees will fail. These programs are worse than a waste of time and money. They crush morale. And what about punishment? Don't even think about it.

Before discussing what to include in your new employment vision, it is important to consider what *not* to include. By dropping ineffective actions, you will promote simplicity as you gain time and energy.

Here are some "motivators" I've heard about in other answering services: useless gifts (as exemplified by a huge bag of plastic Mickey Mouse ears brought back to TSRs after the owner visited Disney World); complicated formulas to award cash bonuses for perfect attendance; "fun" games and rewards for those who attend staff meetings. I've heard of gift certificates for having a "good attitude," and movie theater tickets as prizes for making it through initial training or for "good behavior." Also useless: long, drawn-out conversations with problem employees in which management attempts to reason with them, as in, perhaps, convincing them to show up for work on time.

What do all of these strategies have in common?

First, they have nothing to do with the real, long-term needs of people. Arriving inconsistently, they are of low intrinsic value. They are ineffective Band-Aids.

Second, TSRs perceive motivational gimmicks and heart-to-heart chats for what they are: manipulative and childish, management's thinly veiled efforts to maneuver them into being good little girls and boys. This is insulting in a low-key way. This is carrot-on-a-stick, Bugs Bunny methodology, and within your staff it will breed an underlying disrespect for you because it is disrespectful of them.

GOOD PEOPLE FROM THE START

At Centratel, we have little staff turnover in our operations department. Only occasionally will a TSR call in sick or arrive late. Everyone makes it to staff meetings. These are exceptionally positive, solid, good people— and they were that way before they showed up at Centratel. Our first success is in being able to find people like this and then convince them to work for us.

Rather than attempting to cultivate the attitudes and work ethic we seek, we carefully pick good people and then we don't alienate them.

In addition to giving TSRs what they need for compensation and treating them like the adults they are, we work hard to give them a stability that, occasionally, is in contrast to their lives at home. It may be just a job, but Centratel is a place that is safe, calm, and predictable. This stability is rooted in our rigorous documentation: in exact detail, we have written down what we want and expect them to do.

As a sidebar: in the history of my own business, the ground-shaking paradigm shifts came at the blackest of times. It was usually "do something dramatic right this minute, or file for bankruptcy tomorrow morning." In these on-the-edge times, a huge and immediate change in philosophy and operating policy was exactly what was needed, and our present staff philosophy arrived in exactly that way.

Be thankful, I say, for the hard times we survive.

GETTING SPECIFIC

Please. No more Band-Aids.

What would William of Ockham do if he owned a telephone answering service? What follows is my best-guess list. None of these strategies are new or revolutionary, but what they have in common is that they meet the needs of both TSRs and owners. Remember to presume the good intentions of each TSR.

1. You've already identified the number one item: pay a generous wage. Money is why people come to work. Forget the convenient theory "pay isn't the most important part of a job; it's the feeling of being valued," etc. How '60s is that? Don't ask college campus psychologists and sociologists what is most important to your people. Ask your employees what is most important to them! Long ago, I submitted a written questionnaire to our TSRs asking what was most important to them regarding their positions with Centratel. The overwhelming response was that pay is what is most important—and so I was delighted to find I had "a firm grasp of the obvious." Remember that a high pay scale has benefits that are not always obvious and measurable—high-quality performance from long-term employees. Have faith this nonmeasurable benefit will more than compensate for the extra cost.

2. I'll get some argument on this one, but my bet is that Sir William would propose that there be no part-time people. All staff members should be full-timers. Part-timers won't have the same experience on the phones. They can't get the same workout with the accounts and the techniques. How can a twenty-hour-per-week employee attain the same degree of expertise as a forty-hour-per-week employee? Also, for part-timers, the job tends to rank a too-low priority in their lives. We want career-minded, serious people who consider their jobs important enough so that what we want, and what they get, really matters to them. We don't take our business in a casual way and neither does a full-time employee.

3. No paid sick days. Why? Because paying people when they are not at work is a reward for not being at work! We provide PTO, but it is a cash payment that shows up as TSRs earn it, as a separate line item on their biweekly paychecks. TSRs can take time off—two to three weeks each year, depending on length of employment—but because PTO is paid in advance, there is no pay while they are gone.

4. Should you offer health insurance? Yes.

5. If an employee does a good job, say so publicly. If an employee does a poor job, also say so, but privately.

6. We put shift schedules out to bid and award them by seniority. Inevitably, the most senior TSRs occupy the best weekday day-time shifts, with everyone understanding this is the reward for long service. The less-tenured TSRs will also value their time with the company, seeing their accumulating work histories as assets that grow more valuable every day. The seniority method is logical and fair.

7. Put the job down on paper. This includes a clear and concise operational manual, an employee handbook, and individual job descriptions. It's a stressful occupation as it is: do TSRs also have to be mind readers and fortune-tellers in order to survive? To the very last detail, instructions for performing the work should be recorded in black-and-white, in hard copy, and in electronic files.

8. Implement "pay by performance," with an objective method of measurement. At Centratel, we have a full-time independent quality specialist who rates call quality and reviews performance weekly with each TSR. TSRs can boost their take-home pay by up to 30 percent with this plan. For the TSR, that additional 30 percent is the fun money and/or get-ahead money that lies beyond the necessary money.

Cultivating a long-term, loyal staff begins with a mindset change. Stop looking for the perfect employee, inserting gimmicks, or blathering away with impotent excuses about a declining work ethic or nonsensical theories of human motivation. Instead, per Ockham's razor, "choose the simplest explanation, the one requiring the fewest assumptions," and document a plan that addresses the real needs of your people—people who want to do a good job.

APPENDIX H
Centratel's Procedure for Procedures

FOLLOWING IS OUR MASTER PROCEDURE FOR PROCEDURES, which contains precise instructions for creating a Working Procedure. It is the Mother of All Procedures, the master instructions for creating the several hundred that are necessary for our operation. This document ensures each will share the same tone and format.

Don't be discouraged by the length and complexity of it, and don't get bogged down in what it says. Of all the procedures at Centratel, it's the longest and most intricate. Simply consider its essence and then apply it to your own situation. It begins with a narration. See appendix J for information about Business Documentation Software that will significantly automate the technical details of all Working Procedures.

PROCEDURE FOR PROCEDURES

Overview to staff: We base Centratel's mechanical functioning on Working Procedures (or simply, "Procedures"). With hundreds of human and mechanical operating processes in action at any one time, keeping Centratel organized in any other way would be impossible. Working Procedures guide everything from an emergency relay for a TAS account, to how we deposit payments in the bank, to job descriptions for staff members, to greeting customers at the door.

Strict adherence to written procedure is critical, but we counterbalance this strictness with our eagerness to make instant adjustments should the environment change or should someone come up with a better idea. Whatever your job description, if you have a suggestion for making things better, pass it on. If it's good, we'll change the written procedure and implement it now!

Strict yet easy-to-modify procedures provide a huge degree of freedom to the individual staff member because the guidelines eliminate guesswork. Answers and instructions are right there. Working Procedures are the heart of Centratel's operational model: "Freedom and responsibility within a structured yet flexible business system."

OVERALL GUIDELINES

Is there a recurring problem or task? Then a Working Procedure is necessary. Or if there is already a procedure and a problem arises, we will modify the existing procedure to eliminate the problem. If there is no problem, let's streamline the procedure to make it as efficient as possible. In the earliest stage of creating a procedure, get feedback from those people affected. It is mandatory the creator of the procedure and the relevant department manager be advised of any changes before they are made. In fact, they must be intimately involved with the revision, and each must give final approval to changes.

Create the procedure with an "off-the-street" simplicity. Be simple, concise, and thorough. Remember the overall goal: "Freedom and responsibility within a highly developed system."

How much information should be included?

For narrative procedures: Add as much information as possible, but do it in a way so that the information is easily found. Use alphabetical listings, logical subheadings, numbering and bullet formats, simple and concise sentence structure, etc.

For charts and graph procedures: Design it to be simple, concise, and fast to read. Often it will be necessary to leave out information in order to make it more readable. Limit the typefaces and sizes, special formats, etc.

Per point-of-sale strategy, we will change a procedure instantly. *Betterment of a procedure by modification, addition, deletion, or outright elimination is quick and without hesitation.* We operate within a strict framework, but that framework can be quickly changed by group consent.

Do not assume anything. Every step must be obvious and logical. Especially do not assume the user of the procedure will be knowledgeable regarding the subject or can read your mind: remember the "off-the-street" methodology!

General layout: After the title, if necessary, start the procedure with a concise narrative that provides a quick overall description of the what, why, how, who, and when of the procedure. Follow this, if applicable to the particular procedure, with bulleted or numbered instructions.

Never title a procedure "Procedure for . . ." The title must be concise yet descriptive and make sense to an "off-the-street" staff member. The title must be logical so the subject can be found quickly. Start the title with the subject. For example: "Sales Call Procedure," not "Procedure for Sales Calls." Then start with a brief narrative of what the procedure accomplishes.

Critical: Test the procedure before release! Use an "off-the-street" subject (a staff member who is *not* involved with the procedure).

Post all new or modified procedures on the procedures drive. In the modified procedure, date the change, and show the new information in blue type. Hard copies are immediately printed and placed in alphabetical order in either the Administrative Procedures Folder or the Operations Procedures Folder.

Each affected staff member will review the new procedure. Upon understanding it, the staff member initials and dates the hard copy.

The staff member directs questions and suggestions back to the person who created the procedure. (If there *is* a question, it is evidence that the procedure itself should be further modified so questions will not have to be asked in the future.) Before release, all new or significantly modified procedures must be OK'd by the general manager.

The staff member follows the new procedure exactly. Hear this: IF A PROBLEM ARISES WITH A PROCEDURE, WE INSTANTLY ADJUST THE PROCEDURE. WE DO NOT CIRCUMVENT IT!

SPECIFIC DESIGN

(The complex design specifications that are listed here are embedded in our Business Documentation Software. For information see appendix J and www.workthesystem.com/documentation)

Use template on P: drive titled "Procedures Template" and in the Template folder.

Start with the title, in the Heading 1 style (Verdana bold size 12).

Follow the title with the date, in the Procedure Date style (Verdana regular 10).

For subheadings, use the Heading 2 style (Verdana bold size 10) and for further subdivision within those subheadings, use the Heading 3 style (Verdana italics size 10).

For the body text, use the Normal style (Verdana regular size 10).

For any bullets or numbering, use the default bullets and numbering styles.

Procedures are addressed at the bottom of the last page in this way:

> Select View, Headers and Footers.
>
> Click in Footer.
>
> 1st line: Choose Insert AutoText "Filename and Path."
>
> 2nd line: Choose Insert AutoText "Created by." Add your name. You may have to do this manually, depending on what computer you are using and how it is set up.
>
> 3rd line: Choose Insert AutoText "Created on." Add date and time. Use the Footer style.

Use italics and bold sparingly.

Use the 1-2-3-step format when applicable.

Use bullets or numbers when applicable.

If a relay is involved, use numbering and the same acronyms and methodology used in TAS relays.

Is the above procedure long and complicated? Yes and no. The "Specifics" portion is simple. The "Design" portion is necessarily long because the details are complex—it's the actual mechanical guideline for creating a procedure. But its detail is clear and concise, and therefore not at all complicated. You will note, as with the Thirty Principles document, it is nonlinear.

APPENDIX I

Centratel's System for Communication

At Centratel, based on our Strategic Objective and the efficiency thread that permeates the Thirty Principles document, we employ the latest communications technology. It's an interesting paradox: the simple effectiveness of our internal communications hinges on highly complex technologies. (Somehow our IT manager, Dan, keeps all of it working with rarely any downtime.)

Right at the beginning of our transformation, we developed a Working Procedure for communication among ourselves and with the outside world. Because it's simple and easy, our people communicate a lot.

Every Centratel staff member uses the same protocols. There is no confusion. This procedure has evolved with the technical and even social changes that have occurred in the last half dozen years. Here it is:

INTERNAL COMMUNICATIONS: PROCEDURE AND FUNDAMENTALS

The tools of active communications:

1. Voice Mail (VM)
2. E-mail (EM)
3. Instant Messenger (IM)
4. One-on-one via phone
5. One-on-one in person
6. Hard copy memo/procedure

What method of communication should I use?

1. Routine, not time sensitive: EM, VM

2. Time sensitive: IM, one-on-one in person or via phone

3. "Getting all my thoughts in order," detailed explanations: VM, EM

4. Personal and sensitive issues: one-on-one in person or via phone

5. Documentation is necessary: EM or hard copy

6. Information is complex/detailed: EM, hard copy, one-on-one in person or via phone

7. Procedures: Soft copy on Procedures drive and hard copy

Point-of-Sale

Point-of-sale protocol for our internal communications means, most of all, that when someone asks a question, the response is immediate. For instance, avoid saving a voice mail message for a future response. If you must delay your reply, immediately take the time to answer the message sender to say you will get back with a detailed answer later (and be sure to provide an approximate time he or she can expect your response). Understand this approach is just as applicable to e-mail: the most basic rule is to keep your inbox empty by dealing with the issue *now*, via our point-of-sale mandate.

Microsoft Outlook

The Centratel Microsoft Outlook information system is the heart of our administration's internal communications. The task list, contact list, and calendar are critical to staying organized and maximizing efficiency. Have the program open all day and use it often. Use the task list to remind yourself both of your own tasks and of tasks delegated to others.

Instant Messenger: If you are on the job, it must be active. Be sure to configure it to turn on automatically when you log in.

E-mail: Thoroughly read messages you receive. Reread and double-check each outgoing message before you send it. Is your outgoing e-mail clear, concise, and brief? Are there grammatical errors? Does your message make sense, or are you presuming you are communicating with a mind reader, or maybe someone who is fond of deciphering puzzles?

Giving (Delivering) a Message via Any Medium

Consider quantity before quality. In fact, Centratel's definition of quality communication emphasizes high quantity. But note, *the quantity aspect has more to do with frequency than with volume of content*. Generally, if there is enough communication, quality will evolve. If in doubt about whether to communicate or not, you should communicate.

Rambling dispatches that contain more information than necessary, or messages that keep repeating the same detail, are a waste of two people's time. The voice mail medium is particularly susceptible to fatiguing, inefficient messages. But then, sometimes a voice mail message is faster and more meaningful than an e-mail message. *Sometimes a thirty-second voice mail will deliver the same message as a fifteen-minute e-mail*. Whatever the communication method, remember this when sending a message: "A great message is a short message."

Not many people think about the quality of their communications. At Centratel, since our entire purpose is to provide the very best communication services, we have to be good at it! We are "the highest-quality telephone answering service in the United States" because we unceasingly refine and improve the communication services we provide, as well as our own internal communications. We think about communications all the time. It is a primary system that we relentlessly analyze and refine.

We have many communication tools. At any given time, is the best method being used? Before leaving a message for someone, what preparation is necessary for the message to be complete, clear, and concise? While leaving the message, is too much being said, or too little?

An effective training process is to record and review conversations with callers and clients. For most of us, there is incongruity between how we think we sound and how we actually sound. This self-analysis can eliminate "yeahs" and "ya knows," deepen one's voice, promote conciseness, and point out annoying flaws that otherwise go unnoticed.

APPENDIX J

Business Documentation Software

OPTIONAL TO THE ACADEMY PRODUCT, and as part of the critical system improvement process, is our Business Documentation Software, which is used to create concise and congruent documentation, house it in an orderly manner, and provide routine updating reminders.

Go to businessdocumentationsoftware.com for detailed information.

APPENDIX K

Other Offerings

AUDIO AND PDF VERSIONS OF THE THIRD EDITION *WORK THE SYSTEM*: *THE SIMPLE MECHANICS OF MAKING MORE AND WORKING LESS*

The audio, recorded by Sam, is unabridged. Both versions are available at workthesystem.com and at the usual retail outlets, including Amazon.

WORK THE SYSTEM BOOT CAMP

Held in Bend, Oregon, and sometimes other locations, this one-day program goes to the heart of the process with the intention of launching your business or corporate department into an organized, efficient, and profitable organism. See workthesystem.com/bootcamp for details. Call us at 1-800-664-7448, or e-mail us at info@workthesystem.com.

SPEAKING ENGAGEMENTS

Sam will occasionally travel for presentations. Call us at 1-800-664-7448 or e-mail at info@workthesystem.com.

Kashmir Family Aid

ON SHORT NOTICE, JUST AFTER THE OCTOBER 8, 2005, earthquake that devastated great swaths of Azad Jammu and Kashmir (AJK) and the northwest frontier province of Pakistan, I traveled alone to Muzaffarabad, the capital city of AJK, the epicenter of the quake. Local Kashmiris greeted and housed me, as I tried to help out. Not restricted to a guarded encampment, I was one of few Westerners to roam freely through the area, unattached to an official NGO or the U.S. military. I wrote newspaper articles and took photos in order to publicize the plight of the millions who were homeless, and I gave away cash.

The dazed survivors wandered the tent camps and streets, wondering what to do next. It was devastation, with eighty thousand dead—a disproportionate number of whom were children who had been trapped in schools when the quake struck. Nearly every family I met had lost one or more close family members on that tragic day.

Shortly thereafter, I created Kashmir Family Aid, a 501c3 nonprofit organization. Its narrow purpose is to provide assistance to the schoolchildren of the region. I had been to Pakistan several times on business before the earthquake, and I have returned a number of times since. Linda has traveled with me there, too.

Note that Bend, Oregon, and Muzaffarabad, AJK, have become official sister cities.

We recently extended our reach into India Kashmir.

I invite you to visit the Kashmir Family Aid website (kashmirfamily. org) and view the slide presentations and photos. You will find some of my newspaper articles there, too. Please consider helping us. A school with two hundred students and eight teachers can be totally supported for less than U.S. $500 a month, but any size donation goes a long way. Thank you.

—Sam Carpenter

INDEX

Note: At the end of most chapters is an illustration, a short true story that reflects the *Work the System* methodology. You will find a list of these stories under the main entry, "illustrations." Each chapter also contains sidebars, which will be found under the main entry, chapter sidebars.